THE MENTALLY DISORDERED OFFENDER

THE MENTAL HEALTH FOUNDATION

The *Mental Health Foundation* (MHF) is Britain's leading grant making charity concerned with promoting and encouraging pioneering research and community care projects in the field of mental illness and mental handicap.

The Foundation aims to prevent mental disorders by funding and encouraging research into the causes of mental illness and mental handicap, and to improve the quality of life for mentally disordered people by funding and supporting pioneering and innovative community care schemes.

The Mental Health Foundation has several professional committees which meet at regular intervals to decide upon the allocation of funds to priority areas.

Apart from its interests in offering financial support, the Mental Health Foundation also runs regular seminars and conferences. These provide an arena for the exchange of information for a wide range of professionals working in the field who might otherwise find it difficult to meet.

In 1988, the Mental Health Foundation held a seminar on 'The Mentally Disordered Offender in the Penal System' at Cumberland Lodge, Windsor Great Park. The object was to consider progress in all aspects of the management of the mentally disordered offender since Lord Butler's 'Report of the Committee on Mentally Abnormal Offenders' in 1975 (Cmnd 6244).

John Gunn, Professor of Forensic Psychiatry at the Institute of Psychiatry, University of London was advisor to the Mental Health Foundation on the academic content of the seminar. Dr Katia Herbst is Policy Development Officer for the Foundation and responsible for two of the new specialist grant-giving committees. One of these concerns itself solely with mentally disordered offenders.

THE MENTALLY DISORDERED OFFENDER

Edited by

KATIA R. HERBST
MA, PhD
The Mental Health Foundation, London

and

JOHN GUNN
MD, DPM, FRCPsych

Professor of Forensic Psychiatry, Institute of Psychiatry, University of London

Butterworth–Heinemann
in association with

**The
Mental Health
Foundation**

Butterworth-Heinemann Ltd
Halley Court, Jordan Hill, Oxford OX2 8EJ

 PART OF REED INTERNATIONAL BOOKS

OXFORD   LONDON   GUILDFORD   BOSTON
MUNICH   NEW DELHI   SINGAPORE   SYDNEY
TOKYO   TORONTO   WELLINGTON

First published 1991

British Library Cataloguing in Publication Data
The mentally disordered offender.
  1. Mentally ill offenders
  I. Herbst, Katia Gilhome   II. Gunn, John *1937–*
364.38

ISBN 0-7506-0028-4

Typeset by Latimer Trend & Company Ltd, Plymouth
Printed and bound in Great Britain by Clays Ltd, St Ives plc

Contents

Contributors

Robert Baxter
Assistant Secretary, C3 (Mental Health) Division, Home Office, London

Ian Bynoe
Legal Director, MIND, London

Diana M. Dickens
Unit General Manager, Rampton Hospital, Nottinghamshire

Susan Evershed
Senior Psychologist, Parkhurst Prison, Isle of Wight

Clifford Graham
Under Secretary, Department of Health, London

Adrian Grounds
University Lecturer in Forensic Psychiatry, Institute of Criminology and Department of Psychiatry, University of Cambridge, Cambridge

John Gunn
Professor of Forensic Psychiatry, Institute of Psychiatry, University of London

James Higgins
Consultant Forensic Psychiatrist, The Scott Clinic, Rainhill Hospital, Merseyside

Herbert Laming
Direct of Social Services, Hertfordshire County Council, Hertford

Anne E. Mace
Chief Probation Officer, West Yorkshire Probation Service, Wakefield, West Yorkshire

Joy Major
Justice of the Peace, Birmingham Bench, and Vice-President of the National Schizophrenia Fellowship

Molly Meacher
Mental Health Act Commissioner and Director, Campaign For Work, London

Michael Mustill
Lord Justice of Appeal, Royal Courts of Justice, London

Maggie Pinder
Development Officer (Mental Health), Hertfordshire Council County, Hertford

Adam Sampson
Deputy Director, Prison Reform Trust, London

Michael Selby
Governor, Grendon Underwood Prison, Buckinghamshire

Stephen Shaw
Director, Prison Reform Trust, London

Christopher Stuart-White
Circuit Judge, West Midlands

Nigel Walker
Formerly Professor of Criminology and Director of the Institute of Criminology, University of Cambridge, Cambridge. Former member of the Butler Committee on Mentally Abnormal Offenders

Rosemary J. Wool
Director, Prison Medical Services, London

Preface

The Right Honourable the Lord Butler KG CH was President of the Mental Health Foundation from 1973 to 1982. His concern for the mentally disordered was profound and well informed. When he withdrew from the Mental Health Foundation shortly before his death in 1982, he asked Lord Elwyn-Jones—then retiring as Lord Chancellor—to take over his position. Lord Elwyn-Jones accepted and remained with the Mental Health Foundation until a few months before his death in late autumn 1989. It was under his inspired presidency that the Mental Health Foundation grew to become Britain's largest fund-giving charity concentrating primarily on the promotion and support of academic and community projects concerned with mental disorders.

Lord Butler had a particular interest in mentally abnormal offenders: this group of people met his joint interests of criminology (he had been an outstanding Home Secretary) and of mental health. This concern came to the fore when, in September 1972, he was asked by the Government to chair an inquiry into the legal, administrative, and medical problems of mentally abnormal offenders. To assist him, he chose a distinguished panel of fifteen professionals, including psychiatrists such as Sir Denis Hill (a founder member of the Mental Health Foundation), lawyers such as the Honourable Mr Justice Croom-Johnson (as vice-chairman), Dr Douglas Acres as a magistrate, and Professor Nigel Walker as a criminologist. The 'Butler Report', as the *Report of the Committee on Mentally Abnormal Offenders* (Cmnd 6244) is usually known, was published by Her Majesty's Stationery Office in 1975. It provoked immediate and widespread interest and has become a yardstick for the development of British forensic psychiatry.

The Butler Report made a large number of recommendations. These concerned matters as diverse as the facilities for mentally abnormal offender patients, both in hospitals and in prisons; the dangerousness of patients; the labelling and management of psychopaths; 'inadequate' offenders; discharge and after-care arrangements for offender patients; the law concerning disability in relation to the trial and insanity; medical services to the courts; changes in the Mental Health Acts; probation orders; and interprofessional cooperation. Many of these proposals have since been implemented, some of course have not.

One of the subsidiary functions of the Mental Health Foundation is to provide an independent arena for the exchange of ideas in the rather more contentious areas of psychiatry and related fields. So it was that in September 1988—with great encouragement from Lord Elwyn-Jones— the Mental Health Foundation convened a three-day seminar on the subject of the mentally disordered offender in order to review progress since the publication of the Butler Report. Some forty professionals concerned with the care and treatment of mentally disordered offenders were invited to attend; they included Lord Justices of Appeal, psychiatrists, social workers, nurses, probation officers, and senior representatives from the Home Office and Department of Health.

Initially, when the meeting was planned, there had been no intention of producing a book based on the presentations of those attending: good conferences seldom make good books. However, so unusual was the collection of informed opinion and debate, and such was the excellence of the contributions, that it was generally agreed—there and then—that a book should be produced. Three extra chapters were later commissioned in order to provide a better balance for the text.

As a multidisciplinary group we struggled with terminology—an indication of the difficulties of communication between different professions. For example, on occasion we used the term 'mental disorder' in its legal, Mental Health Act sense to mean mental illness plus psychopathic disorder plus mental impairment plus severe mental impairment; at other times the same term was used in its wider clinical sense to also include other personality disorders, all neurotic disorders, organic mental states, mental handicap, sexual disorders, and substance abuse. The term 'inadequate' proved very difficult to use: it is used in the Butler Report, it is used by lawyers, but it is eschewed by psychiatrists and some others. We have used it in quotation marks in this book to indicate that its sense is that indicated by the Butler Committee. If the reader is conscious of what s/he would regard as terminological inexactitude, or even downright confusion, we crave the reader's indulgence and excuse ourselves on the grounds of good intentions for clarity which cannot yet (perhaps ever) be achieved in a world of changing opinions.

We have tried to present to the reader as balanced a picture as possible of the current problems faced by our major institutions in coping with the needs of the mentally disordered offender. The book's sections follow the mentally disordered offender himself as he passes through the courts, the hospital, the prisons, and/or into the community. But the chapters grouped within each section are written by a range of professionals each of whom has shaped the life of the mentally disordered offender at that stage of his or her 'career'. The whole is masterfully summed up by a Lord Justice of Appeal adjudicating on and explaining the conflicts inherent within the systems.

The recurring theme throughout the volume is one of dissonance: things are out of step with current welfare systems and psychiatry on the one hand, and penology and criminology on the other; anomalies in the law produce anomalies in provision, and anomalies in the condition of offenders actually create problems about what to do for the best. It seems clear that in order to proceed, the courts must work in tandem with the providers of appropriate services; and in order to achieve this, each set of professionals, in turn, must understand better the interests and concerns of the other. We hope this book will help towards that end.

Lord Elwyn-Jones, who attended the meeting and spoke enthusiastically, had agreed to write the Foreword to this book, but died before he could do so. This book is dedicated to his memory and to his work.

Katia Herbst
John Gunn

Section 1
Introduction

1 *Fourteen years on*

NIGEL WALKER

INTRODUCTION

Unlike my school, college and regiment, the Butler Committee does not hold reunions. Some of us are dead, some of us have accepted transportation, some of us are simply disappointed: in the small hours of our wakeful nights we sometimes ask ourselves what we actually achieved.

Our terms of reference were:

(a) To consider to what extent and on what criteria the law should recognise mental disorder or abnormality in a person accused of a criminal offence as a factor affecting his liability to be tried or convicted, and his disposal;

[In other words, what should be done about the insanity defence, diminished responsibility, infanticide and unfitness to plead?]

(b) To consider what, if any, changes are necessary in the powers, procedure and facilities relating to the provision of appropriate treatment, in prison, hospital or the community, for offenders suffering from mental disorder or abnormality, and to their discharge, and after-care; and to make recommendations.

[That is, to overhaul Part IV of the 1959 Mental Health Act and the ways in which disordered and abnormal offenders were being disposed of between Special Hospitals, National Health Service hospitals, prisons and what was optimistically called 'the community'.]

SUBCOMMITTEES

Lord Butler, an experienced and skillful chairman, divided members into two subcommittees charged with producing solutions to these two kinds of problem for approval by the Committee as a whole. The 'legal' subcommittee—which considered point (a) above and of which I was a member— drafted a complete new code. Not one of its features has been adopted, for reasons I shall discuss later. One minor recommendation—that restriction orders should be confined by law to the protection of the public from *serious harm* [Recommendation 108], not just any kind of harm—was incorporated in the Mental Health Act 1983; but by that time few judges were using it for any other purpose. Our recommendation that all restriction orders should be 'without limit of time' [Recommendation 109], which was in line with the Court of Appeal's practice direction, was resisted by some psychiatrists (for reasons which seem to me to be artificial), and was not adopted. Fortunately, most judges have followed the Court of Appeal's practice direction.

Secure units

The other subcommittee fared a little better. Its first fruit was the revival of an idea first mooted by the Emery Working Party in 1961: that the Special Hospitals should be supplemented by smaller and more numerous 'diagnostic and treatment centres' (Ministry of Health, 1961). Although this coincided with a fairly similar recommendation by the Royal Medico-Psychological Association (now the Royal College of Psychiatrists), and although it had the blessing of the Government, it had been left to Regional Hospital Boards to implement; and they thought they had better ways of spending their money. The innovation seemed to us so overdue that we devoted the whole of an Interim Report to it (Home Office and DHSS, 1974). Even then, it seemed likely that nothing would be done, until Butler decided to use his personal political influence to make sure that the Interim Report did not suffer the same fate as the Emery Report. He initiated the debate in the House of Lords which drew public attention to the inertia (or worse) of the Regional Hospital Boards, and the need for special funds to create 'secure units'. The money was provided from central funds. Even then, difficulties were raised wherever the creation of a secure unit was proposed: it would seduce badly needed nursing staff from other National Health Service (NHS) hospitals; it would alarm local residents, and so forth. Eventually, however, these fears were overcome, and now every region—except, for some reason, Wales—has a secure unit.

FORENSIC SERVICES

Later, in the main Report, the Committee recommended the establishment of forensic psychiatric services in each NHS region [Recommendations 69–72]. At that time only London and Birmingham had what could honestly be called a forensic psychiatric service; but now every region has one—except, again, Wales. Some members of the Committee wanted to include a much more ambitious set of recommendations for merging the Prison Medical Service with the NHS, chiefly in order to raise the standard of psychiatry in prison establishments; but it was pointed out that the membership of the Committee was not such that we were properly qualified to pronounce on such an intricate problem. Eventually the Committee settled for some rather vague recommendations which were of lesser importance [Recommendations 126, 127].

PSYCHOPATHIC OFFENDERS

The Committee spent many hours discussing two categories of offender: the psychopath and the 'inadequate' (still the subject of much debate and considered at length in Chapter 5). My own view is that Henderson did British psychiatry a disservice when he popularized the concept of 'psychopathy', with doubtful examples, such as Joan of Arc (Henderson, 1939). It delayed the development of more specific diagnoses, of the kind now found in the International Classification of Disease (ICD) (WHO, 1987). (It is worth noting that Henderson's own country, Scotland, did not use the term in Mental Health (Scotland) Act.) However that may be, by the early 1970s it was considered by many psychiatrists to be an undesirable label. More important—although this was said less openly— offenders with antisocial personality disorders were a nuisance in hospitals, and seldom responded to treatment. The Committee could not accept the suggestion that psychopathic disorder should be excluded altogether from the definition of mental disorder: that would have prevented the compulsory admission, whether civil or criminal, of some people, especially the young, who might well benefit from it. The Committee's compromise proposal was that courts should not be allowed to use hospital orders to deal with 'psychopaths' unless 'satisfied that 1. a previous mental or organic illness, or an identifiable psychological or physical illness, or an identifiable psychological or physical defect, relevant to the disorder, is known or suspected; and 2. there is an expectation of therapeutic benefit from hospital admission' [Recommendation 124]. After a great deal of discussion this was more or less what was incorporated in the 1983 Mental Health Act, with two differences. First, it was considered sensible to apply it to civil as well as to criminal compulsory admissions. Second, it was thought unnecessary to include requirement 1., presumably on the assumption that certifying psychiatrists would not hold out hope of 'therapeutic benefit' unless they had a fairly clear idea of what was wrong with the psychopath (whether this is so in practice I am not qualified to say). In any case, hospital orders dealing with psychopaths were becoming much less frequent than in the early days of the Mental Health Act, and the amendment did little more than add legal force to what had become the practice.

Yet the fewer the 'psychopaths' who were admitted to hospital the greater the number who would have to be sent to prison, usually under determinate sentences. Since some of them presented a danger to members of the public when at liberty, the Committee felt that it had to consider whether determinate sentences provided a sufficient safeguard. Clearly, in some cases they do not; and prison staff are familiar with prisoners whom the law requires them to release but about whose future behaviour they have the gravest misgivings. The only alternative available to the courts was the discretionary 'life' sentence, which judges at that time were very hesitant to use (they are less hesitant nowadays). So the Committee proposed a special 'reviewable sentence' which courts could use when faced with disordered offenders not suitable for disposal under the Mental Health Act and guilty of one of a list of serious offences (which was drawn up). Detention under a reviewable sentence would be reviewed every two years by the Parole Board, whose recommendation for release, like its recommendations for parole, would be subject to the Home Secretary's approval [Recommendations 39–43]. The Committee knew, of course, that the judiciary did not like sentences which exceeded their tariff (flexible as that tariff has always been). Even the 'extended sentence', though determinate, was not popular. But the Netherlands were operating a reviewable sentence (with differences), and the Committee could not take the view that the English sentencing system dealt satisfactorily with the problem of the dangerous disordered offender. But the Committee's recommendation received little support, and the problem remains untackled, apart from a slight increase in the frequency with which judges use the discretionary life sentence.

Certainly the Committee did not solve the problem presented by psychopaths of the kind who continued to be committed to hospital. They continued to be numerous enough to necessitate another working party, which produced a consultative document in 1986 (DHSS and Home Office, 1986). Instead of a single proposal it offered three alternatives:

1. Section 37 of the 1983 Act might be replaced by one giving courts discretion to sentence a mentally disordered offender to imprisonment but *direct* his admission to hospital, as a result of which his status would be that of a prisoner transferred with restrictions on his discharge;
2. The reference to psychopathic offenders might be deleted from Section 37, so that they would simply be sentenced to imprisonment with the *possibility* of being transferred to hospital;
3. Section 37 might be amended so as to allow hospital orders only for psychopathic offenders who would not have merited a restriction order. For others imprisonment would be the outcome.

Need I say that none of these proposals has been pursued. The problems remain unsolved. It seems unlikely that they will be any nearer a solution until we have special establishments designed and staffed to deal with aggressive or sexual psychopaths, and—as the Butler Committee proposed—a special type of sentence to suit.

'INADEQUATE' OFFENDERS

Where 'inadequates' were concerned, the Committee's proposals were less specific and no more successful. Since many 'inadequates' suffer from mild forms of mental disorder the Committee did not think it illogical to urge that the NHS should play a greater part in providing them with sheltered accommodation; but it was perhaps a little unrealistic to expect this to happen. The Committee also emphasized the help which voluntary and probation hostels could give; but mental disorder, even of a mild kind, makes the management of such residents troublesome. Nor are 'inadequates' always willing to 'stay put'. The structured regimens of prisons seemed able to cope with 'inadequate' offenders, many of whom seemed fairly content while inside; but no one could envisage a system which would subject them to long sentences. As for guardianship orders, the legal powers conferred by them seemed suitable, and the Committee was told of a few cases in which they had worked well; but they were little used. Local authorities have no liking for them, and cannot be forced to accept anyone under such an order: a provision which the Committee did not want to see repealed. It expressed the hope that social service departments would be more cooperative where courts were concerned [Paragraphs 15.5, 15.8], but the Committee's hopes were not high, and today guardianship orders are still almost unheard of. Nor has any real solution for disbanding the stage-army of 'inadequate' offenders been produced (see Chapter 5).

REMAND TO HOSPITAL

More successful were the proposals for hospital remands [Recommendations 16–19]. What the Committee envisaged, however, was a type of order that would have covered both remands for diagnosis and remands for treatment, whereas the 1983 Mental Health Act provided a different sort of order for each purpose. For some reason, it was decided that remands for diagnostic reports should be outside the scope of the sections dealing with consent to treatment. Thus a psychiatrist who wants to use a form of treatment to which the remanded patient objects has to rely, not on a clear statute, but on the notoriously obscure common law, or else apply for further powers under the Act, say under Section 3. It became apparent that the Mental Health Act Commission would like to have the two kinds of remand combined, as the Butler Committee originally proposed (Mental Health Act Commission, 1987).

INTERIM HOSPITAL ORDERS

The Committee also proposed what—with minor differences—became the interim hospital order [Recommendations 16–19], designed for cases in which, although the offender was clearly disordered enough to warrant committal to hospital, it was not certain that he would co-operate sufficiently to make this effective. Under an ordinary hospital order the offender cannot be brought back to court for resentencing if he is uncooperative; but under a Section 38 order he can if he absconds. Interestingly, while remands to hospital are now quite frequent, interim hospital orders do not seem popular. One reason may be that remands to hospitals enable staff to predict with confidence—if not accuracy—who will cooperate and who won't, so that interim orders are rarely considered necessary. Another reason, however, may well be that psychiatrists are still reluctant to become involved in the resentencing of someone who has been under their care. Certainly this reluctance is still evident where psychiatric probation orders are concerned. By no means all psychiatrists are happy to report a breach of requirements when a probationer does not cooperate in treatment.

THE PSYCHIATRIC DEFENCES

So much for what might be called 'administrative' reforms. Where the law is concerned with the determination of guilt the proposals of the Committee's legal subcommittee were completely unsuccessful [Recommendations 20–38; 44–55]. First, it was faced with a state of affairs which had more or less killed off the insanity defence. The effect of a successful insanity defence was so drastic—indeterminate commitment to a mental hospital under a restriction order—and so obviously unsuited to the harmlessness of some insane offenders, that an offender's legal advisers would usually regard it as not in his interests to plead insanity as his defence. As for psychiatrists, the insanity defence required them to testify about what was in the offender's mind, not when they talked to him but when he committed the *actus reus*. They were asked not merely whether he was disordered at the time—a sensible and usually answerable question—but also whether he knew 'the nature and quality' of his act, and if he did, whether he knew that it was against the law. Many people who are not disordered would have difficulty in giving a definite and truthful answer to such a question, especially if asked several weeks later. To ask a psychiatrist to answer such questions about the actions of another person, and especially a person who may still be confused, emotional and inarticulate, is to force him into silence or dishonesty.

However, for a century and a half France had successfully operated a much simpler defence. Under the *Code Napoléon* the accused is not guilty if, at the relevant time, he was suffering from *démence*—namely, severe mental disorder. If the Committee adopted this solution psychiatrists would no longer have to testify as to what the accused believed about his action. The Committee agreed, and the psychiatrists provided guidelines as to what constituted *severe* mental disorder. Professor Glanville Williams (a member of the Butler Committee) pointed out that the Committee must not exclude the occasional case in which the accused, although his disorder was not severe, was lacking nevertheless in the necessary *mens rea* as a result of it. (For example, a person whose subnormality was not severe might, nevertheless, because of it, believe that he owned something which he did not.) Lastly, the Committee proposed that a successful defence of this kind should no longer oblige the court to impose a restriction order, but merely permit this, with the alternative of an ordinary hospital order, a psychiatric probation order or other non-punitive disposal. To date, none of the features of this proposal has even been discussed by Parliament, even when they were endorsed by the Criminal Code Team of the Law Commission (Law Commission, 1985).

Since their draftsmanship was of a high order, and since the Report is not on everybody's bookshelves, it may be helpful to reproduce their version here:

(1) A mental disorder verdict shall be returned where
    (a) the defendant is proved to have committed an offence but it is proved on the balance of probabilities (whether by the prosecution or the defendant) that he was at the time suffering from severe mental illness or severe subnormality; or
    (b) (i) the defendant is found not to have committed an offence on the ground only that, by reason of mental disorder or a combination of mental disorder and intoxication, he acted or may have acted in a state of automatism, or without the fault required for the offence, or believing that an exempting circumstance existed; and
    (ii) it is proved on the balance of probabilities (whether by the prosecution or by the defendant) that he was suffering from mental disorder at the time of the act . . . (Clause 38, Law Commission, 1985).

The rest of the clause deals with definitions—for example of severe mental illness.

Professor Gunn (see Chapter 2) wonders why the Committee overlooked a simpler solution. Section 60 (3) of the 1959 Mental Health Act (now Section 37(3) of the 1983 Mental Health Act) allowed magistrates' courts to make a hospital order without convicting the defendant if the Courts are satisfied that the defendant did whatever he is charged with but is suffering from mental illness or severe mental impairment. Why did the Committee not simply recommend the extension of this power to the Crown Court? There are several reasons, some more telling than others:

1. That Section deals only with the making of hospital orders, and we wanted the court to have a wider choice of measures. So considerable redrafting would have been needed;
2. 'Mental illness' can be so mild that it does not excuse but merely

mitigates. The Section would have had to be restricted to 'severe' mental illness; and that would have had to be defined;

3. The Section deals with the state of mind of the offender at the time when he appears in court. What is relevant when excuses are under consideration is his state of mind at the time when he committed the *actus reus*.

But the all-important reason was:

4. The Section merely *permits*: it does not *compel*. This last feature of the insanity defence is often overlooked. It distinguishes it from 'diminished responsibility' and the Sections concerned with hospital and guardianship orders and psychiatric probation orders, which allow the court discretion to use either penal or psychiatric disposals. The crucial point is this. If you believe that there are mental states which excuse a person so completely that it is morally wrong to sentence him or her in a penal way, then you need a defence that will, if successful, rule that out; not one which will leave the decision to the court.

UNFITNESS FOR TRIAL

When the Committee turned to 'disability in relation to trial' (its slightly pedantic term for what is more often called 'unfitness to plead'), the Committee were equally dissatisfied. This is an issue which, nowadays, has to be faced more often than 'insanity'. Yet a finding of 'unfitness' still results in a mandatory restriction order, although some unfit defendants obviously do not need one. In addition, too often the issue is decided without waiting to see whether the defendant can be rendered fit. Further, since the issue is usually raised by counsel before the prosecution have outlined its evidence, there is a possibility (as experience has shown) that a defendant who has really 'no case to answer' will be disposed of as if he had. Finally, the legal definition of 'unfitness' needed overhauling, as the senior judges who gave evidence to us in person conceded. Our proposals included a 'trial of the facts', and it was this which seems to have led to opposition by the Home Office. The Law Commissions' Criminal Code Team were so discouraged by the Home Office's comments on this aspect of the Committee's recommendations that they made no attempt to incorporate any of them in their draft code. Yet none of the other recommendations was controversial, and they could have been incorporated without providing for a 'trial of the facts'.

DIMINISHED RESPONSIBILITY

Surprising as it may seem, I do not regard what the Committee had to say about diminished responsibility as important. Certainly it offered a reworded formula that was an improvement on the slipshod drafting of the Homicide Act 1957 [Recommendations 58–61]. The Criminal Law Revision Committee agreed that it needed rewording and offered their own version. In fact the Committee hoped, and said, that diminished responsibility could be forgotten if the mandatory life sentence for murder were replaced by discretionary powers of sentence [Recommendation 57]. Evidence of mental disorder (or abnormality or stress) could then be given at the sentencing stage, and could persuade the judge to choose a hospital order (for example) instead of a life sentence. In retrospect, I am not sure that the Committee was right. Certainly I agree—as so many committees have—that 'life' for murder should cease to be mandatory. But a verdict of diminished responsibility does not merely set the sentencer free: it removes the stigma which attaches to a 'murderer', and there are cases in which this matters—especially domestic homicides.

What I think the Committee might have discussed, and what I regret not having raised during the discussion of diminished responsibility, is the question 'Why should it apply only to charges of murder?' The fact that it is so restricted is due to mere historical accident: the need to find some workable substitute for the unworkable insanity defence that would save some 'capital murderers' from the death penalty. (The story will be found in Volume I of *Crime and Insanity in England* (Walker, 1968). In reality, any sort of offence—except such things as long-term frauds!—can be committed by persons in states of 'diminished responsibility'. So why should they not then have the chance of pleading it? In Italy, for instance, the equivalent plea (*vizio partiale di mente*) can be used to compel the court to award a more lenient sentence than the tariff provides for the offence. English lawyers have argued that it would be meaningless or ineffective to extend diminished responsibility to offences other than homicide, partly because none is subdivided like homicide into two sorts (murder and manslaughter). This is not invariably true. We distinguish grievous bodily harm according to the 'intent' with which it is committed; and judges sentence it accordingly. Even when it is true that no similar distinction is made by law, it could be provided that in cases of diminished responsibility the court must sentence more leniently. To answer that courts already do this when given evidence at the sentencing stage that the offender was suffering from an abnormality of mind is only a partial counter: a verdict of diminished responsibility would reduce the stigma in many cases. Finally, can any lawyer defend a defence which applies to murder but not to attempted murder?

MAGISTRATES' COURTS

Joy Majors' Chapter (Chapter 4) is a much-needed reminder of magistrates' problems, which receive less attention in these discussions than do those of the higher courts. Yet magistrates deal with far more cases involving disordered offenders: they are responsible for most of the involving disordered offenders: they are responsible for most of the remands to hospital, most of the hospital orders and most of the psychiatric probation orders. They are not supposed to find anyone 'unfit for trial', but in practice they use Section 37 (3) of the Act to make hospital orders without convicting the offender when they cannot make head or tail of what he has to say or interpret his silence. Occasionally magistrates use the same Subsection 37(3) for an offender who seems insane, although most lawyers doubt whether magistrates can consider an insanity defence. (Traditionally the defence was confined to capital crimes: see Hale's *Historia Placitorum Coronae* (Hale, 1736).)

The Committee proposed that it should be made clear that both insanity and unfitness to plead could be accepted by magistrates' courts. What the Committee could not solve is the magistrates' chronic problem: the petty offender who is remanded for psychiatrict reports only to reappear with an assessment of 'no apparent disorder' (NAD). Other assessments which present difficulties are that the offender is mildly mentally ill, impaired or psychopathic and that the psychiatrist is unable to offer him a bed or even outpatient treatment, or that he has been mentally ill. Adrian Grounds (personal communication) has pointed out that consultants are often faced with offenders whose history includes psychotic episodes—sometimes more than 'mild'—but who no longer show acute symptoms. Once more we find ourselves baffled by the psychopathic or 'inadequate' stage-army.

PSYCHIATRIC PROBATION ORDERS

Nowadays we are much less optimistic about the efficacy of psychiatry in dealing with offenders who are only mildly disordered. The psychiatric probation order, with a requirement of in- or outpatient treatment, seems tailor-made for such people; and the Mental Health Act of 1959 expressly stated that these orders were not to be used for offenders whose mental condition warranted hospital orders. But whether this rule is being observed or not we do not know. Remarkably little research has been focused on psychiatric probation orders. (An excellent exception is Lewis' study of the operation of such orders in one city (Lewis, 1980).). However, what we do know is that while the Butler Committee was sitting more than 1000 outpatient orders and about 500 inpatient orders were being made each year; although by 1987 these numbers had fallen to 870 and 150, respectively. Yet nobody seems to have noticed, or suggested a reason. Were they being overused in those days, or are they underused nowadays? We need to know, too, whether there is collaboration between the psychiatrist and the probation officer (Anne Mace (Chapter 16) suggests that the answer varies.) Do psychiatrists tell probation officers if the patient ceases to cooperate (as he not infrequently does)? One of the Committee's recommendations [Recommendation 93] was that he should be obliged to do so; but again it has not been implemented.

The Committee made some other recommendations [Recommendations 88–95]—for example, that there should be close and efficient cooperation between the psychiatrist and probation officer—but we were handicapped by the paucity of research. 'Efficiency' is not the same thing as 'efficacy'. Measuring 'efficacy', whether in terms of reconvictions or of improvement in mental condition, would obviously be very difficult (the main problem being the satisfactory selection of controls). But efficiency is not so hard to measure. Sensible questions include 'What percentage of such orders terminate in premature abandonment of treatment?'; 'In what percentage of such cases is the court given the opportunity of disposing of the offender in some other way?' Yet at the moment this is what I call a 'paved area'. It looks nice and tidy because it is covered with smooth flat stones, which nobody wants to turn over because of what they might find underneath!

DECISIONS TO PROSECUTE

I have confined this chapter to what I regard as the Committee's important recommendations. Others may feel that I have been too selective, or selected wrongly. However that may be, my final point concerns an undeniably important subject: the decision to prosecute mentally disordered offenders. The Committee's recommendations were that

Chief officers of police should review their policy and practice . . . and the Director of Public Prosecutions should give them guidance . . . In general the presumption should be against bringing charges which may result in the ordeal of court appearances and the stigma of conviction, with no compensating advantage. Prosecution should be seen as a last resort, and should not be embarked upon where it is not clearly in the interests of the patient or the community.

(Recommendations 6 and 7)

It took the Director of Public Prosecutions (DPP) nearly seven years to give prosecutors the guidance which the Committee thought they needed, and when he did he made more reservations than it had envisaged:

(i) The defence solicitor, knowing that the police are investigating his client's conduct, may sometimes send to the DPP a psychiatric report to the effect that the accused is suffering from some sort of mental illness and that the strain of criminal proceedings will lead to a considerable and permanent worsening of his condition. This is nearly as worrying as, say, a report that the accused has a weak heart and that the shock of prosecution may be fatal.

(ii) Once again, the DPP will normally try to arrange for an independent examination and will in any event give anxious consideration to such reports as he may receive. This is a difficult field because in some instances the accused may have become mentally disturbed or depressed by the mere fact that his misconduct has been discovered, and the DPP is sometimes dubious about a prognosis that criminal proceedings will adversely affect his condition to a significant extent.

(iii) The DPP does not normally think it is right to pay much regard to evidence of mental instability which is not coupled with a prognosis as to the adverse effect of proceedings, as such mental instability may increase the likelihood that the offence will be repeated. The accused's mental state will, of course, be relevant in considering any issue of *mens rea* or fitness to plead.

(*Criteria for Prosecution* (DPP, 1982))

Although elsewhere the DPP's guidance refers to 'the public interest', it does not do so in the context of the mentally disordered offender. The all-important difference is that, in effect, the Butler Report said 'Don't prosecute unless the public interest requires it', whereas, in effect, the DPP said 'Prosecute unless you are sure that you will do harm'. Like most of the advice in the DPP's document, it was drafted plainly with serious offences and Crown Court trials in mind, but, as we have seen, it is magistrates' courts that have to deal with the majority of the offenders with whom we are concerned. As Adrian Grounds says in Chapter 3, we need to know far more about what happens to unprosecuted offenders.

In the Pantheon of English politics Lord Butler was an Olympian. If only he could descend from Olympus for just one more Parliamentary session we would see more action than we have these last 14 years.

REFERENCES

Home Office and Department of Health and Social Security (1975). *Report of the Committee on Mentally Abnormal Offenders* (The Butler Report) Cmnd 6244. London: HMSO.

Henderson D. K. (1939). *Psychopathic States*. New York: Norton.

World Health Organisation (1987). *International Classification of Diseases, (ICD) IO 1986 Categories F00–F99. Mental, Behavioural and Developmental Disorders. Clinical Descriptions and Diagnostic Guide Lines*. Geneva: WHO (Division of Mental Health).

Home Office and Department of Health and Social Security (1974). *Interim Report of the Committee on Mentally Abnormal Offenders*. London: HMSO.

Department of Health and Social Security and Home Office (1986). *Offenders Suffering from Psychopathic Disorders*. Consultative Document. London: HMSO.

Mental Health Act Commission (1987). *Second Biennial Report 1985–1987*. London: HMSO.

Ministry of Health (1961). *Special Hospitals: Report of a Working Party* (Chmn. D. Emery). London: HMSO.

Law Commission (1985). *Criminal Law: Codification of the Criminal Law: a Report*. London: HMSO.

Walker N. (1968). *Crime and Insanity in England*. Vol. I: *The Historical Perspective*. Edinburgh: Edinburgh University Press.

Hale M. (1736). *Historia Placitorum Coronae*. London: Nutt and Gosling.

Lewis P. (1980). *Psychiatric Probation Orders*. Cambridge: Institute of Criminology, Cambridge University.

Director of Public Prosecutions (1982). *Criteria for Prosecution*. (Not for sale.)

Director of Public Prosecutions (1987). *Code for Crown Prosecutors*. London: HMSO.

Section 2
The Mentally Disordered Offender in the Courts

2 The trials of psychiatry: insanity in the twentieth century

JOHN GUNN

INTRODUCTION

Forensic psychiatry has developed from two slightly different routes: a public interest in the social and legal problems posed by the insane, and from the development of services for offender patients.

Walker (1985) has pointed out that the notion that madness excuses—at least partially—the actions it explains can be traced far back into European history. He believes that the earliest reference to madness being treated as an excuse for crime is Justinian's *Digest* in the sixth century AD. This early view may have been based on the idea that the mad are sufficiently punished by their madness. Eventually this idea became the first mechanism by which the insane were able to be treated more leniently than the sane. The notion that the madman has impaired volition came later.

Walker also tells us that he finds no English examples of *acquittal* on account of insanity until the beginning of the sixteenth century. By the seventeenth century the concept had broadened to include excusing 'idiots' for murder on the grounds that they do not have sufficient knowledge of good or evil, nor sufficient felonious intent or will to do harm. By the middle of the eighteenth century there was a sharp increase in the frequency with which the insanity defence was attempted. This increase was not the result of medical empire building—as it was usually not the medical evidence, but the testimony of relatives, friends or spectators that persuaded the court that the defendant had been mad at the time of his crime. The use of doctors in the court is, in historical terms, quite recent. The first time such testimony was used in Britain was probably in 1760 at the trial of Earl Ferrers. Dr John Monro, physician superintendent of Bethlem Hospital, London, testified on the subject of insanity in general— not actually on the defendant's condition *per se*. In the event, the defence of occasional insanity was unsuccessful and the Earl was convicted and executed (Eigen, 1986).

In the following 35 years, namely up to 1815, the Old Bailey became more familiar with the insanity defence—not as a result of charges of murder or violence, but through experience with routine, run-of-the-mill thefts. Further, the overwhelming majority of insanity pleas in this period were without the support of corroborating medical testimony (Eigen, 1986).

At the beginning of this century, Oppenheimer (1909) undertook a survey of as many national laws as he could find. He noted only two countries, China and Montenegro, that made no allowance for lunacy as a defence to criminal responsibility. However, in China that was modified by a rule whereby the insane escaped the death penalty and were, for example, imprisoned with fetters instead.

The second development in forensic psychiatry came much later and it has produced a range of specialist services. These services began alongside the nineteenth century enthusiasm for institutions and asylums.

For example, in England, Broadmoor Hospital was opened in 1863. In parallel, there has been an increase in the amount of medical care offered to prisoners. The culmination of this particular trend in Britain was the East Hubert Report of 1939 (East and Hubert, 1939) which, in turn, resulted in Grendon Prison.

In recent years, we have seen a number of significant developments in Britain. There has has been a plethora of official reports—the most important being the Butler Report of 1975 (Home Office and DHSS, 1975). There has also been the development of what was called by a World Health Organisation (WHO) seminar on forensic psychiatry in 1975 the 'new forensic psychiatry with less emphasis on diagnosis and more on treatment' with particular attention being given to community treatment, primary prevention and crisis intervention (World Health Organisation, 1977).

Forensic psychiatrists are, then, the inheritors of two different historical themes: an ancient theme which has its roots in the commonsense philosophy of responsibility and insanity, and a much more up to date and somewhat pragmatic theme of providing services for the mentally disordered even though they may be antisocial. Many forensic psychiatrists encompass both aspects of this inheritance in their work, but inevitably some emphasize one aspect more than the other. In some countries, important groups of forensic psychiatrists become ever-increasingly involved with the philosophical and legal issues, some going so far as to regard forensic psychiatry as a branch of law! But this is a view unlikely to be shared by many lawyers. For example, Gerber, an Australian barrister, wrote recently in a textbook of forensic psychiatry:

Looking back over my years of legal practice, I have little doubt that the cross-examination of psychiatrists offered me the greatest forensic challenge. It was a kind of blood sport. English gentlemen like to hunt, shoot or fish, my hobby was catching psychiatrists ... I rarely had any logistic problems in convincing a jury—or even a judge—that the accused was or was not insane, schizophrenic or not schizophrenic, potentially violent or not, the result depending merely which side I was on ... Like police manufacturing evidence, I was not, at times, above using psychiatry for my own ends.

(Gerber, 1984)

INSANITY

An older textbook of forensic psychiatry (Wiley and Stallworthy, 1962) sums up the issue of insanity thus:

Insanity, madness and lunacy are synonymous for an imprecise concept which can only be defined in practical terms and which, while convenient to the lawyer, has little value to the doctor. They also have colloquial meanings far removed from the technical. What amounts in law to insanity for the purpose of a successful defence against a criminal charge has little to do with insanity in medical terminology.

(Wiley and Stallworthy, 1962)

In English common law, insanity had remained undefined for several centuries, but in the nineteenth century when public opinion began to be a force to be reckoned with definitions were demanded. The particular event which precipitated a definition was the McNaughton trial. In 1843, Daniel McNaughton killed the Prime Minister's secretary, but was acquitted with the special verdict of not guilty by reason of insanity. When he was acquitted the public was outraged. *The Times* published this little ditty:

> Ye people of England exult and be glad
> For y're now at the will of the merciless mad.
> Why say ye that but three authorities reign
> Crown, Commons and Lords?
> —You omit the insane.
> They're a privileged class whom no statute controls
> And their murderous charter exists in their souls.
> Do they wish to spill blood they have only to play
> A few pranks—get asylum's a month and a day
> Then Heigh! to escape from the mad doctor's keys
> And to pistol or stab whomsoever they please.
> Now the dog has a human-like wit in creation.
> He resembles most nearly our own generation.
> Then if madmen from murder escape with impunity
> Why deny a poor dog the same noble immunity?
> So if a dog or man bite you beware being nettled
> For crime is no crime—when the mind is unsettled.

(West and Walk, 1971)

It is worth noting in this poem the scorn poured on the concept of mental incapacity as a defence: for crime is no crime when the mind is unsettled.

As a result of the outcry, the Law Lords were asked to explain the criteria on which insanity was based. After three months, they produced answers to the five specific questions that had been put to them and thus produced the rules of insanity which we still know as the McNaughton Rules. The rules state, among other things, that every man is presumed to be sane and to possess a sufficient degree of reason to be responsible for his crimes until the contrary is proved to the satisfaction of the jury and

that to establish a defence on the ground of insanity it must be clearly be proved that, at the time of committing the act, the accused was labouring under such defect of reason, from disease of the mind, as not to know the nature and quality of the act he was doing, or, if he did know it, that he did not know he was doing what was wrong.

(West and Walk, 1977)

In other words, the McNaughton Rules are largely about *knowing*: knowing the nature and quality of the act and knowing that it was wrong. What another person knows is of course a mystery and subjective judgments are made about this using inferences from the defendant's behaviour and from what the defendant says was in his mind at the time. It is apparent nowadays that judges, and juries also, like to know whether one or more doctors think the individual suffers from a mental disorder; equally, it is apparent that such evidence is not sufficient or even necessary evidence. Indeed, the McNaughton Rules do not mention mental disorder. Thus, it is theoretically possible for a jury to decide that someone is insane even though doctors would not call him or her mentally disordered, although this is unlikely. Furthermore, decisions about responsibility are not attached to particular diagnoses or to levels of severity of mental disorder. For example, Peter Sutcliffe (the so-called 'Yorkshire Ripper') was found to be fully responsible and guilty in spite of being severely schizophrenic (Gunn, 1981).

It is conceptually possible for a defendant to be:

1. Mentally normal and insane
2. Mentally disordered and insane
3. Mentally disordered and fully responsible

Medical evidence is therefore not crucial because the decision about responsibility is by laymen (jurors) using perceptions which do not depend exclusively upon medical evidence.

These McNaughton Rules apply to the defence of insanity in any type of case. However, in practice, in England now, they are more often used in murder cases. This seems to be because murder is one of the few crimes in

England which has a mandatory sentence—the death penalty until 1965; now, life imprisonment. A mandatory sentence obviously excludes all court discretion and therefore any debate about moral responsibility, culpability, lesser degrees of liability, or impaired mental capacity, in the sentencing phase of the hearing. The insanity plea is therefore one way round the mandatory sentence. However, it is an unsatisfactory way round because it, too, has a mandatory outcome. Under English law, if you are insane, you go to a mental hospital under indefinite detention—although that is not necessarily a long detention.

DIMINISHED RESPONSIBILITY

To bring in some more discretion and flexibility, English law has developed two other ingenious devices: infanticide and diminished responsibility. Both are also means of circumventing the mandatory sentence, and their increasing use has meant that the defence of insanity is used less and less.

Diminished responsibility was first introduced into Scotland in 1867 (Walker, 1968) as a common law means of reducing the charge of murder—with its then mandatory penalty of death—to culpable homicide. In England, parliamentary abhorrence of the execution of women who had killed their own young children spilled over into the first Infanticide Act of 1922. The effect of this and the subsequent Act of 1938 was to reduce the offence of child killing from murder to manslaughter in those cases where a mother killed her own infant whilst the balance of her mind was disturbed by the birth or subsequent lactation. In effect, criminal responsibility had been diminished although not removed. The woman was not taken away as insane, but convicted of a lesser offence—a lesser offence for which mitigation of her moral responsibility could be heard, and for which every possible sentence became available: from probation and hospital orders to life imprisonment.

Precisely the same principles were introduced for a wider range of killings by the 1957 Homicide Act. This states that:

where a person kills or is party to the killing of another he shall not be convicted of murder if he was suffering from such abnormality of mind as substantially impaired his mental responsibility for his acts and omissions.

'Abnormality of mind' is defined in a Court of Appeal Judgment as 'a state of mind so different from that of ordinary human beings that the reasonable man would term it abnormal'. Note the use here of the civil law concept of the reasonable man. Who is the reasonable man? Certainly not a psychiatrist! In theory, he is the juror, although this is an oversimplification.

In England debates about mental responsibility and insanity are unusual, and largely confined to homicide cases; yet even in these the McNaughton Rules are almost never raised. Most killers with a psychiatric defence try the diminished responsibility route and only sometimes does this lead to oral psychiatric evidence being given in court. If the prosecution and defence agree before the trial that the evidence for diminished responsibility is sufficiently strong, then the judge is invited to accept the plea of guilty of manslaughter. Usually, he does, although he does not have to. In the normal way only when the prosecution psychiatrist says one thing and the defence psychiatrist says another is the matter hammered out in front of a jury for a decision.

This means that in England most of the questions of mental capacity are now dealt with in the sentencing phase. During that phase the doctor is able to argue the connection, as he sees it, between the offending behaviour and any mental disorder. He can further argue for a pure psychiatric disposal, such as a hospital order, or for an element of psychiatric care during another type of sentence such as a probation order or a period of imprisonment. This system reduces the conflict between doctors and lawyers to a very great extent.

RESIDUAL SOURCES OF CONFLICT

However, matters are not always harmonious. A number of cases have produced severe clashes between doctors and lawyers in court and some remarkable results. Smith (Smith, 1981) has outlined a series of important nineteenth century cases where clear evidence of mental illness was ignored or summarily dispatched by judges and where juries determined that particular individuals, especially in highly emotional cases, should not escape punishment no matter what the doctor said. It seems that insanity is a concept which the mind of the public finds difficult to separate from wickedness, and that part of the problem is that insanity is accepted as a medical concept *provided* it does not cause bad, violent or dangerous behaviour; if it does, then it becomes wickedness. The outcry mentioned earlier relating to McNaughton's acquittal may well be attributable to this confusion.

In 1979, Lord Justice Lawton said: 'We cannot stress too strongly that these cases of homicide are to be tried by judges and juries and not by psychiatrists' (*R v Robinson*), and in 1980 the Sutcliffe case reminded psychiatrists of some political realities. The facts are that a seriously psychotic man, who could probably have fulfilled the English criteria for being unfit to plead and who did not know that what he was doing was wrong, was found guilty of murder by a jury after a most extraordinary trial. The defence decided that in the emotional climate the safest course was to argue for diminished responsibility. Not a difficult task in ordinary circumstances because all the doctors who had ever seen this man agreed about his florid psychosis. Nevertheless, the judge exercised his right to put this matter to the jury—even though nobody could find conflicting medical evidence. The prosecution spent several days arguing with psychiatrists about the diagnostic criteria of schizophrenia.

The most important medical matter to be discussed was the issue of malingering, but the level of debate on this point was not very high. The jury, in the midst of a storm of publicity, found Peter Sutcliffe guilty of murder 13 times, although the verdict was not unanimous. How is it that from time to time the legal system produces such apparent anomalies?

There are probably four reasons.

1. The laws relating to insanity have little to do with science or medicine. The legal concept of insanity is determined not by doctors but by judges and juries. Insanity is what the layman says it is. Psychiatrists did not invent insanity, and they are not allowed to define it. Most importantly, but hardest of all for psychiatrists to swallow, neither schizophrenia nor any other mental illness equals insanity. Schizophrenia is a medical concept, insanity is a legal one, they overlap, interact, but that is all. Wing (1978) summarizes the conceptual dichotomy neatly in his book *Reasoning About Madness*:

> . . . the term 'illness' can have two quite distinct connotations. In one usage, someone is regarded as sick (or regards himself or herself as sick), because of some experience or behaviour that departs from a standard of health generally accepted in that community. Such standards vary widely. . . . In the second usage, . . . 'disease', a limited and relatively specific theory about some aspect of mental or bodily functioning is put forward because it is thought to be relevant to the reduction of some recognisable impairment . . . these two usages represent two different types of theory . . . The term 'madness' should be used only in the first of these two ways. It is a lay term, covering a wide range of experiences and behaviours; from wit to delusion, mild foolishness to total senility.
>
> (Wing, 1978)

2. Lay jurymen: may still believe that 'not guilty by reason of insanity'— or even a diminished responsibility verdict—amounts to a let-off freeing the accused to continue with his dangerous activities.
3. Semantic confusion exists about wickedness and insanity which are sometimes thought to be mutually exclusive and sometimes synonymous. The faulty reasoning may be along these lines: If terrible deeds are carried out they are clearly 'bad', or 'wicked', or 'evil'. Yet if they are bad they cannot be mad; if the deeds are not mad they cannot originate from mental disorder!
4. It may be that on these occasions, the layman falls back on to a concrete view of *mens rea*—namely he falls back on to a simple notion of intent

uncluttered by psychiatric arguments. The layman simply asks himself: Did the accused intend to carry out the murder? Did he plan it? Mr Sutcliffe, for example, carefully planned all his killings for excellent psychotic reasons: he is, therefore, an intentional murderer in the ordinary sense of the word.

The press commentaries on the verdict are illuminating. The morning after the trial *The Times* commented [my emphases]:

Did the Attorney General show a sound instinct at the outset when he offered to accept a plea of diminished responsibility? . . . there would have been considerable saving in public money and much that was harrowing and repulsive in the evidence need never have been publicised . . . In addition, Mrs Sutcliffe, an innocent party who has been seriously ill, would have been spared the worst of an ordeal that can scarcely be imagined. The Attorney General was wrong. He would have been wrong even if the jury had found that Sutcliffe was mad. The whole course of the trial showed that the question of his sanity could not be left to the professionals. *No responsible doctor could have declared on oath his absolute certainty that this secretive and crafty man was not pretending to be mad.* Even though the question did not materially affect his own fate, there is more at stake in a trial of this exceptional character than the fate of the prisoner . . . From a common sense point of view, it is pure nonsense even to ask whether Sutcliffe was sane. *It is . . . an abuse of language to apply the term 'normal' to a person who committed violent murders for years on end for no tangible gain* . . . The poor showing of the psychiatrists in the witness box is less evidence of incompetence than the fact that in these remote areas of psychology, ordinary criteria simply do not apply. The verdict satisfies a symbolic wish for retribution.

(*The Times*, 23 May 1981)

The *Daily Mail* was more succinct:

There will be widespread satisfaction at the jury's majority verdict that Peter Sutcliffe, the Yorkshire Ripper, was found guilty on all counts . . . The judge . . . deserves congratulation for the way he resisted the deal which the Attorney General was prepared to accept of manslaughter on grounds of diminished responsibility.

(*The Daily Mail*, 23 May 1981)

Henry Russell Douglas, in the *News of the World* was the most candid:

At the end of it all, the question for the jury was stark and simple. Was Peter Sutcliffe bad and mad? Or was he just bad? . . . Only the courage of Mr Justice Boreham prevented the cosy little arrangement by which the monster Sutcliffe would have been cocooned away for a time as crazy: mad rather than bad . . . Cynical, calculating, he (Peter Sutcliffe) told his wife 'If I can make him believe I'm mad, I'll only get ten years in a loony bin'. He may well have been right. And had that happened, and had he been freed and killed again, it would not have been the first premature 'cure' of a murderous lunatic.

(News of the World, 24 May 1981)

When the trial was over, it became possible under the English Mental Health Act, 1983, to transfer Mr Sutcliffe from prison—where he was untreated because of his lack of insight and consequent refusal of medication,—to hospital to a maximum security special hospital. Several doctors, including psychiatrists, recommended this course of action, although for two years the Home Secretary ruled that it was in the public interest to leave this man untreated in prison.

Fortunately, we do not have many Peter Sutcliffe trials, but his case illustrates all too clearly how medical time and manpower can be consumed in futile argument. The battle in court, which, here, the psychiatrists clearly lost, is of small moment, for the outcome is the same: Mr Sutcliffe is in a secure psychiatric hospital where he should be. If justice has been better done to the wretched victims of this terrible psychosis by convicting Mr Sutcliffe of murder rather than of manslaughter then so be it. On the other hand, it is equally valid to argue that the expenditure of large amounts of precious forensic psychiatry resource was not worthwhile in this case. Lawyers would have been quite capable of arguing about the question of justice all on their own. They are trained to do that, they do it anyway and will probably always do it.

HUSBANDING RESOURCES

The issue of the husbanding of resources leads to the proposition that the psychiatrist should leave the trial and direct most of the scarce psychiatric resources available toward treatment and management. But does this also mean that the psychiatrist should quit the courtroom completely? No, for the argument is about the role of the psychiatrist in respect of questions of responsibility in court. A minimal role may need to be retained (for example, in diminished responsibility trials) by the presentation of a medical report stating whether or not the defendant has a mental disorder, the nature of the disorder, and how it might manifest itself. Written evidence is not acceptable in the trial phase, but for this purpose it could be given by sworn affadavit. In the sentencing phase the psychiatrist has a much more relevant role and can usefully present detailed reports with clear, practical recommendations about disposal. Ideally, of course, the main psychiatric evidence about sentencing should come from the psychiatrist who is proposing to supervise or treat a particular patient, or who has the facilities to treat but is declining to do so.

The psychiatrist could leave the trial phase almost entirely if all mandatory sentences were abolished. The mandatory life sentence for murder is the only reason that British psychiatrists are still called to murder trials. Without a mandatory sentence psychiatric evidence could be confined to the sentencing phase for mitigation in a such a trial—just as it is in all other cases.

In these days of serious scarcity of resources in the public sector, practitioners must be extremely careful about the way they spend their time. Psychiatric utilitarianism may be going too far, but forensic psychiatrists do have to think of ways of maximizing the assistance they can give to patients. They have to try and undertake tasks that will help the greatest number of patients for any given level of resource input. In any other type of enterprise, this would probably be called high productivity.

CAPITAL PUNISHMENT

It has to be acknowledged, however, that it would be extremely difficult to pursue the forgoing argument were the death penalty still a real possibility in Britain. As long ago as 1874, Henry Maudsley said: 'Abolish capital punishment and the dispute between lawyers and doctors ceases to be of practical importance'. There is no doubt that when a successful psychiatric defence can make a difference between life and death then the pressures on psychiatry during the trial are enormous, and unreasonable.

The role of psychiatry in mitigating capital punishment was highlighted in a television programme on the Bianchi case in America. A serial murderer who had tortured, raped and killed his young female victims was finally caught. He denied all knowledge of the offences but under hypnosis he produced another personality with a different name who knew all about the killings including the fact that some were committed together with his cousin. Several psychiatrists and psychologists turned up to argue the pros and cons of a diagnosis of multiple personality. Some were confident that such a disorder is a truly separate category of illness and that its presence clearly constitutes evidence for insanity. Others were more sceptical and with time began to penetrate the histrionic facade. It came away completely when a plea bargain was struck, such that if the offender testified against his accomplice, the death penalty would not be pursued. After that, the defendant walked into court to plead guilty. The judge said that psychiatrists had nearly perverted the course of justice! What the judge had forgotten, or failed to notice, was that psychiatrists do not control the legal drama, nor do they write its rules.

A disconcerting feature of the programme was that the general impression given was that if the defendant did not suffer from multiple personality, then he was normal. There were mutterings about him being a sexual psychopath, but none of the psychiatrists seemed interested in how this man came to be a sadist, nor did we see any advice given to the court about disposal and management.

Psychiatry is closely involved with capital punishment cases for perhaps two reasons. First, there is a view that every effort must be made to exclude mental abnormality on the basis that it would be immoral to execute an unhealthy man—even though it is not immediately obvious why it is acceptable to execute a healthy man and save a sick one! Second, and perhaps more important, is an unexpressed desire to use psychiatry to provide an excuse for circumventing the death penalty: the implication of some referrals for assessment just prior to a capital sentence is: 'Please find an abnormality that will enable us to reprieve this man/woman', or, worse: 'Please join with us and sanitize this killing'.

Does the intervention of psychiatry between court and executioner really make sure that sick people are not killed? No. Lewis *et al.* (1986) looked at 15 death row inmates (13 men and 2 women) in five different US states. Of the 15, 13 had exhausted all avenues of appeal and all 15 were close to death. Obviously none of them had been found not-guilty by reason of insanity, or even guilty-but-insane. In clinical terms, however, they all had significant pathology: one patient had auditory hallucinations and believed that Christ made him commit the murder, another felt controlled by outside forces, yet another thought his victim was trying to poison him, and so on; two patients had a history of seizures, more than half of them showed neurological abnormalities on examination or computed tomography (CT) scan of the brain. The authors speculated as to why it should be that so many serious disorders were not identified in the prisoners' trials. They discovered that most of the subjects did not consider themselves sick and did not request specialized evaluations. One said he did not think his symptoms of blackouts were relevant. A woman had evidence of a childhood head injury which she had never spoken about: 'It's so ugly, I try to hide it' she said. In one case, the defence lawyer did not obtain a medical examination because the neurologist for the prosecution found 'no evidence of organic impairment'. Yet the prisoner actually had complex partial seizures, xanthochromic cerebrospinal fluid, abnormal brain waves on electroencephalogram (EEG), and atrophy of the frontal lobes. The authors do not tell us anything about the socioeconomic or ethnic background of the prisoners, but it would not be surprising if on such social parameters these condemned differed from others charged with murder but escaping the death penalty.

The Lewis study shows very clearly that even when the death penalty is in operation, forensic psychiatry does not necessarily protect the defendant: sick people are still found guilty and executed. In these circumstances two important strategies for forensic psychiatry are first vigorously campaign for the abolition of the death penalty, and second, refusal to participate in court proceedings leading up to a death sentence.

OTHER APPROACHES

In an attempt to moderate potential clashes between psychiatrists and lawyers over mentally disordered people, a very few common law jurisdictions have opted for a verdict of: 'Guilty but mentally ill'. This has some advantages and even some sense, but still it is argued out in the trial phase in front of a jury as a means of avoiding a mandatory sentence.

A more radical approach was suggested some years ago by the English lawyer, Glanville Williams (1954). Williams was profoundly disturbed by the amateurness of the insanity enquiry and he proposed to replace the system by a panel of doctors and a pre-trial judicial inquiry. Two of the panel would examine all serious offenders at the time they are charged. If the defence intended to raise a psychiatric argument then three experts should do the examination and report directly to the judge, who would then decide on the question of insanity (or whatever), in the absence of the jury, and without necessarily following the McNaughton Rules.

To find a common law system which even approaches this radical proposal necessitates a visit to Queensland, Australia. There, the Australians have devised a Mental Health Tribunal which sits outside, and largely in advance of, the criminal hearing in an attempt to remove most of the mentally abnormal from the court process altogether. A Mental Health Tribunal has been set up, consisting of a judge of the Supreme Court advised by two psychiatrists. There are also several patient review tribunals consisting of a district court judge, also advised by two psychiatrists. Any person charged with an indictable offence and awaiting commital who is thought to need psychiatric treatment can be referred to the Tribunal. In practice, referral comes from a number of sources— doctors, lawyers and prisons. The Tribunal may determine three separate matters: that the person was of unsound mind at the time of the alleged offence; in the case of murder, that the person was not of unsound mind but was suffering from diminished responsibility; that the person was not of unsound mind but is not fit for trial. Where the opinion is that the medical facts in regard to either the first or the second disposal are in dispute, the person's fitness for trial must be determined in court.

During the course of any trial, the proceedings can be stopped and a patient sent to the Tribunal if this is thought to be appropriate. Tribunal decisions can be appealed against in the Court of Criminal Appeal. These procedures were deliberately designed to reduce the amount of adversarial conflict in the giving of psychiatric evidence and to shift forensic psychiatry into a more inquisitorial setting.

BUTLER PROPOSALS

As already indicated, the main stumbling block for murder trials in Britain is the mandatory sentence. Without it, murder cases could be dealt with much like other serious cases, where medical evidence is largely confined to the sentencing phase of the hearing after the determination of guilt by the court using non-medical criteria. In its comprehensive review of British forensic psychiatry, the Butler Committee (Home Office and DHSS, 1975) proposed that the verdict of diminished responsibility and the mandatory life sentence be abolished. As they pointed out, the two matters are entirely linked because the 1957 Homicide Act, which introduced diminished responsibility, was largely a device for circumventing the mandatory sentence for murder (being the death penalty at that time). The Butler Committee examined the arguments against abolition—the main one being that, in effect, it would merge the offences of murder and manslaughter creating one offence. They pointed out that public opinion, allegedly, would be strongly against such a merger because it would remove the special stigma attaching to a conviction for murder. The Committee countered with the view that it would still be possible to continue with murder and manslaughter as separate offences, and it might even be possible to differentiate the penalties for the two by making murder punishable with a discretionary life sentence, whereas manslaughter could carry other sentences.

The Butler Committee did not content themselves with the simple recommendation of abolishing the mandatory sentence for murder. They went on to discuss the concept of insanity and the McNaughton Rules. This is perhaps surprising because at the moment these Rules are only used about half a dozen times a year in the whole country and it seems highly likely that if the mandatory life sentence for murder were abolished then their use would wither even further. The problem is that it seems unjust ultimately that a severely mentally ill person—someone whom doctor and layman alike would regard as 'not responsible'—should be convicted of a serious crime. On the other hand, such scruples are only rarely expressed. To deal with these few cases, the Butler Committee proposed a complex, revised special verdict in which the current 'not-guilty by reason of insanity' should be replaced by a new verdict of 'not-guilty on evidence of mental disorder'. They were particularly keen to drop the McNaughton 'knowledge of wrong' test. They also wanted statutory exemption from punishment for defendants, who, although they were suffering from severe mental disorder at the time of the act or omission charged, did not come within the compass of the new special verdict because they were able to form intentions and carry them out. But all this amounts to rather complex law for dealing with a small problem—which would, anyway, wither further if their proposal to abolish the mandatory sentence were adopted.

In all their deliberations, the Butler Committee experts seem to have overlooked a mechanism which is already available to courts. The law would need very little alteration in order to make provision for the two or three cases a year which they are concerned about. Under the English 1959 and 1983 Mental Health Acts there is a special provision, (Section 37(3)

MHA, 1983), which states that where a person is charged before a magistrates' court with something which could lead to a conviction and be followed by a hospital order because he is mentally ill or severely mentally impaired then, 'if the court is satisfied that the accused did the act or made the omission charged, the court may, if it thinks fit, make such an order without convicting him'. This is a neat device used by magistrates' courts to make sure that the mentally ill or severely mentally impaired individual who has been proved to have committed a criminal offence is in fact sent to hospital without the stigma of a conviction. All that is required is for the power to be extended into the Crown court and poor old Daniel McNaughton would be left in peace.

ACTUS REUS

Most of this chapter has been concerned with the issue of the guilty mind or *mens rea*; some consideration should also be given to the issue of whether or not the accused person actually committed the act or omission charged.

Most practitioners are aware of the dangers of finding someone 'unfit to plead'. For, under the 1964 Criminal Procedure (Insanity) Act that, too, has a mandatory disposal and individuals can be sent to hospital for indefinite periods without testing the question of who actually carried out the killing, rape, arson, or whatever. Here, the best safeguards against error would be to introduce the arrangements proposed by the Butler Committee. These, in brief, would allow the judge discretion to postpone the trial for six months. If disability was still an issue after this time then the judge would be allowed to determine the question (unless the defence objected), and to have a trial of the facts in every case to determine whether there is evidence beyond a reasonable doubt that the defendant actually did what he is charged with having done. It would also help if the issue of mandatory disposal was discarded, thus allowing the judge to exercise discretion about placement after hearing medical and other evidence.

Even more worrying is the issue of confessions. This is an area where psychologists and psychiatrists may have an increasing rather than a diminishing role to play—a role which may even be carried into the trial. The responsibilities lie not only in dealing with mental issues but also with the central question of facts, which are so important to establish; this comes before all the esoteric niceties relating to intentions and guilty minds.

Many trials and convictions turn entirely on a confession. At first glance, this may seem reasonable for who would say they had done something if they had not? But, strangely, the answer is, many. The list includes people who do not understand what they are saying because of mental handicap, mental illness, or even intoxication; those with a neurotic drive to confess because of intense guilt feelings related to something entirely different, or to a mental disorder, such as depression; those who are drawing attention to unrelated neurotic problems by dramatic means; those who are highly suggestible and succumb to leading questions; those who are under great duress (for example, captivity in a police station); and those who gradually lose their resolve to stick to the facts and acquiesce to a false description in the hope of ending the ordeal of interrogation. In a study conducted for the Royal Commission on Criminal Procedures, Irving (1980) estimated that less than half of police suspects have a normal mental state at interview. The judgments of the suspects' mental states in 60 witnessed cases are shown in Table 2.1.

One important effect of that Royal Commission has been the 1984 Police and Criminal Evidence Act. This came into force in 1986 and gives force of law to the Judge's Rule that anyone who is thought to be mentally ill or mentally handicapped must have an appropriate adult with him or her during any interview. An appropriate adult may be a relative, but others are eligible, including psychiatrists.

The role of the psychologist and of the psychiatrists in respect of suggestibility and duress during interrogation has been reviewed by Gudjonsson and MacKeith (1982). The special problems posed by mental illness at the time of interrogation are, however, not well documented. Theoretically, the police should exercise discretion and in some cases drop charges. The new Crown Prosecution Service should also exercise discretion in some cases, and some should be dealt with in court as unfit to plead.

Nevertheless, there is a potential medicolegal conflict which needs attention. A case may illustrate:

A professional man of good character suffers from recurrent mania. He travelled to the West Country to visit a friend. When he arrived he was in the throes of another manic episode. He behaved wildly, staying up all

Table 2.1   The mental state of interviewees*

	No	%
Affected by drink or drugs	11	18
Mentally handicapped	1	2
Mentally ill	5	8
Frightened	8	13
Withdrawn	5	8
Aggressive	7	12
Friendly	9	15
Nothing noted	14	23
Total	60	100

*This table is taken from the Royal Commission on Criminal Procedure Research Studies No 2 (Irving, 1980).

night, rushing in and out of nightclubs, accusing someone of making homosexual advances and generally being a nuisance. That night six fires were set, two in clubs where he had visited. His strange behaviour was noted and he was arrested and questioned. No one could have had any doubt that he was mentally abnormal. A priest was called to be present during the interview. The defendant recalls being in the presence of the Holy Trinity (three policemen) in order to interrogate the priest about his faith and his rectitude. In reality he was asked the questions

Q 'Did you start the fire?'

A 'Yes'

Q 'How did you start the fire?'

A 'Because I am a saint. Well I went in with a cigarette and a flaming torch . . . It was the light of the world. The torch of Jesus Christ.'

There are pages of transcript like this. The defendant was charged with six counts or arson.

Later the defendant was examined by a psychiatrist who took the view that the defendant was 1. mentally ill at the material time, 2. had started the fires, and 3. would therefore be likely to end up in a special hospital on a restriction order. Still in an abnormal mental state, the defendant was reluctant to have medical evidence called at his trial. The defence, therefore decided to let the trial proceed without medical evidence, the defence argument being that the confession (which was never signed) was manifestly unreliable. In the trial, the defendant tried to explain to the jury that he suffered from manic depressive psychosis, but this was discounted on the grounds that it is hearsay evidence, the defendant not being an expert. No corroborative evidence was brought to court, everything depended upon the confession and upon whether or not the jury believed it. They had difficulty in making up their minds. After four and a half hours of deliberation they returned not-guilty verdicts on three counts and guilty verdicts (by a majority of 11 to 1) on three counts.

Before passing sentence, the judge insisted on a psychiatric report. The new psychiatrist was somewhat aghast at what he found and clearly upset both the judge and the defence counsel by stating in his report that the patient 'appears to be convicted solely on his admissions made when psychiatrically ill without any psychiatric evidence being heard during the course of the trial'. He went on to say that he thought the patient 'would probably have been acquitted had psychiatric evidence been heard as part of his trial'. The judge said he found this 'a little worrying' in the sense that if he made a hospital order 'it looks as though the defendant will be in the care of somebody . . . who is really saying the verdicts of the jury are wrong ones'. To deal with this the defence counsel rose to tell the judge that he had ticked off the psychiatrist for saying such naughty things. The judge went on to make a hospital order but he also added a restriction order.

The patient steadfastly protested his innocence—the more so as his mental state improved. Ten months later, a Mental Health Review

Tribunal released him from hospital. Slowly he pieced his life together, and sought new legal advice. A number of psychiatric opinions were obtained on the nature, quality, and reliability of the interview recorded by the police on which he was convicted. All said much the same thing: the interview gives a splendid account of manic speech; it cannot be relied upon because manics are distractible, suggestible, acquiescent, largely inattentive to content. Armed with this new data, a new defence team was granted leave to appeal out of time. It took four years for the appeal to be heard. Heard is hardly the word, however, for the patient's counsel was stopped early in his submission by the chairman of the bench pointing out that there was no affadavit from the previous defence lawyers explaining why they had chosen not to submit psychiatric evidence at the trial. The defendant and his mother were in court but were not called to give evidence on this point which proved crucial. Law books innumerable were consulted, jargon flew, heads were shaken, but in the end it came down to the fact that psychiatric evidence on the confession interview could have been available at the time of the trial, therefore it must have been deliberately excluded. As it was a leading counsel who defended the patient, the psychiatric option must have been excluded for good reason, therefore, it cannot be re-entered at the appeal stage—that would be to 'have two bites at the cherry'. The judgment quoted a 1969 warning in which it was said that 'public mischief would ensue and legal process could become indefinitely prolonged were it the case that evidence produced at any time will generally be admitted by this court when verdicts are being reviewed . . . there must be some curbs' (Stafford and Luvaglio 1969, 53, CrimApp R.1,3). It concluded: '. . . we do not think that in the absence of any sort of misconduct on the part of the defence team we should readily interfere in a case now four years old when the jury had the opportunity of seeing and hearing and making their own assessment of this appellant in the witness box and also, of course, had before it the police evidence as to his behaviour during the course of the interrogation'. The appeal was therefore dismissed; evidence from two psychiatrists and one psychologist was not called. The defence was advised that its best course of action was to ask the Home Secretary to refer the case to the Court of Appeal.

Presumably, 'public mischief' has been prevented by the court failing to re-examine this case. That is obviously a matter on which opinions will divide. What is clearer is that at no point was the husbanding of resources given any consideration. The mounting of a full-scale appeal with expert and other witnesses coming from all over the country is an expensive business. The psychiatrists and lawyers involved in the case could have spent their day (and the time on preparation) more profitably, and surely they should either have been allowed to put the arguments, or told at a much earlier stage that the defendant was not going to be allowed a chance to put his case in a rational state of mind.

The lessons from this case pertain to both legal and psychiatric professions. In legal terms, it is clear that the new rules in the 1984 Police and Criminal Evidence Act are very important. (This case was first heard before they came into force.) Judges should have power to order expert examination of evidence, even if the defence declines to do this. The Court of Appeal should have much greater flexibility in its ability and willingness to review important issues.

The lessons of this case for the psychiatrist are several. For the moment, like it or not, psychiatrists increasingly may be asked questions about the veracity of confessions. For this reason it is important to withhold any advice about disposal until everybody, especially the defence, is satisfied that the man or woman to be sentenced is actually the person who committed the alleged offence. Further, when dealing with courts, evidence should be confined to specific issues. In the case quoted above, raising the spectre of a special hospital and a restriction order seems to have panicked the defence. Raising doubts about the veracity of the convictions after the trial upset the lawyers. In a paradoxical way, this case also reinforces the earlier point that it may be better for psychiatrists to stay out of the court room. At the Court of Appeal the psychiatrists were plainly rank outsiders to the legal process even though matters of mental illness were involved. To recap: 'these cases . . . are to be tried by judges and juries and not by psychiatrists', that is a political reality, a reality which should be accepted by everyone. A further political reality is that resources are limited and dwindling: British public services are impoverished, this means that uncomfortable decisions about priorities have to be made.

CONCLUSION

The role of the psychiatrist in the court is not always satisfactory. It would be quite wrong to exaggerate, however. The unsatisfactoriness is confined to a minority of cases—those cases where passions are raised. However, improvements which would benefit society, patients, and professionals alike could be effected without much radicalism. Changes needed come in two categories: changes to the law, changes to attitudes.

The following points highlight the legal changes that cover most of the issues mentioned in this chapter.

- The mandatory sentence for murder should be abolished.
- Higher courts should have the same power as lower courts to try a suspect in respect of the facts of a case and then, when properly recommended, be able to send him or her to hospital without recording a conviction.
- Crown courts should also be obliged to try the facts of the case in respect of suspects where it is considered that they are unfit to plead, before the suspect is sent to hospital.
- The mandatory disposal following a finding of unfitness to plead should be removed, thus giving judicial discretion as to disposal.

- The Court of Appeal should be more flexible to allow the presentation of relevant new evidence to a case, and thus acknowledge that defence counsels, even leading ones, can make errors of judgment about the presentation of evidence.

Changes in attitudes, equally desirable, are more difficult to list. The main changes seem to be required of psychiatrists. Psychiatrists need to understand more clearly the politics of the court system and not puff themselves with the belief that it is only they who can judge matters of insanity and responsibility—matters which are also philosophical questions for lawyers and laymen. Psychiatrists should educate themselves more fully in matters of philosophy. They should also be clearer about their role in society, the realities of their power, and the priorities of serving patients. Tempting legal wrangles, especially those where publicity is involved, should be eschewed wherever possible.

Forensic psychiatry education should not only take note of medicolegal politics. It should also take note of current NHS resource realities and teach doctors how best to deploy their time and effort to assist the greatest number of patients to the best possible advantage.

Finally, and perhaps most importantly, there needs to be better mutual education between law and psychiatry and more frequent opportunities for informal exchanging of views.

REFERENCES

East W. N., Hubert W. H. de B (1939). *The Psychological Treatment of Crime*. London: HMSO.

Eigen J. P. (1986). Intentionality and insanity: what the eighteenth-century juror heard. In *The Anatomy of Madness*: Vol. II: *Institutions and Society* (Bynum W. F., Poster R., Shepherd M., eds). London: Tavistock.

Gerber P. (1984). Psychiatry in the dock—a lawyer's afterthoughts. In *Mentally Abnormal Offenders* (Croft M., Croft A., eds). London: Ballière Tindall.

Gudjonsson G. H., MacKeith J. A. C. (1982). False confessions. Psychological effects of interrogation. In *Reconstructing the Past* (Trankell A., ed). Stockholm: Nersteat & Sons.

Gunn J. (1981). Questions of responsibility and the Sutcliffe case. *Poly Law Review* 66–70.

Home Office and DHSS (1974). *Interim Report of the Committee on Mentally Abnormal Offenders* Cmnd 5698. London: HMSO.

Home Office and DHSS (1975). *Report of the Committee on Mentally Abnormal Offenders* Cmnd 6244. London: HMSO.

Irving B. (1980). *Police Interrogation: the Psychological Approach. Royal Commission of Criminal Procedure Research Study No. 2*. London: HMSO.

Lewis D. O., Pincus J. H., Feldman M., Jackson L., Bard B. (1986). Psychiatric, neurological and psychoeducational characteristics of 15 death row inmates in the United States. *American Journal of Psychiatry*, **143**, 838–45.

Maudsley H. (1874). *Responsibility in Mental Disease*. London: King.

Owen D. (1988). *Our NHS*. London: Pan.

Oppenheimer H. (1909). *Criminal Responsibility of Lunatics, A Study in Comparative Law*. London: Sweet & Maxwell.

Smith R. (1981). *Trial by Medicine*. Edinburgh: Edinburgh University Press.

Walker N. (1968). *Crime and Insanity in England*. Vol. 1: *The Historical Perspective*. Edinburgh: Edinburgh University Press.

Walker N. (1985). The insanity defence before 1800. In *Annals of the American Academy of Political and Social Science—The Insanity Defence* (Moran R., ed). Beverely Hills: Sage.

West D. J., Walk, A. (1977). *Daniel McNaughton: His Trial and the Aftermath*. London: Gaskell Books.

Williams G. (1954). The Royal Commission and the defence of insanity. *Current Legal Problems* 16–32.

Wily H. J., Stallworthy K. R. (1962). *Mental Abnormality and the Law*. Christchurch, NZ: Peryer.

Wing J. K. (1978). *Reasoning about Madness*. Oxford: Oxford University Press.

World Health Organisation (1977). *Forensic Psychiatry—Report of a Working Group*. Copenhagen: WHO, Regional Office for Europe.

CASES

R. *v.* Robinson [1979]—1 Cr.App.R.(S) 109.

R. *v.* Stafford & Luraglio [1969]—53Cr.App.R. 1,3.

3 The mentally disordered offender in the criminal process: some research and policy questions

ADRIAN GROUNDS

BACKGROUND

The problems currently faced by courts in dealing with mentally disordered offenders need to be seen against the background of historical changes in 1. penological thinking and practice, and 2. the philosophy and organization of psychiatric services.

Garland (1985), in his impressive survey, traces the transformation that began to occur at the turn of this century from the Victorian system of penal sanctions, which provided a limited range of legal punishments with prison having a central role, to the modern 'penal-welfare complex' in which courts have an extended range of dispositions, and reform and control of the individual become of central importance. However, the 'post-rehabilitative era' of recent decades has been characterized by a decline in the idea of reforming offenders through the penal process, and the goal of rehabilitation as an aim of sentencing has been criticized on grounds of ineffectiveness and injustice. This change raises possibilities of conflict between medical and penal perspectives (Chiswick et al., 1984), and highlights the contrast in current approaches and statutory frameworks for the sentencing of mentally disordered and normal offenders.

Changes in the philosophy and organization of psychiatric services during recent decades have been associated with a continuing decline in the number of hospital beds, from 150 000 in 1954 to 110 000 in 1971 (Bransby, 1974). Between 1971 and 1986 the number of occupied beds fell by a further 37 per cent in mental illness hospitals and units, and by 35 per cent in mental handicap hospitals and units (Central Statistical Office, 1988). Many traditional mental hospitals are being replaced by district general hospital units and community based services. Bowden (1975) demonstrated that reductions in the number of psychiatric beds and the loss of closed wards lead to fewer admissions of mentally disordered offenders under the Mental Health Act, and Coid (1988) reported that consultants from district general hospital units are less likely to accept mentally ill remanded prisoners than consultants from older mental hospitals. Thus, offending behaviour, particularly violence, can lead to exclusion from psychiatric care.

These various changes have contributed to a conflict between the expectations of the courts and the realities of psychiatric practice. As Chiswick *et al.* (1984) point out:

> Psychiatric thinking in the 1960s was that not only could advice be given to the criminal justice system about offenders with mental problems, but also that a solution could be given: psychiatrists took a wide view of their remit and would accept the alcoholic, the sex offender, the personality-disordered who 'belonged' to medicine rather than to criminal justice. Now things are out of step. The criminal justice system has come to accept the wider view of the offender's responsibility and seeks to make the psychiatrist accept the responsibility for that offender's care. But since then psychiatry itself has changed. Mental hospitals now seek to provide treatment and cure rather than containment, and many of the problem offenders are no longer considered as being treatable.
>
> (Chiswick *et al.*, 1984, p. 97)

The problem of the mentally abnormal offender in court should not be considered simply as one of disposal. Underlying the present difficulties are complex and conflicting sets of attitudes and expectations, together with unresolved questions about the aims of sentencing in the criminal justice system. Furthermore, the simple view that in principle all those who are mentally disordered ought to be diverted from the criminal justice system into psychiatric care in the health service is both impracticable and fails to take into account the heterogeneity of psychiatric conditions and clinical needs. It is an aspiration with a long history of failure. The policy question cannot be framed as: 'How can we achieve the diversion of the mentally disordered from the criminal justice system?', rather, the questions are 'What kinds of mentally disordered offender should be diverted?' 'Under what circumstances?' 'At what stage in the criminal process?' 'Within what legal framework?' 'To what provision?' and, crucially, 'What should be done to meet the needs of those who are not diverted and remain either in the penal system or are simply released back to the community?' With these questions in mind, a selective examination will be made of issues arising at different stages of the criminal process. The approach taken will be deliberately sceptical rather than even-handed—in the hope of provoking controversy.

THE CRIMINAL JUSTICE PROCESS

Overview

A schematic outline of some of the ways of dealing with mentally disordered offenders is given in Figure 3.1 together with statistics relating to their use in 1985 (Home Office, 1985; 1986a; 1986b; 1988).

Prior to criminal proceedings

The question of whether mentally disordered people are more likely than others to commit criminal offences is unanswered. Whether the 'dark figure' of unreported crime is proportionately greater for the mentally

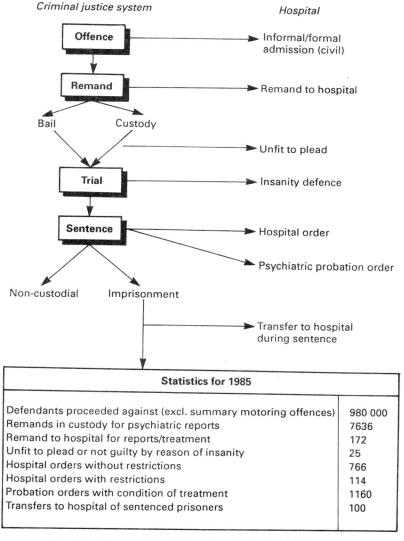

Statistics for 1985	
Defendants proceeded against (excl. summary motoring offences)	980 000
Remands in custody for psychiatric reports	7636
Remand to hospital for reports/treatment	172
Unfit to plead or not guilty by reason of insanity	25
Hospital orders without restrictions	766
Hospital orders with restrictions	114
Probation orders with condition of treatment	1160
Transfers to hospital of sentenced prisoners	100

Fig. 3.1 *The mentally disordered in the criminal justice system*

disordered is a matter for speculation. Little is known and there is a need for research on police contacts and decision-making concerning mentally disordered offenders who come to their attention. The police have discretion to seek a psychiatric opinion, and it is not known how many mentally disordered individuals enter criminal proceedings because prior attempts to obtain hospital admission have failed.

It is probable that the decision to prosecute is affected by the presence of recognized mental disorder. Mental health is a matter which may be taken into account by Crown Prosecutors in deciding whether a prosecution is in the public interest, and there may be a higher threshold, in terms of gravity of offence, for deciding to initiate proceedings in some cases involving mentally disordered people. There is a large gap in research knowledge of this area. Little is known about what happens to mentally disordered offenders who do not enter criminal proceedings, and these gaps need to be filled if a complete picture is to be obtained. Such research might also indicate whether more mentally disordered offenders could, or should, be diverted away from criminal proceedings.

Pretrial stage

About 1 per cent of those proceeded against in the criminal courts (excluding cases of summary motoring offences) are remanded in prison custody for medical reports. The 1983 Mental Health Act introduced new powers for courts to remand mentally disordered defendants to hospital as an alternative to prison. Defendants with any category of mental disorder could be remanded for a report (Section 35), and the mentally ill and severely mentally impaired could be remanded for treatment (Section 36). A further provision, the interim hospital order (Section 38), became available for cases where the court considered a hospital order might be an appropriate eventual disposal. The provisions came into operation in October 1984, and were preceded by a ministerial statement that the new arrangements were becoming available because the government believed:

... the mentally ill should be treated in hospital, wherever possible, and they did not wish the courts to have to send sick people to prison.

(*Hansard*, Written Answer, 23 October 1984)

Within the prison medical service there was a similar hope that the new powers would achieve a significant reduction in the number of mentally disordered people held in prison on remand. To what extent has this hope been realized?

As the above figures show, during the first calendar year of operation (1985) the contribution made by this new legal avenue for psychiatric remands was numerically small, although the new powers may have contributed to a small but significant shift towards the NHS as the source of reports for hospital orders (Grounds, 1988). The underuse of the provisions following their introduction was noted by the House of Commons Social Services Committee (1986), the Interdepartmental Working Party on Mentally Disturbed Offenders in the Prison System (1987), and the Mental Health Act Commission (1987), whose own research suggested that cases suitable for hospital are being unnecessarily remanded in custody. As I have previously noted:

Clearly, no conclusions can be drawn about the likely future use of these provisions on the basis of the first year's figures, and it is to be expected that the number of orders made under the new Sections will increase as hospitals and courts become more familiar with them. However, there remains the question of whether the underlying intention of the new powers, namely to divert substantial numbers of remanded mentally disordered defendants from prison to hospital, is likely to be realised. The above statistics emphasise that the bulk of the psychiatric screening and assessment of people requiring custodial remands, and their selection for hospital orders, has been done in the penal system rather than the health service, and it would require a substantial shift in practice to divert this work to the NHS. Moreover, the Prison Medical Association, in its evidence to the Social Services Committee (1986) stated the view that local prisons,

'. . . act in effect as acute psychiatric assessment centres for those whose behaviour has brought them into conflict with the law, and the use of the 'remand to hospital' facilities introduced in the 1983 Mental Health Act cannot be widely applied until there has been a period of assessment in conditions which ensure the safety of both the defendant and the public.'

(*Minutes of Evidence*, p. 32)

The new provisions are to be welcomed for the flexibility they allow in assessing and treating mentally disordered defendants, but whether they can provide an alternative to prison for the majority of psychiatric custodial remands is less certain. The policy of diverting the mentally disordered from prison to hospital appears laudable in principle, but can it really be translated into practice?

(Grounds, 1988, p. 126)

Trial stage

The idea that the insane offender should not be held liable to punishment has a long history in the criminal law, and the criteria for acquittal on the grounds of insanity are formulated in the McNaughton's Rules (see Chapter 2). Walker (1981) described the insanity defence as in need of a heart transplant: 'Its moribund state, with only one or two gasps a year, may not worry judges and psychiatrists ... but it should worry those who want to see mentally disordered offenders properly disposed of' (p. 596). In practice, the defence is very rarely used. As the figures given above indicate, the venerable principle represented by the insanity defence is not effectively applied in practice in the criminal courts: the issue of mental disorder is usually raised at the sentencing stage, and severely ill defendants may be advised to plead guilty to enable suitable medical disposals to be achieved.

In contrast to the view put forward by the Butler Committee (Home Office and DHSS, 1975) that the correct way forward would be to expand the scope of the insanity defence, it could be argued that abolition of the special defence and the ideas underlying it would enable legal theory to catch up with legal practice, and also limit some possibilities of injustice.

The traditional insanity defence has two functions which need to be clearly distinguished. The first is to provide criteria for excusing the mentally disordered from criminal conviction on the basis that the insanity negates the mental element necessary for the act to be counted as a crime; thus an acquittal results. The second function is to enable a psychiatric disposal. A finding of acquittal on the grounds of insanity results in mandatory commitment in hospital with restrictions on discharge. The sane person who is acquitted because he lacks *mens rea* goes free, the insane person in the same condition is also acquitted but is detained. It is, as Morris (1982) remarks 'a strange defence ... whose purpose is confinement of those who could not otherwise be confined' (p. 61). In the case of *R. v. Sullivan* (1983), Lord Diplock made this function quite explicit in his judgment in the House of Lords:

the purpose of the legislation relating to the defence of insanity, ever since its origin in 1880, has been to protect society against the recurrence of the dangerous conduct.

One of the main criticisms of the M'Naughton Rules is that they are too restrictive. If their purpose is to open a door leading to the acquittal of severely mentally ill offenders, the opening is too narrow and excludes too many. Only a small minority of severely mentally ill offenders could be said to be suffering from a defect of reason which prevented them knowing the nature and quality of their acts or knowing that what they were doing was wrong. In practice the use of the defence is restricted only to the gravest crimes, such as homicide, and it is not used for the broad range of mentally ill offenders before the courts. The solution envisaged by the Butler Committee to meet this criticism of narrowness was to reformulate and expand the scope of the insanity defence. The Committee recommended that a new verdict of 'not guilty on evidence of mental disorder' should be brought in by a jury in two alternative circumstances. First, the defendant could be acquitted if he was found to be mentally disordered, and this mental disorder negated the state of mind necessary for the offence. This, however, would still exclude some people with severe mental disorder who were nonetheless able to form the requisite intent. To deal with such cases the Butler Committee recommended their second basis for a not-guilty verdict. This could be brought in if the jury was satisfied on the balance of probabilities that at the time of the offence the defendant was suffering from severe mental illness or severe subnormality. The criteria for severe mental illness were carefully laid out by the Committee and were in effect restricted to clear cases of psychotic illness. Thus, there would be a specific exemption from conviction for any defendant who at the time was suffering from severe mental illness or severe subnormality, and no direct link between the offence and the disorder would have to be established. As various critics have noted, the jurisprudential basis for these proposals is weak (Wells, 1983), and there could be difficulties in deciding who falls within and without the classification of 'severe' mental disorder (Ashworth, 1975).

The best epidemiological study of the relationship between mental disorder and offences of grave violence also points to the need to rethink traditional beliefs about criminal responsibility and mental disorder. Häfner and Böker (1982) argue that the risk of serious violence is no greater in the severely mentally disordered than in the normal population. Factors of personality and situation frequently outweigh the importance of the illness in governing the criminal act. In view of this, two questions arise. First, is it justified to have a social and penal policy that provides specific measures for mentally disordered offenders to be detained preventively for longer than non-disordered offenders? Second, should the mentally abnormal be regarded as more similar to normal offenders in relation to criminal responsibility?

... exculpation, based solely on diagnosis takes no account of the fact that a chronically deluded patient may still preserve considerable portions of his personality intact. The delusional motivation of a violent crime does not mean that the person committing it had at the time no insight into the culpability of his delusionally motivated act and was incapable of behaving in accordance with that insight. It is quite conceivable that even when the patient has no insight into the morbid state of his delusions, insight and self control are still maintained so far as his criminal aggressive desires are concerned.

... we found that several mentally abnormal violent offenders admitted responsibility for their crime and would have preferred severe punishment to internment in a psychiatric hospital. We make no apology for expressing our doubt as to whether this facile exculpation, which is applied now to increasingly trivial mental illnesses, is really humanitarian. We would again draw attention to the fact that many abnormal offenders do not by any means share that view.

(Häffner and Böker, 1982, pp. 333–4)

These various strands of evidence suggest that one could take a view opposite to that adopted by the Butler Committee. The Butler Committee held that it was safest to assume that the severely mentally ill should be regarded as exempt from criminal responsibility. In contrast, it could be suggested that there are fewer dangers in generally assuming that in the case of the mentally ill offender *mens rea* is present. This would be more in keeping with the evidence indicating greater similarities than differences between mentally disordered offenders and their non-disordered counterparts. Morris (1982) has strongly argued that *mens rea* may be necessary to preserve the moral infrastructure of the criminal law, but the insanity defence is not, and 'operationally the defence of insanity is a tribute to our hypocrisy rather than to our morality' (Morris, 1982, p. 64).

Sentencing stage

The abandonment of the assumption that mental illness should be a specific defence against conviction would also provide a way forward for those who would wish to argue that considerations of 'proportionality' should enter into the framework of sentencing for mentally disordered offenders (Ashworth and Gostin, 1984; Parker, 1980). If maximum periods of detention are to be related to the gravity of the offence, this needs justification in terms of a theory of 'limiting retributivism', and retributive principles can not be applied if at the same time it is held that the mentally disordered are not culpable. In contrast to Butler, an assumption that *mens rea* is likely to be present not only fits the empirical data better but is more consistent with current understanding of the nature of mental illness and the determinants of criminal behaviour.

It must be emphasized that these remarks should *not* be taken to imply that I believe imprisonment instead of psychiatric care is appropriate for mentally disordered offenders. I would reject such a view emphatically and believe every effort should be made to ensure that those who need it are treated in a therapeutic environment during any sentence imposed. The argument above is explored in order to show that the *principles* of sentencing for mentally disordered offenders require re-examination. The view that indeterminate sentencing for the dual purposes of treatment and public protection is appropriate for the mentally disordered is strongly held:

In the Government's view the law should continue to enable society to protect itself from certain dangerous mentally disordered offenders by detaining them in hospital for a period longer than would be justified by the gravity of their offence. (DHSS *et al.*, 1978, para. 5.26.)

The validity of this belief requires critical examination, from both a criminal justice point of view, and from the standpoint of empirical research.

REFERENCES
Ashworth A. J. (1975). The Butler Committee and criminal responsibility. *Criminal Law Review*, 687–96.

Ashworth A. J., Gostin L. (1984). Mentally disordered offenders and the sentencing process. *Criminal Law Review*, 195–212.

Bowden P. (1975). Liberty and psychiatry. *British Medical Journal*, 4, 94–6.

Bransby E. R. (1974). *Health Trends*, 6, 56.

Central Statistical Office (1988). Social Trends 18. London: HMSO.

Chiswick D., McIsaac M. W., McClintock F. H. (1984). *Prosecution of the Mentally Disturbed*. Aberdeen: Aberdeen University Press.

Coid J. R. (1988). Mentally abnormal prisoners on remand: I—Rejected or accepted by the NHS? *British Medical Journal*, 296, 1779–1782.

Department of Health and Social Security, Home Office, Welsh Office, and the Lord Chancellors Department (1978). *Review of the Mental Health Act 1959*.

Garland D. (1985). *Punishment and Welfare: a History of Penal Strategies*. Aldershot: Gower.

Grounds A. T. (1988). The use of the remand provisions in the 1983 Mental Health Act. *The Bulletin of the Royal College of Psychiatrists*, 12, 125–6.

Häfner H., Böker B. (1982). *Crimes of Violence by Mentally Abnormal Offenders*. Cambridge: Cambridge University Press.

Home Office (1985). *Report on the Work of the Prison Department 1984/85* Cmnd 9699. London: HMSO.

Home Office (1986a). *Report on the Work of the Prison Department 1985/86* Cmnd 11. London: HMSO.

Home Office (1986b). *Criminal Statistics England and Wales 1985* Cmnd 10. London: HMSO.

Home Office (1988). *Statistics of Mentally Disordered Offenders, England and Wales, 1985 and 1986*. London: Home Office Statistical Department.

Home Office and Department of Health and Social Security (1975). *Report of the Committee on Mentally Abnormal Offenders* Cmnd 6244. London: HMSO.

House of Commons Social Services Committee (1986). *Third Report: Prison Medical Service*: Vol. I. London: HMSO (paras 55–85).

Interdepartmental Working Group of Home Office and DHSS Officials on Mentally Disturbed Offenders in the Prison System in England and Wales (1987). *Report*. London: DHSS and Home Office.

Mental Health Act Commission (1987). *Second Biennial Report*. London: HMSO (paras 13.1–13.3).

Morris N. (1982). *Madness and the Criminal Law*. Chicago: Chicago University Press.

Parker E. (1981). Mentally disordered offenders and their protection from punitive sanctions. *International Journal of Law and Psychiatry*, 3, 461–9.

Walker N. (1981). Butler v. The CLRC and Others. *Criminal Law Review*, 596–601.

Wells C. (1983). Whither insanity? *Criminal Law Review*, 787–97.

CASE

R. *v.* Sullivan [1983] 2 All ER 673.

4 *What can a magistrate do?*

JOY MAJOR

INTRODUCTION

The title 'Justices of the Peace' derives from 1361, in the reign of Edward III. Whereas the Bethlem Hospital was established in 1377 as a place for those who were seen as insane rather than as criminal, the first special legislation for the detention of dangerous, 'furiously mad', lunatics on the order of magistrates was under the 1744 Vagrancy Act, and most ended up in prison. In 1800, the first piece of legislation specifically for mentally abnormal offenders was passed. This was the first Criminal Lunatics Act. Thereafter a new breed of criminal lunatics accumulated in the Bethlem and elsewhere, leading Parliament to recognize the need for a special institution for their care. The result was the passing of the 1860 Criminal Lunatics Act, and the opening of Broadmoor.

Dr John Hamilton provides a splendid summary of the history of mental health legislation (Hamilton, 1983) spanning the 600 years between the establishment of the Bethlem and the enactment of the 1983 Mental Health Act. Sadly, many acts and many years have passed, and the plight of mentally ill people imprisoned when they should be receiving other treatment has still not been resolved.

TRAINING

Magistrates are laymen and have no legal qualifications. Further, in common with most people, the majority of magistrates come to the Bench with little or no knowledge of mental illness; they are totally reliant on the Clerk's knowledge of mental health law. However, training programmes exist which focus on issues of current concern and aim to maintain a good level of practice throughout the magistracy. Although not all will choose to attend a session on mental health, such has been the recent concern over the difficulty in getting mentally abnormal offenders into hospital, that a day course in Birmingham on the 1983 Mental Health Act was oversubscribed, and repeated twice.

Training sessions for magistrates can be theoretical, or can include practical exercises drawn from real cases. One such training evening, described in a letter to the National Schizophrenia Fellowship by a

London magistrate, was held in London for magistrates who sit in the Crown Court. (A judge may sit in some instances with magistrates, usually on appeals from magistrates' sentences.) They were told of a defendant aged 24 who had 14 previous court appearances for dishonesty, which had been dealt with variously by borstal, prison, hospital order, suspended sentence and probation. All matters concerned stealing bicycles, two of which he sold, one worth £100 for £3, and the other worth £106 for £12.

The medical report stated that the defendant was of lowish intelligence, suffered from chronic schizophrenia, was receiving voluntary treatment, and that there was no justification for a hospital order. The psychiatric report pointed out that nothing could be done about the defendant's mental condition, and that in his voluntary treatment the hospital tried to guide him away from delinquency. The report stated that he was more a nuisance than a criminal, and the sentence proposed and largely agreed by all the magistrates on this training exercise was for a probation order, with a condition of residence and continued outpatient treatment. The training judge, however, stated that the sentence should be 15 months' imprisonment, and referred to a High Court Ruling that this sort of behaviour should be punished in the same way when carried out by a chronic schizophrenic as by a mentally normal person.

The original High Court Ruling proved elusive, but a number of judges' Rulings on Appeal show that 50 per cent of the judges agree with the High Court Ruling, and 50 per cent do not (Thomas, 1982, pp. 1055–8). Court training cases are often chosen for their complexity, but such are the complexities surrounding the mentally abnormal offender that it was perhaps, unfortunate that the magistrates were instructed in this way without qualification.

THE MAGISTRATE'S DILEMMA

Magistrates have a double duty: to protect the public, and to rehabilitate the offender. Purely punitive measures are unlikely to achieve the latter, and it is fair to say that once they realize that a medical element is involved, magistrates will lean over backwards to obtain a medical report and to cooperate with the recommendations in it. Two aspects of this will now be considered.

Prison or hospital

Magistrates may only act on the information they receive. If the mentally disordered offender has forbidden his solicitor, probation officer, or anyone else to plead illness in mitigation for his offence, and he behaves normally in court, the magistrates will not realize there is a psychiatric problem and will take the case as a straight criminal charge. This type of offender will prefer to be fined or bound over, or, indeed, to go to prison. This could come as a surprise to a magistrate, who is likely to assume that everyone would rather go to hospital than to prison. Many minor offences are committed as a cry for help, from people unable to care for themselves independently. Failing to find, or rejecting the support offered in the community, they see reception into prison as the only route to adequate care or treatment. This is borne out in the retrospective survey of mentally abnormal prisoners on remand over the five years 1979–83 (Coid, 1988).

But why should a mentally disordered offender seek to conceal his illness and choose to go to prison rather than to hospital? The general view of a group of people who have experienced schizophrenia, some of whom had been imprisoned while ill is that *while ill* prison is preferable to hospital. This is because the length of sentence is known, as opposed to an indefinite period in hospital; also they felt the after-care from prison is superior to that from hospital; and while in prison one is mixing with mentally normal people. But unlike the group above, these people had not been seeking help, and now that they were well, most felt that their decision had been wrong, and that it would have been better for their illness if they had had treatment in hospital. Most had not requested treatment in prison for the reasons they had given, and, they said, because they had found the military precision with which prisoners are marched in to see the doctor inhibiting.

Considerable thought was put in to the 1983 Mental Health Act to try to ensure that offenders who meet the criteria are dealt with wherever possible through the hospital, and not the prison system. Rather unfairly, courts have come in for a lot of criticism for not making more use of these measures. There are regular press reports of frustrated judges and magistrates, compelled to remand in custody, or to give custodial sentences, because of the non-availability of hospital beds. The tragic suicide of Mr Michael Flynn, debated in the House of Lords (Hansard, 4 March 1988, pp. 402–18), is a striking example of such failure to provide a hospital bed. Flynn was moved 16 times while on custodial remand from a London court, and had to be accommodated not even in prison, but in police cells as far afield as the Midlands, under conditions which made it impossible to prepare a psychiatric report. Serious mental illness carries an increased risk of suicide, which is probably exacerbated among mentally abnormal offenders, many of whom are alienated from family and friends, destitute, and unable to find asylum (Robertson, 1987). Thirty per cent of inmates who committed suicide in prison department establishments in 1987 had undergone psychiatric assessment or treatment before coming into custody (Hansard, 1989).

Mental Ability to Plead

Where the defendant's behaviour is disturbed or bizarre in court, a psychiatric report will clearly be required. Before this, however, the mode of trial has to be decided, and the defendant's plea taken. For this, the magistrates have to be satisfied that the defendant can understand what is happening, and is fully aware of the implications of his/her plea to the charge. Whenever there is any doubt as to the defendant's ability regarding this, magistrates must first obtain a medical report on the defendant's present mental state, irrespective of the state of mind at the time of the offence. A defendant's ability to participate in the proceedings in court is, perhaps, one of the most difficult things for a magistrate, inexperienced in mental health, to understand. For example, a man charged with criminal damage thought he was a dog, and refused to leave his kennel; the magistrates had to go down to his cell (the kennel). They requested a report on the defendant's mental state. Seven days later, the report stated that the man was fit to participate in the court proceedings. The magistrates immediately and angrily requested a second opinion. The nature of the defendant's illness was not explained. Formal tests of fitness to plead are rare. Such cases can only be settled by a jury in a higher court. Home Office statistics from 1976 to mid-1986 average 20 cases per annum only [extrapolations made by the Home Office for the author on Criminal Procedure (Insanity) Act, 1964, returns]. These people must go to wherever the Secretary of State directs. The majority are charged with comparatively minor offences, and go to ordinary NHS hospitals. Only about five a year go to special hospitals, with restrictions that make discharge difficult.

A full psychiatric report is not requested usually until after the mode of trial has been established, and the defendant's plea entered. The medical report on a defendant's current mental state is not a prerequisite to the psychiatric report but will precede it when felt necessary to determine the mode of trial. It would seem, however, that a seven-day remand in custody for a report on a defendant's ability to participate in the court proceedings is too much time wasted. Studies by Roesch and others show that 75 per cent of such evaluations need only take half an hour, and this is generally accepted (Roesch *et al.*, 1984). Surely, it is unnecessary and uneconomic to subject these people to a week's custodial remand for a quickly established assessment, particularly when the sequel is to remand again for three or four weeks to obtain a full psychiatric report. Even though psychiatrists are busy, and cannot drop commitments at short notice to come into court to provide an assessment, the actual number of cases is few. In Birmingham's Magistrates' Courts for example, 22 mentally abnormal offenders were remanded in custody during the months of February, March and April in 1988, of whom 13 were requiring medical reports. Although there are quite wide regional variations, it would seem that Benches remand about 2 per cent of the total court turnover for medical reports (Roesch *et al.*, 1984). Would it not be possible for local psychiatrists to agree a rota to be on-call to cover this infrequent need, with the entitlement to claim expenses for the service? This would be infinitely cheaper and more humane than a week's custodial remand. Alternatively, Ann Barker suggests preliminary evaluations could be the work of the duty probation officer or the duty solicitor using a suitable test (Barker, 1988).

POWERS OF THE MAGISTRATE

When an offence is punishable on summary conviction with imprisonment, an alternative option is open to magistrates. If, having regard to all the circumstances, the court considers a hospital order to be the most suitable disposal for the case, the magistrates may make an order authorizing admission to, and detention in, hospital under the conditions set out in Section 37 of the 1983 Mental Health Act, either with or without recording a conviction against the defendant, provided that the court is satisfied that the defendant did the act.

The 1983 Mental Health Act

Mentally abnormal offenders include those who are detainable under the 1983 Mental Health Act, and those who are not. All cases first come to the magistrates' courts. Decision-making for the magistrates is not so difficult when the offence is very serious, or when the patient is treatable under the Act, and very ill. Of much more concern to magistrates are offenders who are not detainable or treatable under the Act, and whose illness has made them socially incompetent. (These people are sometimes referred to as socially 'inadequates' and are discussed at length by Christopher Stuart-White in Chapter 5.) Many will have committed minor offences, such as breaking a window or causing a disturbance, and would normally be dealt with in the courts by a fine or a bind-over, but they are remanded because a medical report is needed. Some are remanded on bail, but those with no fixed abode, or whose family cannot cope, or who the NHS hospital consultants and staff will not admit because they are disruptive, are likely to be remanded in custody. In coming to a decision concerning disposal, magistrates will be looking for considerable guidance from the psychiatric report. The Magistrates. Association drew up a paper entitled 'Dealing with Mentally Disordered Offenders in Magistrates' Courts' in November 1987, and wrote asking the Home Office to consider revising the form which goes to the prison governor from the court, requesting a medical report when remanding in custody. The Association suggested a revised version which would ensure more information being given to the court than the one currently provided (see Appendix A). The suggested version and other recommendations of the Association (see Appendix B) are still being considered by the Home Office. Doctors, too, may find little help in the minimal background information provided with some requests for a medical report.

The Sections of the 1983 English Mental Health Act of most use to magistrates are Sections 35, 37, 38 and 39. There are various reasons why some of these are underused or impracticable to implement. Section 35 is used by magistrates requiring a psychiatric report to remand a defendant, where bail is inappropriate, to hospital for medical assessment without treatment. Section 36, involving the remand of an accused person to hospital for treatment, is for Crown Courts only; magistrates may not use it. As magistrates may make a hospital order or an interim hospital order under sections 37 and 38, respectively, both of which involve treatment, their exclusion from Section 36 seems strange. Sections 35 to 38 are, in any case, all subject to the written or oral evidence of medical practitioners who are registered under Section 12 of the Act, and approved by the Secretary of State as having special experience in the diagnosis or treatment of mental disorder (Section 54 (1)). If magistrates remand to the Crown Court with Section 36 in mind, the hearing is likely to be delayed for several weeks, and, where bail is inappropriate, the accused will spend these weeks in custody.

Reluctance to accept mentally disordered offenders on remand

The question of treatment has a bearing on the use, or not, of Section 35, which may be underused in some areas due to the lack of suitable provision within the health service. To treat the patient could disguise the symptoms of illness which the Court requires to be assessed. Furthermore, NHS consultants and nursing staff may be reluctant or unable to accept patients on remand who, although not gravely ill, can nevertheless be disruptive, and can create management problems where staffing ratios are low, and where the patient may easily abscond. Is it, indeed, fair on staff to ask them to accept disruptive people into open wards whom they cannot treat? According to the Mental Health Act Commission's Second Biennial Report, the difficulty appears to be the embargo on treatment without consent imposed by Section 56 (1) (b) of the 1983 Mental Health Act. The Commissioners found evidence that the reluctance to accept patients on remand under Section 35 is, in large part, attributable to the uncertainty surrounding treatment of psychiatric patients at common law. While Section 35 is being used in some areas, in others it is scarcely used at all. In Birmingham's Magistrates' Court for example, it was used not more than five times in 1988, and only twice in the first three months of 1989.

The retrospective survey over five years (1979–83) by Dr Jeremy Coid of all mentally abnormal offenders remanded to Winchester Prison for psychiatric reports shows that one in five was rejected for treatment by the NHS consultant psychiatrist responsible for their care (Coid, 1988). Those unable to cope independently in the community were the most likely to be rejected, being commonly described by consultants as too disturbed or potentially dangerous to be admitted to hospital, or as criminals and unsuitable for treatment.

Where, then, do those considered a danger to themselves or others go? Most charges were burglaries or theft, but many of these were minor incidents involving hungry and destitute men. Some would break a window, and sit below it till the police arrived. If the police took too long, they would go round to the police station and report themselves. Out of 334 men, 197 were of no fixed abode on arrival in prison, and of these, the prison doctors considered 136 to be incapable of caring for themselves independently in the community at the time of their arrest. One has only to visit large railway stations to see that matters are no better now.

With the rundown of mental hospital beds, doctors may also fear that accepting a patient on remand may risk his return as a long-term patient. Dr Coid raises the point which was one of the main findings of the 1982 Home Office/Cheadle and Ditchfield study (Home Office and DHSS, 1982): that psychiatrists were unwilling to provide care in the long term (Coid, 1988).

To implement Sections 35 to 38 of the 1983 Mental Health Act, the written or oral evidence of the registered medical practitioner must state that arrangements have been made for the admission of the patient to hospital. If the registered medical practitioner has been unable, for any reason, to make these arrangements, there is no question of the court being able to make an order under these Sections. Different hospitals can specialize in the treatment of different forms of mental disorder. For this reason, the legislation provides that the consent of the receiving hospital is required before the courts may order an offender's admission. It is unlikely that courts would fill hospitals with unsuitable patients, as both Crown and magistrates' courts make their decision to remand to hospital based on the written or oral evidence of registered *medical* practitioners. In any event, it seems totally wrong that NHS hospitals should be able to refuse to accept patients who are offenders, while overcrowded prisons have no option but to accept offenders who are patients. The courts are not the final arbiters in this respect.

Courts do have one card they can play called Section 39. Unfortunately, it is not an ace, and it cannot touch Sections 35 and 36. What it can do, is to require the Regional Health Authority to furnish the court with information as to the hospital where arrangements can be made for the admission of the patient under Sections 37 and 38 of the Act—the two sections concerning hospital and interim hospital orders. Section 39 can be quite effective in producing a bed, although it cannot oblige a hospital to accept a patient. It would be useful to see Section 39 extended to cover Sections 35 and 36 also.

Psychiatric bail hostels

In addition to the hospital order, Section 37 also gives provision for guardianship, which could involve local authority placement as an alternative to hospital. Resource issues restrict its use. In all four Sections (35 to 38), doctors' recommendations may be influenced by their knowledge of the resources available—and in resources lies the key. These four Sections can only be implemented if there are adequate resources in the health service to meet the needs of the courts. There is an urgent need, therefore, for the provision of remand centres in the community for those requiring psychiatric assessment. A Psychiatric bail hostel, or one particular ward in a NHS hospital, adequately staffed, could meet the needs of quite a large area. Providing a health rather than a penal setting would surely be better for the patients, would greatly relieve the prisons and be more suitable and convenient for assessment.

The Home Office and DHSS *Report on Mentally Disturbed Offenders* (The Home Office and DHSS, 1987) indicates (para. 6.7) that from 1 April 1985 to 31 March 1986, Brixton Prison prepared some 3000 psychiatric reports to court, and Holloway Prison prepared 500. It is pertinent that the Interdepartmental Report also comments that 'the degree of overcrowding and pressure of facilities in our local prisons and remand centres is at a level which militates against the promotion of health care, both physical and mental' (para. 5.1). A group coordinated by the Law Society, which includes the Criminal Bar Association, Justices' Clerks' Society, Crown Prosecution Service and—as observers—the Association of Chief Police Officers, is calling for increased funding for existing and new bail hostels, and for special accommodation, preferably in hospitals, for those requiring medical or mental treatment (*The Times*, 12 December 1988).

Probation orders

Further options open to magistrates include fining and binding-over, but some magistrates may give an absolute discharge rather than adding to the mentally ill offender's problems. This may be a mistaken kindness. While the circumstances of each case are particular to that person, and one should not generalize, where a mentally ill offender's action has brought him or her before the court, an opportunity has been lost if no constructive action is taken. The offender will be returning from court to exactly the same circumstances which provoked the incident which led to his arrest, and it will not be long before he is in court again. This situation highlights the present inadequacies in community care (discussed by Maggie Pinder and Herbert Laming in Chapter 15) and our increasing need for and reliance on the probation service (see Chapter 16).

The responsibility for care and supervision often shifts from the health and social services to the probation service after a mentally disordered person is arrested and brought before the courts. Probation orders requiring treatment for mental conditions come under the 1973 Powers of Criminal Courts Act, and not the Mental Health Act. Appendix C to this chapter is an extract from Section 3-243 3 of the 1973 Powers of Criminal Courts Act, referring to probation orders requiring treatment for a mental condition. While magistrates' courts are accustomed to psychiatric probation orders involving treatment as described in (2) (b), they are not making use of the provision in (2) (c), which allows the treatment to be carried out *under the direction of* the duly qualified medical practitioner, and not by him personally. The sort of case which could be helped by this is, for example, a patient who is able to cope in the community while receiving medication from his general practitioner (GP), and has neglected this and suffers a relapse which may readily be put right when medication is restored. Such a case was a man who appeared before me in court charged with the theft of a Mars bar. He was a discharged mental patient and he said he felt he was becoming ill again, he had asked for help but none was forthcoming, so he went into a newsagent, picked up a Mars bar, held it up and said, 'I'm stealing this'.

Eventually, the police were called. We asked for a medical report, and the man was able to be remanded on bail. The report said he was fine when he took his medication, but that he had neglected to get his prescription from his GP. We wished to encourage this very minor offender to consult his GP monthly for a while, and this is possible under (2) (c) of the Section above, which allows treatment to be carried out under the direction of the duly qualified medical practitioner and not by him personally. In other words, the duly qualified medical practitioner could direct that the patient consult his GP, and if the offender agrees to do so in court, the magistrates may make such an order. It would be very helpful if this could be spelt out to magistrates, and even more so be brought to the attention of Justices' Clerks, and even to the duly qualified medical practitioners themselves. At present, this very simple form of support is not being used.

GENERAL PRACTITIONERS

General practitioners (GPs) are said to deal with 95 per cent of the public's psychiatric problems (Goldberg and Huxley, 1980) and magistrates with 90 per cent of criminal offences (Barker, 1988). *The Independent* (31 March 1989) puts this figure at 98 per cent. Perhaps with the present emphasis on community care, discussion between their respective Associations could be beneficial. Mentally ill patients can be time-consuming, but the numbers, overall, are comparatively few, and it is unlikely that an individual GP would find one of his patients being referred to him as in the Mars bar case more than once in a very great while. A study on the use of Section 136 (of the 1983 Mental Health Act) in the London metropolitan area found only 63 per cent of mentally abnormal offenders to be registered with a GP compared with 97 per cent of the general population (Rogers and Faulkner, 1987).

DIVERSION FROM CUSTODY

The effect of custody

What is the effect of custody on mentally ill people? Each relapse will take its toll. Prison hospital staff do a wonderful job, but a man in prison is first and foremost a prisoner. He will be disciplined for behaviour which, in a NHS hospital, would be treated as part of his illness. And what about the need for space? It is accepted by the Government that clarification is required in identifying prisoners for whom punishment—that is cellular confinement—would be contraindicated on medical grounds. Yet the Government rejects the recommendation of the Social Services Select Committee for the amendment of Prison Rule 17 to permit a second medical opinion to be sought in relation to either a medical diagnosis, or to fitness for cellular confinement, by any prisoner (HMSO, 1987). At present, Prison Rule 17 applies to remand prisoners only.

Diagnosis

Has the term 'personality disorder' become a facile description which disguises true illness, and denies treatment? Five years ago, 200 of the 600 prisoners at Winson Green Prison, Birmingham, were said to be suffering from some form of personality disorder. Over the last twelve months, the prison's figures for personality disordered inmates have fluctuated from between 20 and 25 per cent of its 1056–1120 prisoners (personal communication). Over the five-year-period covered by Dr Coid's survey, mentioned earlier, the large number of men remanded from magistrates' courts to Winchester Prison for psychiatric reports included sufferers from mania, depression and, mainly, schizophrenia (75 per cent) (Coid, 1988). Dr Coid's survey was concerned only with men who could have been admitted to hospital under the Mental Health Act; it did not include those suffering from personality disorder. Diagnoses of schizophrenia and personality disorder are not mutually exclusive; both can exist at once. But to refer only to personality disorder in prisons gives concern that a label is being used which disguises the true number of mentally ill people in prison who should be in hospital. The then governor of Stafford Prison, Ian Boon, in a training session for magistrates concerning the care and treatment of patients said that his greatest problem was prisoners with 'personality disorders': they occupied a full landing, and he was at a loss to do anything for or with them.

'A PLACE OF SAFETY'

Although all cases start in the magistrates' courts, the story actually begins when an incident involves the police. The role of the custody officer at the police station is critical. Under the 1984 Police and Criminal Evidence Act, the custody officer is obliged to treat a person as mentally ill or handicapped if there is any suspicion at all that this may be the case. A certain set of procedures must then come into play. It is unfair to expect the police to diagnose mental illness: a disruptive and disturbed person may be under the influence of drugs or drink and may not necessarily be mentally ill. Some officers prefer to play safe, and to use the police cell as the place of safety overnight, bringing the offender before the court in the morning. The offender is then on the conveyor belt to the criminal justice system. Research carried out by MIND (The National Association for Mental Health) into the operation of Section 136 of the 1983 Mental Health Act shows that when the police *do* consider mental illness to be present, then at least 90 per cent of these assessments are subsequently confirmed as correct on psychiatric examination (Rogers and Faulkner, 1987). The London metroplitan area has the advantage of emergency assessment units as well as hospitals and police stations from which to make psychiatric referrals. Many areas employ police surgeons on fulltime appintment. Other regions, such as Oxford, employ practising GPs to take on the role on a part-time basis, so that their everyday clinical skills are brought to bear in the police station (Sichel, 1988).

Birmingham has now evolved a procedure which is proving effective in channelling offenders out of the criminal justice system at this stage. When it is realized that a psychiatric problem may be involved, the magistrate can ask for a stand-down report from the liaison probation officer, and the case is put back while this is prepared within the precincts of the court. The liaison probation officer is the direct link between Birmingham's law courts and All Saints Hospital, and works closely with consultant psychiatrists both at the hospital and at Reaside Secure Unit. In conjunction with the psychiatrist (who does often agree to come into court at short notice) the liaison probation officer has often been able to persuade the patient to go into hospital voluntarily, and then to persuade the prosecution to drop the charge. With more serious illness, a Section 2 admission, under the 1983 Mental Health Act, may also be possible at this stage. A similar procedure also exists in Peterborough, where a duty consultant psychiatrist will attend the courthouse on call, and immediately begin to prepare a report, which is normally available to the court the same day. This scheme has enabled defendants to be admitted to hospital under Section 35 of the 1983 Mental Health Act.

THE MULTIDISCIPLINARY ASSESSMENT PANEL

In coming to a decision about sentencing, magistrates will be conscious that minor offenders, unable to cope with life in the community, will require considerable support if they are not to re-offend. Of great interest is the multidisciplinary assessment panel now being practised and promoted by the Hertfordshire Probation Service. In addition to the consultant psychiatrist, the Assessment Panel can include a number of professionals in the community, for example, a community psychiatric nurse, a probation officer, a social worker, a clinical psychologist, and a general practitioner. A psychiatric bail hostel would provide an ideal venue for such assessments. A modest number of beds could accommodate the constantly changing remand population over quite a wide area for this difficult but needy type of offender. As the problems of these minor offenders, who are not detainable under the Act, are part medical, part social, this should be far more beneficial to their rehabilitation and successful resettlement than a remand in prison.

THE CASE FOR CUSTODY

Magistrates will make very effort to keep a mentally abnormal offender out of prison, but factors do exist which are beyond their control. This chapter has concentrated on minor offenders on remand who are not treatable under the Mental Health Act—some of whom will not even be convicted. It is good that the research, commissioned by the Home Office as a national survey of mental illness in prisons, has now been extended to cover prisoners on custodial remand in addition to the sentenced prisoners.

'Criminalization' of Patients

A trend which is beginning to cause concern to the National Schizophrenia Fellowship—and about which they are receiving an increasing number of letters from relatives—is the bringing to court of patients detained in hospital who commit a criminal offence (often of a trivial nature) either within the hospital, or, having absconded, in the community. The patient is subsequently charged with the offence, and brought before the court. This has caused considerable distress to the families, who feel that their relative was known to be ill and Sectioned to be detained in hospital, and that the hospital has consequently failed in its duty to care for the patient. As a result of this failure, their relative has been 'criminalized'. In some minor cases which took place within the hospital (for example breaking a window), the police have felt that hospital staff should have been able to contain the situation themselves. The Fellowship is also hearing of cases where courts are being involved either as a 'lesson' to the patient, or because a transfer to a regional secure unit is considered to be more quickly achieved through a Court Order.

Protection of the public—and the patient

Perhaps out of concern for people who have committed offences under the stress of mental illness which they would never have been likely to commit in good health, it may seem that the implication is that such people should be 'kept out of prison at all costs'. This would be wrong, however. In their handbook, *Sentence of the Court*, magistrates are advised on their powers to deal with 'offenders who are not so mentally disordered as to be absolved from criminal responsibility for their actions, but are nevertheless, in need of psychiatric treatment' (12.1) (Home Office, 1986). It may well be that the mentally ill offender knew his act to be wrong, and committed it with full understanding of all the implications and consequences involved. Mental illness is no respecter of persons, and no doubt shares its proportion of delinquents with the mentally fit. How long should the public be asked to tolerate nuisance or hazard from someone not ill enough to meet the criteria for admission to hospital under the 1983 Mental Health Act—and, indeed, be frightened by them?

Cases from the *Encyclopedia of Current Sentencing Practice* on proportionality of sentence make interesting reading (Thomas, 1982). There are frequent references to the lack of secure hospital accommodation. Typical, is the case of *R. v. Scanlon* (p. 1058). The appellant was convicted of causing damage to the door of her flat and possessing an offensive weapon. When she came before the court, there was no hospital prepared to take her because, when in hospital, she was allegedly 'very difficult, a great nuisance, and liable to violence'. Her condition was not considered sufficiently serious to justify a place in a special hospital, but in the doctor's view, 'she should be in a hospital where conditions are secure'. Her appeal against a prison sentence of three years was dismissed as it was felt necessary to protect the public from the risk of her being free. *R. v. Arrowsmith* (p. 1057) also concerned a woman sentenced to three years' imprisonment for causing £18 damage to a flat by flooding. Again, no hospital bed was available. The appeal heard before Lord Chief Justice Widgery and Justices O'Connor and Goff was dismissed. They accepted the submission that for the offence three years was too long, but felt that:

When the matter is looked at in the round (because the fact is that since she has been in prison, she has improved so far as it is in her nature to improve—she is quieter, she is more rational), in fact in her own interests, it is better that she should remain in the secure surroundings from which she cannot go off on these mad escapades which she has done for so much of her life. When all those matters are weighed together, then the importance of protecting the public from her, and the importance of seeking to alleviate her own condition, outweigh any criticism that three years is too long for the offence of which she was found guilty.

(Thomas, 1982, p. 1057)

In coming to their decision, magistrates too, must weigh all the circumstances surrounding the case they are considering, including *mens rea*—guilty intent. Is the defendant ill? Where is there a place for her/him? What course of action will help both him and the public with whom he must live? Has this happened before? How can one protect both him and the public from this happening again? What can a magistrate *do*?

CONCLUSION

The law makes provision for various courses of action which magistrates can only implement if resources match the requirement. The present lack of suitable accommodation in ordinary psychiatric hospitals is a factor which undoubtedly needs to be rectified if sick people who are too disruptive for an open ward but not ill enough for a secure unit are not to be locked away in prison, either for being a nuisance or as their only route to care. *Sentence of the Court* points out (12.18) that although some offenders receive psychiatric treatment in prison, the court has no control over the allocation of prisoners to prisons which are able to provide treatment; and further, that it is not considered correct sentencing practice for a court to pass a sentence of imprisonment on the assumption that the offender will receive treatment while serving the sentence (Home Office, 1986).

It is surprising, perhaps, to end on a quote from Russia. Dr Vladimar Kozinev, Chief Doctor of Kashchenko Psychiatric Hospital in Moscow, in an interview in *The Independent* (25 March 1989), said: 'The level of a society's development can be determined by how it treats the mentally ill. ... The humanisation of psychiatry will only be achieved when a discharged patient can rely on a safety net of compassion and after-care in the world outside. Of course, a patient's rights must be protected. But the whole of society must be educated as well.'

ACKNOWLEDGEMENTS

I would like to thank the National Schizophrenia Fellowship, Dr David Tidmarsh, consultant psychiatrist at Broadmoor Hospital, and Mr Mervyn Walker and Mr David Summers, Clerk and Deputy Clerk to the Justices of Birmingham Magistrates' Court, all of whom helped this magistrate to understand.

REFERENCES

Barker A. (1988). Mentally disordered offenders and the courts: some aspects of the problems as seen by a beak and a quack. *Justice of the Peace*, **152**(4), 55–7; 71–4; 100–104.

Coid, J. W. (1988). Mentally abnormal prisoners on remand: I—Rejected or accepted by the NHS? *British Medical Journal*, **296**, 1779–84.

Goldberg D., Huxley J. (1980). *Mental Illness and the Community*. London: Tavistock Press.

Hamilton, J. R. (1983). Mental Health Act 1983. *British Medical Journal*, **286**, 1720–5.

Hansard (1989). Written answer by Mr Douglas Hogg, *Hansard* 15 March 1989 Colm. 230.

HMSO (1987). *The Government Reply to the Third Report from the Social Services Select Committee Session 1985–1986* Cmnd 115. London: HMSO.

Home Office (1986). Sentence of the court. *A Handbook for Courts on the Treatment of Offenders*, 4th edn. London: HMSO.

Home Office and DHSS (1982). Report of a study carried out by John Cheadle and John Ditchfield. Home Office Research and Planning Unit.

Home Office and DHSS (1987). *Report of the Interdepartmental Working Group Between the Home Office and DHSS on Mentally Disturbed Offenders in the Prison System in England and Wales.* London: HMSO.

Rahman, F. Personal communication with Dr F. Rahman, Senior Medical Officer, Winson Green Prison, Birmingham.

Robertson G. (1987). Mentally abnormal offenders: manner of death. *British Medical Journal*, **295**, 632–4.

Roesch R., Jackson J. A., Sollner R., Eaves D., Glackman W., Webster C. D. (1984). The fitness to stand trial interior test: how four professions rate video-taped interviews. *International Journal of Law and Psychiatry*, **7**, 115–31.

Rogers A., Faulkner A. (1987). *A Place of Safety.* London: MIND.

Sitchel J. (1988). Paper presented at the National Schizophrenia Fellowship Annual Conference at Oxford on Forensic Psychiatry and the Mentally Ill Offenders, 1988.

Thomas D. ed. (1982). *Encyclopaedia of Current Sentencing Practice.* London: Sweet and Maxwell.

APPENDIX A

Present form

(a) On exercising the power conferred by section 30 of the Magistrates' Courts Act 1980 by remanding the accused in custody, the court is required, by Rule 24 of the Magistrates' Courts Rules 1981, in PART V: STATUTORY INSTRUMENTS, ante. to send to the institution to which he is committed a statement of the reasons why the court is of opinion that an inquiry ought to be made into his physical or mental condition and of any information before the court about his physical or mental condition. Home Office Circulars Nos 113/1973 and 1/1975 recommend that the following form should be used for this purpose—

*Remands in custody under Magistrates' Courts Act 1989, ss 10/3; and 30.
Statement of reasons for medical enquiry (Rule 24)*

Name of defendant. . . . .

Court . . . . .Date . . . .

Offence. . . . .

Section under which remand is ordered . . . .

. . . .

Dear Sir,

This defendant has been remanded for a medical report. To assist the Medical Officer I give below the information available.

1. Type of report (eg on physical or mental condition or suitability for particular treatment).
2. Reasons which led the Court to request the report.
3. Previous medical history of offender and family history, so far as known.*
4. Particulars of circumstances of offence (including, if the offender is of no fixed abode, the place where it was committed, if known).*
5. Previous conduct, including previous convictions if known.*
6. Address and home circumstances of offender.*
7. Name and station of police officer concerned with case.
8. Name and telephone number of any probation officer appointed to or having knowledge of the case.
It would be helpful to the court if your report could indicate—
a. Whether the defendant suffers from any form of mental disorder, if so:
b. whether he is in need of or capable of gaining benefit from treatment, if so—
c. where and by whom this treatment can be given,
d. whether it should be as an in-patient or out-patient, and
e. prognosis where possible

Yours faithfully,

The Governor,
HM Prison

. . . .   *Clerk to the Justices*

*Where the required information can best be conveyed by attaching a copy of a report or statement in the court's possession, all that need be entered here is "See attached . . . . ".

APPENDIX B

Suggested form

Our Ref: The Clerk to the Justices

Your Ref: . . . .

. . . .

. . . .
Tel: . . . .
Date: . . . .

Remands in custody under Magistrates' Courts Act 1980 ss 10(3) and 30.
Statement of reasons for medical enquiry (Rule 24)

Dear Sir

This defendant has been remanded for a medical report. To assist the Medical Officer I give below the information available.

1. Type of report (eg on physical or mental condition or suitability for particular treatment).
2. Reasons which led the Court to request the report.
3. Previous medical history of offender and family history, so far as known.*
4. Particulars of circumstances of offence (including, if the offender is of no fixed abode, the place where it was committed, if known).*
5. Previous conduct, including previous convictions if known.*
6. Address and home circumstances of offender.*
7. Name and station of police officer concerned with case.
8. Name and telephone number of any probation officer appointed to or having knowledge of the case.

*Where the required information can best be conveyed by attaching a copy of a report or statement in the court's possession, all that need be entered here is 'See attached . . . .'.

It would be helpful to the court if your report would indicate—

a. Whether the defendant suffers from any form of mental disorder, and if so:—
b. which form of mental disorder;
c. bearing in mind that treatment includes nursing, care, habilitation or rehabilitation under medical supervision, whether you feel that he/she is in need of or capable of obtaining benefit from treatment under:—
   1. a probation order with psychiatric treatment as a condition and if so whether this should be as an in-patient or as an out-patient;
   2. a hospital order under section 37 of the 1983 Mental Health Act;
   3. a guardianship order under section 37 of that Act;

4. a remand to hospital for a report on his/her mental condition under section 35 of that Act;

5. an interim hospital order under section 38 of that Act.

d. whether it would be appropriate for him to be remanded on bail to hospital.

e. the name and address of the consultant responsible for the relevant catchment area;

f. that you have forwarded a copy of this letter to that consultant;

g. the Regional Health Authority responsible for providing the defendant with treatment should the court wish to seek information under the provisions of section 39 of the Act about hospitals to which the patient might be admitted;

h. whether you have any reason to believe that the accused will be unfit to plead.

APPENDIX C

Summary and recommendations

1. Magistrates' courts should be encouraged to:
   a) Establish an effective liaison with local psychiatrists with a view to greater understanding of each other's problems (3.1 and 3.2) and establishing a policy with regard to probation orders with a condition of treatment (6.3.).
   b) Ensure that full information is provided when requesting a psychiatric report (3.3).
   c) Wherever possible remanding on bail or remanding to hospital in order to obtain a psychiatric report (3.4).
   d) Where difficulty is experienced in securing the admission to hospital of a mentally ill defendant the opportunity provided by Section 39 of the Mental Health Act should be considered (4.1).
   e) Consider the possibility of making a Hospital Order without proceeding to a conviction (4.3).
   f) Consider the use of an Interim Hospital Order (5.5).

2. The Home Office should be asked to consider:
   a) The adoption of a revised form for requesting a psychiatric report when remanded in custody (3.7 and Appendix 'B').
   b) In consultation with the Department of Health & Social Security the possibility of providing for a Community Treatment Order and Non-Consential Order for Treatment within the Community (4.5 and 7.1/2).
   c) How the Prison Department might make better provision for dealing with those mentally disordered offenders who are committed to prison (5.7).
   d) The setting up of a Working Party to review the establishment of community establishments to accommodate mentally disordered offenders not coming within the provisions of the Mental Health Act 1983 (5.10 to 5.17).

3. The Department of Health and Social Security should be asked to review the policy of the closure of psychiatric hospitals and discharge to care in the community (5.9).

The author recommends that further to the suggestions of the Magistrates' Association, possibly the following might be considered:

1) The extension of Section 39 to cover Sections 35 and 36 also.

2) Speedier provision of mental state assessments.
3) Secure provision by increased staffing for mentally abnormal offenders not treatable under the Act should be provided in every Health District or Region, such as the establishment of Remand Hostels, where such people may stay short-term during the preparation of a medical report.
4) Better medical and social care for mentally disturbed offenders on release from prison or custodial remand. e.g. For those of no fixed address, an offer of accommodation.
5) In large Courts, the designation of a Probation Officer as Liaison Officer between the Court and the local psychiatric hospital.
6) Education for local authorities, Councillors and the general public.
7) The provision of training programmes for Police, Court Clerks, Prosecution and Solicitors. Encourage local dialogue between them.

APPENDIX D

1973 Powers of Criminal Courts Act

Probation orders requiring treatment for mental condition.—(1) Where the court is satisfied, on the evidence (a) of a duly qualified medical practitioner approved for the purposes of section 12 of the Mental Health Act 1983, that the mental condition of an offender is such as requires and may be susceptible to treatment but is not such as to warrant his detention in pursuance of a hospital order under Part III of that Act, the court may, if it makes a probation order, include in it a requirement that the offender shall submit, during the whole of the probation period or during such part of that period as may be specified in the order, to treatment by or under the direction of a duly qualified medical practitioner with a view to the improvement of the offender's mental condition.

(2) The treatment required by any such order shall be such one of the following kinds of treatment as may be specified in the order, that is to say—

(*a*) treatment as a resident patient in a hospital within the meaning of the Mental Health Act 1983 or mental nursing home within the meaning of the Nursing Homes Act 1975, not being a special hospital within the meaning of the National Health Service Act 1977;

(*b*) treatment as a non-resident patient at such institution or place as may be specified in the order; or

(*c*) treatment by or under the direction of such duly qualified medical practitioner as may be specified in the order

but the nature of the treatment shall not be specified in the order except as mentioned in paragraph (*a*), (*b*) or (*c*) above.

5 The 'inadequate' offender: a view from the courts

CHRISTOPHER STUART-WHITE

INTRODUCTION

The problem of the social 'inadequate' who offends is a perennial one for the police, the social services, the medical profession, the legal profession, and the courts. It has exercised many minds over many years, and it is not the intention of this chapter to analyse even, let alone to suggest solutions to this problem. The scope of this chapter is limited to the strictly legal aspects of 'inadequacy' and of 'inadequates' as they present themselves to the criminal justice system.

It is most important to bear in mind that only a limited number of 'inadequates'—probably a small minority—commit offences and find

Editors' note

This chapter was commissioned after the Cumberland Lodge meeting had finished. It was clear at the meeting that members of the judiciary used the concept of 'inadequates' in a special, semitechnical, sense and believed that particular attention should be paid to their needs. This view is in line with the Butler Report which devoted Chapter 6 to 'Provision for Inadequates'. The Butler Committee said 'In recent years there has been an increasing public awareness of the considerable numbers of rootless and often homeless persons in London and other large conurbations who are incapable of living in the community without continuous supervision and support, and who are loosely labelled 'inadequates'. Among this group are to be found individuals suffering from distinct psychiatric disorders, often personality disorder, chronic schizophrenia or organic psychosis, a number who are subnormal and many others on the borderline of mental disorder or dependent to some degree upon drugs or alcohol. Most have some experience of institutional treatment, whether in hospital, voluntary hostel or government reception centre, and while some may by temperament be natural 'loners', others are completely institutionalised and quite unable to cope with life on their own.' The Butler Committee acknowledged that the word 'inadequate' could be regarded as pejorative, but they intended it as a term of compassion.

themselves before the courts. The exact number is unknown because, as will become obvious, if it is not already so, statistics cannot be provided.

It is a remarkable fact that so many people, presented with social, financial and medical problems with which they are constitutionally unable to cope, avoid turning to crime and never trouble the criminal courts, or do so only on rare occasions. Speculation about why some 'inadequates' offend, while so many do not, is fascinating but outside the scope of this book. Equally, it is no part of the task of this chapter to express views on the current policy of encouraging 'care in the community' rather than care in institutions, save to observe that, with more 'inadequates' living in the community, it will be surprising if more do not find themselves in criminal courts. Only time will tell whether this forecast proves to be correct.

In one sense there are no 'legal aspects of inadequacy' because the terms 'inadequate' and 'inadequacy' have never been defined by statute nor, so far as I have been able to discover, by authoritative judicial pronouncement. However, there are a number of questions which it seems could, with profit, be addressed, though some of them may turn out, in the event, not to be readily answerable. These questions are:

1. Is a legal definition of the terms 'inadequate' and 'inadequacy', as they are used within the context of the criminal justice system, necessary, desirable, or, for that matter, possible?
2. Are there some practicable means, for example by executive decision not to prosecute, by which such offenders may be diverted from the criminal justice system? If such means exist, ought they to be implemented?
3. Are 'inadequates', more than other categories of defendant, held in custody unnecessarily before trial; and, if so, what should be done to prevent this?
4. What is the precise nature of the problems with which courts are presented when they have to pass sentence on 'inadequates'?
5. What might be the characteristics of a form of disposal suitable for 'inadequate' offenders?
6. To what extent do currently available forms of disposal possess these characteristics; and what legal or other restraints are there on the use of those that do?
7. Would it be desirable (or possible) to remove these restraints, or even to seek to devise some new form of disposal combining the characteristics already identified?

DEFINITION OF TERMS

It is necessary to define any category of offender if it is proposed to provide for that category alone some type of disposal different from (and perhaps either more or less severe than) the types of disposal available for offenders who fall into different categories. If there is a class of individual which in law is to be treated differently from other classes, then that class must be precisely and realistically defined. In this chapter it will be suggested, however, that such a precise legal definition is, in relation to 'inadequates' and 'inadequacy', an unattainable goal. But, quite apart from legal definition, any rational discussion of a topic requires definition of the terms in which the discussion is to proceed. In that sense and for that purpose, it is suggested that definition is perfectly possible.

The terms 'inadequate' and 'inadequacy' are in everyday use throughout the criminal justice system but, as pointed out, they have never in fact been defined. It is significant that, in the Butler Report, 1975, they appear in inverted commas. Whether they are found in social inquiry reports, in articles in the literature of penology or in the judgments of the Court of Appeal, they sometimes seem to signify little more than a coded indication of the intractability of the problem which the particular case, situation or individual presents. There seems to be little doubt that one can readily recognize an 'inadequate' when one encounters him (or her) in the course of professional work; furthermore, one would, if asked to describe the individual, have little difficulty in pointing out the characteristics which make the appellation 'inadequate' appropriate. But, if the task is to define 'inadequates' in general, then there would be almost as many suggested definitions as persons invited to supply them.

The reason for this is that the term 'inadequate', in the context which concerns us, could be defined by reference to a large number of possible individual characteristics, either singly or in combination. These might include reference to intelligence, mental health, general behaviour, social circumstances or criminal history. Some would add to this list; others might delete some items from it. The possibilities, in the order in which they have just been posed, will be examined briefly. From now on, in referring to 'inadequates', the masculine gender, will be used—partly to avoid grammatical convolutions; partly because similar considerations apply, in this context, to both men and women; and partly because, though there are, no doubt, just as many female as male 'inadequates', the majority of those who appear as defendants in criminal courts are men.

Intelligence

An offender might be said to be an 'inadequate' if his intelligence quotient, as assessed objectively, indicates that he would have been classified as 'subnormal' within the meaning of the 1959 Mental Health Act, or as possessing an 'arrested or incomplete development of mind' within the meaning of the 1983 Mental Health Act; or if his intelligence, so assessed, fell below some other level specified for the purpose of the sought-after definition. However, whilst it may well be that many individuals, readily recognizable as 'inadequates', do have low intelligence quotients, ex-

perience indicates that this is not by any means a universal characteristic of
such persons.

Mental health

Plainly, not all mentally ill persons are 'inadequate', nor are all 'inadequates' mentally ill. But nobody can sit, or practise, in the courts for any
appreciable time without encountering obvious 'inadequates' who are
diagnosed as suffering from, for example, schizophrenia. If alcoholism or
drug dependency can be regarded as mental disorders, then a very large
number of 'inadequates', in our sense, are mentally disordered.

We have all encountered individuals whom we would regard as 'inadequates' although their intelligence is within normal limits and they cannot
be regarded as mentally ill. Such persons may habitually sleep rough or—
as the Vagrancy Acts put it—'wander abroad'; they may habitually abuse
alcohol or other drugs; they may be constitutionally unable to manage
money; they may be dishevelled, unwashed and smelly; they may move
from hostel to hostel or lodging-house to lodging-house; they may behave
in a variety of socially unorthodox ways. But, equally, persons who behave
in some of these ways may well not be recognizable as 'inadequates'.

Social circumstances

Individuals might be categorized as 'inadequates' by reference to their
social circumstances. Some 'inadequates' are homeless; some have no ties
of family or friendship; some may be affected by other circumstances
which are not of their own making. They may be people who, if not so
affected, might never have appeared to be 'inadequate', but whose
'inadequacy' consists, if at all, in their inability to overcome these problems
or to overcome them unaided.

Criminal record

Many individuals are regarded by the courts (and, no doubt, by the police
and others) as 'inadequates' because they have committed repeated petty
offences. Often there will be frequent convictions for drunkenness;
sometimes for drug abuse. Many shoplifters are no doubt 'inadequates';
sometimes 'inadequates' break into premises to steal food or to obtain
shelter.

Sometimes their offences will be much more serious. Criminal damage,
often to a substantial value, may be committed by 'inadequates'—
especially those who sleep in, and subsequently burn down, barns. Some
sexual offences, notably offences against children, are committed by people
who might, from their other characteristics, be so classified. However,
where serious offences of this kind are committed, the prime consideration
of the courts is likely to be the protection of the public; thus lengthy

custodial sentences may be essential, and nothing that is said in the rest of this chapter is intended to apply to persons who have committed such offences.

It can readily be seen that no single one of these methods of categorization would be sufficient to produce an acceptable legal definition, nor is it easy to see how any combination of them would achieve this result. However, though legal definition may be impossible, a common characteristic of 'inadequates' is their inability to cope unaided with the ordinary problems of everyday life; I shall use the terms 'inadequate' and 'inadequacy' in the rest of this paper without any real concern that the lack of a more precise definition will lead to confusion.

SHOULD 'INADEQUATES' BE DIVERTED FROM THE CRIMINAL JUSTICE SYSTEM?

There can be very little doubt that 'inadequates' are already being diverted from the criminal justice system to a very significant extent. The police will not arrest and seek to prosecute familiar drunks unless they feel they have no alternative. If persons of borderline subnormal intelligence take goods from shops without paying for them, the management will often be persuaded not to prosecute. A real question arises whether greater use might be made of this executive power, and, in particular, whether there is any screening process which might profitably be employed by the Crown Prosecution Service. There is a superficial attraction in this idea which, if it were to be carefully and consistently implemented, might at least have the advantage of reducing court lists. However, I am uneasy about the constitutional desirability of any extension of the executive power to prevent prosecution where there is clear evidence of the commission of a criminal offence. Furthermore, the public money saved by reducing court lists would be largely offset by that required to operate a satisfactory screening process. And, at a practical level, the Crown Prosecution Service is already overstretched, and would, I guess, be most unwilling to take on this further responsibility.

Moreover, it seems very doubtful whether it would necessarily be in the interests of the 'inadequates' themselves to divert them from the courts. It would be different if the sole objective of prosecution were the punishment of the offender. But in fact it may often happen that the appearance of the 'inadequate' before the court is the catalyst which leads to some form of disposal, other than mere punishment, which is of benefit to the inadequate himself and which, but for his appearance at court, might not have been made available to him.

It is suggested, therefore, that this aspect of the matter is best left, as at present, to the good sense and experience of the police.

BAIL AND CUSTODY

It is a feature of our criminal justice system that large numbers of unconvicted persons are held in custody. It is no part of the task of this chapter to discuss whether these numbers are too large. It may, however, be the fact that 'inadequates', more than other categories of defendant, are held in custody before trial unnecessarily, and worse, that they, more than others, are held in police cells rather than in remand prisons. Statistics are, of course, unavailable, but experience suggests that this may be the case. If it is, there are a number of possible reasons for it. The 'inadequates' may not ask for, or insist that they receive, legal representation from an early stage. Magistrates' courts may not always be ready to provide such representation unless pressed by defendants to do so. Duty probation officers may not identify the problem presented by the 'inadequate' at a sufficiently early stage and may not make sufficiently urgent enquiries about places, including bail hostels, where defendants might live if granted bail. Medical and psychiatric reports may take too long to provide, resulting in repeated remands. None of these problems admits of an easy solution. They all need to be kept in mind by those whose responsibility it is to do so.

WHAT IS THE PROBLEM WHICH CONFRONTS THE COURTS?

If the current system operates properly, as, with the possible exception of bail provision, it generally does, the 'inadequate' presents the court with no unusual sentencing difficulties on his first few appearances before the court. Social or medicopsychiatric problems should have been identified by the probation service, which will have recommended some suitable form of disposal. It may turn out that the 'inadequate' person will make, in the course of a lifetime, only a few court appearances if he makes any at all; for 'inadequates' do not necessarily become offenders, habitual or occasional. If existing systems prove insufficient in practice this is not because of any *legal* constraint on their use. There may be constraints in terms of resources, but that is outside the scope of this chapter. In short, the inadequate who is an occasional offender presents no problems which are not common to all offenders.

The real problem is that of repeated offences. Every court becomes familiar with lists of petty convictions extending back over many years and covering many pages. When judges and magistrates complain about the problem of 'inadequates' this is usually what they mean.

The legislature has in the past sought to answer this problem by providing for lengthy periods of incarceration for repeated petty offenders. Imprisonment under the Vagrancy Acts and sentences of preventive detention were examples of this. Extended sentences still provide, in theory, one way of keeping frequent offenders out of public circulation and away from the courts for long periods, but the stringent qualifying conditions coupled with the obvious undesirability of imprisoning petty offenders for lengthy terms effectively prevent the use of such sentences in the type of case under consideration. The Court of Appeal has repeatedly stressed that it is contrary to principle to imprison an offender for a term longer than that merited by the instant offence simply because of a pattern of repeated offences. In any event, the imposition of long terms of imprisonment for petty offences is now generally regarded as unjust, expensive, wasteful of scarce prison accommodation and unlikely to produce any long-term beneficial effect—either for the offender or for the public.

Unhappily, the preferred alternative—that of repeated short terms—suffers from all the above-mentioned disadvantages—save perhaps that it is not so obviously unjust. Why, then, is so plainly unsatisfactory a method of disposal in such common use? The reason, of course, is that almost all non-custodial disposals by their nature depend on the cooperation of the offender, and, if that cooperation is not forthcoming the ultimate sanction is normally a disposal, namely a custodial sentence, which does not require such cooperation. Unhappily, 'inadequates' are often people who find the greatest possible difficulty in cooperating with currently available non-custodial disposals. They probably do not have the means to pay fines, nor the ability to arrange their affairs so that even small regular payments can be made. They may well cooperate at a superficial level or even more deeply, with a probation order, but experience shows that even this is far from certain to prevent their reoffending during the currency of the order, thus rendering an eventual custodial sentence virtually inevitable. The same applies to other forms of non-custodial penalty.

It follows that the core of the problem may lie in the fact that virtually every non-custodial penalty for adults has a custodial penalty held in reserve. Where there have been repeated failures by the offender to co-operate with the non-custodial penalty the pressure on the court to implement the reserve, custodial sanction may become irresistible. Courts, it is reasonably said, cannot function if their orders are repeatedly flouted. Unhappily the 'inadequate' may well be incapable of appreciating that failure to cooperate with a non-custodial penalty is likely to land him in prison; or, worse, he may not regard prison as a deterrent; he becomes resigned to it and used to it; he looks on it as a normal, if intermittent, part of his existence—easier, perhaps, to cope with than the demands of living in the community.

Thus, the problem which confronts the court is that of the repeated, probably petty, offence committed by the 'inadequate' recidivist, and the difficulty of disposing of his case in some way which will not lead inexorably to repeated short sentences of imprisonment.

THE CHARACTERISTICS OF A DISPOSAL SUITABLE FOR 'INADEQUATE' RECIDIVISTS

A phrase frequently found in social inquiry reports is 'a suspended sentence/probation order/conditional discharge will be a constant reminder of what is in store if he re-offends'. This may be true of some offenders, but experience suggests that it is in the highest degree doubtful whether it is ever true of 'inadequate' offenders, one of whose characteristics is that they tend not to think before they offend. It follows that deterrence of the offender will not figure significantly in an ideal disposal. This is not to say that such a disposal should not contain a punitive element. The public and the victims of crime demand this, and no system of criminal justice can function unless punitive sanctions form a central feature of it. But there can, and in many cases should, be other elements as well, and these should include, in the case of 'inadequate' recidivists, elements of some or all of the following kinds.

First, there might be measures designed to address and, if possible, alleviate the particular social, health or other problems which confront the 'inadequate' person and with which, because of his 'inadequacy', he cannot cope on his own. Such measures might include the provison of treatment for psychiatric or physical ailments (whether self-induced or not), supervision and counselling; training in elementary social skills; and the provision of facilities for meeting and mixing with others in reasonably civilized and comfortable surroundings.

Second, there might be measures designed to lessen the temptation to offend and the opportunity of offending. In this connection, it is important not to be unrealistic. The majority of 'inadequate' recidivists will not only reoffend but will do so on frequent occasions. Whilst measures that would have a chance of preventing this would, of course, be highly desirable, a much more limited objective might well be worth striving for. That objective would be to keep 'inadequates' from serving unnecessary prison sentences; to avoid disposals which will actually increase the likelihood of reoffending; and, if possible, to do something which will diminish this likelihood.

Current social trends, including the notorious shortage of accommodation for homeless single persons, are commonly, and perhaps correctly, blamed for the problem of crime committed by 'inadequates'. It is my subjective view, gained, it is true, from experience in the Crown Courts (the position may be different in magistrates' courts) that it is not lack of resources, but constraints of different kinds which prevent the passing of sentences which include, in suitable proportions, elements of this kind. Such constraints include those which will be referred to in discussing currently available disposals, and in particular the notion that failure of a non-custodial penalty must ultimately lead to a custodial one. The Home Office Green Paper *Punishment, Custody and the Community* puts forward the view that suitable non-custodial measures can be properly repeated even if they have not entirely succeeded and even if the offender reoffends during their currency (Home Office, 1988). Whilst the primary concern of the Green Paper is not with 'inadequate' recidivists, this concept seems to be particularly important in relation to such persons, in whose cases it is to easy to despair and impose counterproductive custodial sentences when other types of disposal appear to have failed.

DISPOSALS CURRENTLY AVAILABLE

Before considering whether any new form of disposal, or any new method of implementing existing forms, would be desirable, it would be sensible to consider: 1. what disposals are at present available; 2. the extent to which they conform to the criteria just suggested, namely 'Does it help to alleviate the offender's problems, and does it lessen his temptation to offend and his opportunity of offending?'; and 3. what are the legal constraints upon their use?

Imprisonment

In the absence of some radical alternative this is likely to continue to be used regularly. It fulfils none of the criteria just mentioned. Furthermore, suspended and partly suspended sentences are almost equally inappropriate, being likely to lead before long to actual incarceration.

Community service order

Such an order, though like imprisonment and fines it includes a substantial punitive element, may also have a rehabilitative effect. I am not sure how often it is recommended for, or imposed on, 'inadequates', because, due to the lack of definition of 'inadequacy', statistics are not available. However, experience suggests that it is often not recommended, perhaps because the provision of suitable work and supervision would cause problems for the organizers. This may be a pity, because the performing of some useful work within their powers and under supervision may have a beneficial effect on some 'inadequates'. It may be that further investigation of this area would be worthwhile. It should, of course be noted, that like nearly all of the other non-custodial disposals which shall be mentioned, this suffers from the drawback that non-compliance by the offender is likely to lead to his imprisonment.

Probation order

Probation orders are frequently used for 'inadequates' in an attempt to avoid a custodial disposal. They may provide simply for supervision, in the form of more or less regular contact with the supervising probation officer, coupled with the threat that if the offender fails to cooperate, or commits any offence during the currency of the order, some sentence which is likely, in the event, to be a custodial sentence, will ensue. It is arguable that this type of order, while it may provide a helpful point of contact for the 'inadequate' offender, and may enable some of his more pressing medical, social and financial problems to be addressed, it is of itself most unlikely to prevent his further offending, and because of the 'breach' provisions, may well lead to a longer sentence of imprisonment on his next appearance before the court.

Probation orders with special conditions

Under this heading I refer not to negative conditions, such as prohibitions against consuming alcohol or resorting to public houses, which are now generally agreed to be unenforceable and unhelpful, but positive conditions which can provide, among other things, for psychiatric treatment either as an outpatient, or as an inpatient, for residence at a named hostel or 'where the probation officer directs', and for attendance for a limited period at a day activity centre. Orders of this general kind are, on the face of it, much more likely to be of benefit to 'inadequate' offenders since they can, in theory at least, be 'tailor-made' to their needs. It may therefore be helpful to explore their limitations, and the constraints upon their use.

Orders requiring the offender to submit to psychiatric treatment can only be made on medical evidence to the effect that the offender's mental condition both requires and may be susceptible to treatment. Such evidence will, in the case of 'inadequates', not always be forthcoming: but, if it is, such orders can be helpful. It is to be observed, however, that many clinics for alcoholics and drug abusers will not accept patients who attend as a condition of a probation order, taking the understandable view that success depends largely upon treatments being both undertaken and persisted in entirely voluntarily. Whilst understandable, this may lead to potentially helpful courses of treatment being unavailable for numbers of offenders who could benefit from them. Some investigation of the availability of clinics and treatment centres which will accept patients who attend in accordance with terms of probation orders, leading to the preparation of lists of such clinics and centres, might be useful.

Whereas conditions requiring residence in a hostel do not by law have to specify approved probation hostels, such hostels are, in general, the only ones willing to accept offenders to reside therein as a condition of a probation order. Approved probation hostels are not very numerous, nor do they always welcome the arrival of 'inadequate' recidivists, among their often young inmates. Some such hostels whose regimen specifically caters for 'inadequate' recidivists do exist and some extension of these facilities could only be beneficial.

Attendance at day activity centres can only be ordered, at the moment, for a maximum of 60 days. The regimen available at such centres tends to be geared to the young offender, and is not always suitable for the older 'inadequate' recidivist, whose presence at the centre might well be regarded as disruptive and inappropriate. There do exist, of course many 'drop-in centres' and similar establishments at which 'inadequates' can, if they wish, spend time in relative warmth and comfort during the day. However, attendance at such centres is not normally made a condition of probation orders. Perhaps some extension of this type of facility, coupled with a greater degree of supervision, some useful activities for the offenders to perform and, possibly, the ability to order attendance as a condition of a probation order, might be a useful part of the sentencer's armoury.

At the moment, it is almost unknown, though not unlawful, for terms as to psychiatric treatment, hostel residence and day centre attendance to be combined in a single order. It is interesting to note that the proposals in the Home Office Green Paper do move some way towards such a combination of conditions, either as terms of traditional probation orders or as parts of a new sentence which could also include provisions for community service, tracking, tagging and other restrictions of liberty (Home Office, 1988). It is, however, also to be observed that the Green Paper does not appear to envisage the combination of a requirement for psychiatric treatment with other such requirements or restrictions. In relation to 'inadequates' this may be an unfortunate omission from the proposals, though there may well be some good reason for the omission in relation to other classes of offender.

Conditional discharge

Conditional discharge is frequently recommended for persistent inadequate offenders. However, it seems to suffer from the disadvantages inherent in all conditional penalties: namely, that, in the all-too-probable event of a breach, imprisonment is likely to follow, but to have none of the rehabilitative potential of other forms of non-custodial sentence. It is hard to believe that any 'inadequate' offender who is about to commit a further offence has ever stopped to say to himself 'I am subject to a conditional discharge so I will not offend after all'.

Hospital orders

The criteria for the making of a hospital order are that the offender is suffering from mental illness, psychopathic disorder, severe mental impairment or mental impairment of a nature and degree which makes it appropriate for him to be detained for medical treatment, and, in the case of psychopathic disorder or mental impairment, that such treatment is likely to alleviate, or prevent a deterioration of his condition. It is important to note that dependence on alcohol or drugs is specifically excluded from the statutory definition of those mental disorders which can bring the compulsory powers of the Mental Health Acts into operation.

Plainly, some 'inadequates' will, from time to time, fall within this category of offender, and will thus be candidates for hospital orders; but the ordinary run of 'inadequate' offenders will not. Furthermore, it is very doubtful whether such offenders need, or would benefit from, detention in hospital. Hospital orders, then, are an essential part of the sentencer's armoury, but are not often likely to be appropriate for the 'inadequate' offender.

Guardianship orders

The criteria for the making of guardianship orders are identical to those for the making of hospital orders, save that the mental disorder must be 'of a nature and degree which warrants his reception into guardianship'.

The effect of the order is to place the offender under the guardianship of the local social services authority or of some other named person, and empowers the guardian to require the offender (*inter alia*) to reside at a place specified by the guardian, and to attend at specified places and times for medical treatment, occupation, education or training. The authority of the guardian subsists for six months and is renewable thereafter on the recommendation of the responsible medical officer, in the same way as authority to detain under a hospital order.

There is no provision for the offender to be brought back before the court if he does not cooperate with the guardian, or if he reoffends (except, of course, to be dealt with for the fresh offence).

In many ways, therefore, the guardianship order seems tailor-made for the 'inadequate' recidivist. It keeps him out of prison; it provides for his accommodation; it provides for occupation and training; it provides for medical treatment; and, most importantly, it does not suffer from the defect of so many non-custodial orders, that its breach renders custody inevitable. However, such orders, first introduced in a slightly different form by the 1959 Mental Health Act are seldom, if ever, used. During twenty years in practice at the Bar and twelve years on the Circuit Bench, I cannot recall a single case in which such an order has been recommended or in fact made. Nor has the experience of a number of colleagues been any different. No doubt such orders are made, but they seem to be a rarity, in the context of criminal proceedings.

The reason for this is far from clear. It is possible that the fact that the financial burden of caring for an offender under guardianship will fall on the local authority, whereas that for the offender in hospital will fall on the Department of Health and that for the offender in prison will fall on the Home Office, is of some significance. Perhaps the criteria for reception into guardianship are too stringent, so that persons who fulfil them find themselves in hospital or prison. If this is so, it seems to be unfortunate. The criteria were, no doubt, strictly drawn because the guardianship order involves a restriction of liberty; but if the effect of this is that, in many cases, a far more serious—and less beneficial—restriction of liberty ensues, perhaps the time has come to rethink the criteria. If the problem is that local social services departments do not wish to shoulder the burden of acting as guardians for 'inadequate' mentally disordered offenders, then perhaps this aspect of the matter should be investigated and reconsidered.

If the lack of enthusiasm for this type of order is because there is no sanction for its breach, this view is misconceived for the reasons which have already been put forward.

A NEW OR MODIFIED FORM OF ORDER

All existing forms of order, with the possible exception of the guardianship order, suffer from disadvantages when considered in the context of the 'inadequate' recidivist. And it has to be assumed, from the fact that it is virtually never used, that the guardianship order also has some overwhelming disadvantages, though these are not readily identifiable.

I propose, therefore, that the vital ingredients for a new type of order suitable for the 'inadequate' recidivist might be:

1. Abandonment of the idea that, if the order 'fails' imprisonment is the inevitable next step;
2. The possibility of combining in the same order requirements that the offender shall, for a significant period
   a) reside in a hostel or other approved accommodation
   b) carry out specified activities inside or outside the hostel or other accommodation
   c) remain under the close and continuous supervision of a probation officer or similarly trained person
   d) submit to specified treatment for any relevant physical or psychiatric condition, including dependence on alcohol or other drugs;
3. Recognition of that fact that some offenders will fail to comply with some, or perhaps all, of these requirements, but that their return to court for *breach of requirements* is unlikely to be productive, as is the imposition of a sentence for the offence which gave rise to the order, if a further offence is committed during its operational period. It is suggested that, if the order is 'breached' in either of these ways, the supervising officer should have unfettered discretion whether or not to bring the offender back before the court which made the order, and that the court's options should consist *only* of power to revoke the order or to add, delete or alter any term. The fact of the order, and of the offenders' response to it would, of course, form part of the antecedent history of the offender when he was dealt with for any subsequent offence, committed either during or after the conclusion of the operational

period of the order, but in no other respect would the breach of the order put him in further jeopardy.

There will be objections. It will be said, first, that it would be expensive in terms of scarce resources of accommodation and supervision. No doubt it would be, but before this objection is allowed to prevail some effort should be made to cost, on a daily or weekly basis, the regimen under such an order and to compare it with the cost of imprisonment.

Second, it may be contended that the proposal has the odour of the workhouse about it; such an objection would be based on prejudice rather than fact. There is no reason at all why the proposed regimen should not be both civilized and humane; in any event it would be preferable to imprisonment.

Third, some members of the judiciary, and no doubt of the press or public, will object that it has no 'teeth' in that the offender can breach it with impunity. This, no doubt, is true; however, no court would be obliged to impose such an order; traditional orders with in-built sanctions for breach would remain available if the court, after mature consideration, were of the view that their imposition was to benefit the public.

Fourth, attention will be drawn to the difficulty of selecting suitable cases for the imposition of the order. This, I concede, is a genuine problem. It would be designed for 'inadequates' and as we have discovered, accurate categorization of individual offenders as 'inadequate' is difficult if not impossible. It must be a genuine alternative to custody; its whole point would be lost if it were used as a substitute for other non-custodial sentences.

It could be safely left to the courts, with the help of those who advise them, to select the cases and the offenders for whom such an order would be *suitable* and to devise its precise terms. However, it would also be necessary to restrict the categories of offender for whom it would be *legally availabe*. Its use might therefore be restricted by reference to an offender's criminal history.

CONCLUSION

The problem of the 'inadequate' recidivist is not going to go away. The idea that it is possible to prevent such persons from offending repeatedly is a mere pipe-dream. But to imprison them again and again will not deter them, nor will it deter other 'inadequate' recidivists. It will prevent their offending for the duration of each sentence, but it is expensive, wasteful of resources and likely to increase rather than diminish the chances that they will reoffend.

Non-custodial sentences, whether those currently available or of some new kind will not, in most cases, prevent reoffending either; but, if they are imaginatively and carefully worked out, if they address the real problems of

the individual 'inadequate' offender, and if they are sensitively implemented, they may diminish the frequency of reoffending; if they do not
include custodial sanctions for breach, they will not increase the pressure
on the prison population; and, whatever they do, or do not, achieve in
penological terms, they may do something to diminish the sum of human
misery, and thus be of some benefit both to the individual offenders and to
the public.

REFERENCE

Home Office (1988). *Punishment, Custody and the Community*. Cmnd. 424.
London: HMSO.

Author's note
Since this chapter was written, the Green Paper (1988) 'Punishment,
Custody and the Community' has been followed in February 1990 by the
White Paper 'Crime, Justice and Protecting the Public' (1990, Cmnd 965)
and in October 1990 by the publication of a Criminal Justice Bill based in
large part on the proposals in the White Paper. Some of the concerns
expressed in this chapter, notably that relating to repeated custodial
sentences for petty offences, appears to be addressed although it remains to
be seen whether any alternative disposal, suitable for the specific needs of
'inadequate' recidivists, is to be provided.

Section 3
The Mentally Disordered Offender in Prison

6 *A brief review of the current status of, and provision for, the mentally disordered offender in prison, and suggestions for changes, action and research*

ROSEMARY J. WOOL

INTRODUCTION

Mentally disordered offenders cannot be considered in isolation; they can only be considered within the context of the whole prison service milieu.

Each prison is a separate community, and mentally abnormal offenders within the establishment are members of that community. Within this context they are subject to the same conditions caused by overcrowding, the transfer of responsibility for management from headquarters to regional level, the new working arrangements for prison officers to a salaried service, and the new reality of budget constraints.

The total number of prisoners within the prison system increased over the last decade from an average daily population of 41 570 in 1977 to 48 428 in 1987 decreasing during 1990 to 45 000. The number of unsentenced prisoners, largely on remand, has increased over the same period from 5281 to 10 625. The estate, and particularly that part of the estate holding the remand population, has not increased correspondingly. Consequently, prisoners in the local prisons and remand centres are living in very overcrowded conditions. Furthermore, the prison hospitals have acquired no further accommodation, and in some local prisons beds have been lost.

REMAND PRISONERS

As more prisoners are held in custody there will obviously be proportionately more mentally abnormal people among them. Due to shortage of space, many of them cannot be accommodated in the hospitals of the local prisons and remand centres. They are therefore put on to normal location or on to designated 'medical wings' which are the responsibility of discipline officers and not hospital officers.

The Butler Report recommended remanding mentally disordered persons to hospital for assessment and treatment, and the 1983 Mental Health Act made this possible by the use of Sections 35, 36, and 38. The number of these hospital orders has increased from 40 in 1984 to 248 in 1986; but though the subjects of these orders are subsequently transferred to hospital, the majority are remanded in the first instance to prison. The general district psychiatric hospitals do not help to any significant degree in this respect. One has the impression that many of the general psychiatric hospitals have divorced themselves from any responsibility for those mentally abnormal patients who come into the judicial system.

The half-yearly returns completed by prison medical officers of detainable mentally disordered offenders do not reflect the actual situation in the local prisons (see Table 6.1). It seems that when a hospital disposal cannot be found, no medical recommendation is made to the court, and the prisoner is not included in the returns. It would appear that the Section 39 (of the Mental Health Act) provision, in which the courts can ask for help from the regional medical directors, is not used sufficiently.

A particular cause for concern in the case of mentally disordered remand prisoners is the length of time they spend in prison before a disposal is effected. For example, recently in one local prison there were 23 mentally ill patients in the hospital and on the 'medical wing', who had been there for periods ranging from one to seven months. General psychiatrists who had treated them in the past seemed reluctant to visit, taking up to four weeks to respond to a prison medical officer's request. Due to open-ward policies and contracting inpatient facilities, the psychiatrists are rarely in a position to offer patients in prison on remand hospital beds; but they do offer the courts outpatient supervision. Forensic psychiatrists appear more cooperative, and will, subject to availability of beds, eventually take patients who need the degree of security which they are able to offer.

SENTENCED PRISONERS

The present situation of mentally disordered offenders in the sentenced population is more encouraging. Professor John Gunn has commenced his

Table 6.1 Detainable mentally disordered offenders

	1979	1980	1981	1982	1983	1984	1985	1986	1987
Unsentenced prisoners	206	204	157	160	198	192	150	196	188
Section 48* transfers	16	19	22	18	23	47	41	53	77

Under Section 48 of the 1983 Mental Health Act, removal to hospital of remand and civil prisoners who are suffering from mental illness or severe mental impairment is outlined.

research will also include consideration of the adequacy of the present treatment provision, and he will be making recommendations for improvements.

The number of mentally disordered inmates notified by prison medical officers as meeting the criteria of the Mental Health Act, and the number of Section 47 transfers over the past decade are shown in Table 6.2. Thus in 1987 those transferred under Section 47 accounted for 84 per cent of those identified in the six-monthly returns. The remainder were probably awaiting assessment and/or admission. This is a considerable improvement on the 1979 transfers which at 84 represented only 24.2 per cent of the total estimated as needing admission under the Act.

In times past, most of the sentenced prisoners who were mentally ill were held in local prison hospitals. Given the increasing problems of overcrowding in these local establishments, the medical directorate is developing a policy in which each region will have designated Medical Care Centres. These centres will have psychiatric support, and be complemented with a high percentage of mental-nurse qualified hospital officers.

In addition to the acutely mentally ill, the penal system holds chronically mentally ill offenders and socially and intellectually inadequate prisoners who need asylum and special care. Units for this category are now being established. Thus, there is a response, albeit belatedly, to the Butler recommendations regarding the care of the inadequates.

Young offenders

The Butler Report recommended the provision of psychiatric care for borstal trainees in the North of England comparable to that in the South-East (Feltham). Since then, Youth Custody has replaced borstal. In the mid-1970s Glen Parva Borstal (later Young Offender and Remand Centre), opened, and was designated a psychiatrically supported national resource. The hospital has established acute psychiatric wards, a therapeutic community, and wards for the socially and intellectually inadequate.

During 1988 a committee considered the allocation of trainees with

Table 6.2 The number of mentally disordered inmates and Section 47 transfers

	1979	1980	1981	1982	1983	1984	1985	1986	1987
Sentenced prisoners	347	250	175	139	160	144	124	137	156
Section 47 transfers	84	87	86	85	92	108	100	107	131

special psychological needs. Since January 1990 a pilot scheme has been operating in the Midlands and if successful it will be adopted nationally.

Personality disordered offenders

Grendon remains the one national resource for the treatment of those with personality disorders within therapeutic communities (see Chapter 8 by Michael Selby). Increasing use is being made of Grendon for life-sentence prisoners, of whom the penal establishments now hold over 2000.

Two years ago, in response to a Home Office committee recommendation, Grendon began to accept psychiatric patients into its hospital. It now has about 20 mentally ill at any one time. The two limitations are in the areas of consent to treatment, as medication cannot be administered without consent except in an emergency, and in rehabilitation, because trips outside prison giving the opportunity to assess progress are not possible.

Special units have been opened at Parkhurst, Lincoln and Hull for the treatment of psychopaths who have exhausted all other prison department outlets. Other such units, which hold small numbers of inmates in a high staff/inmate ratio, are anticipated. The Parkhurst unit alone at present has psychiatric oversight (see Chapter 7 by Susan Evershed). Another unit, having psychologists on the staff overseeing, is proposed. These units fulfil recommendation 127 of the Butler Report relating to the treatment of psychopaths.

Sex offenders

There is an upsurge in interest in the treatment of paedophiles at present. Also, concurrent with the feminist lobby to standardize sentencing for rapists come demands for the treatment of these offenders while they are in prison. Treatment in the minds of most pressure groups implies medical treatment; and the prison medical service is expected to 'do something'. In fact, many visiting prison psychiatrists are quietly giving considerable psychotherapeutic support to very many sex offenders. Twenty per cent of Grendon's population at any one time are sex offenders, and the Annexe at Wormwood Scrubs treats sex offenders. Feltham's psychologists continue to help 'inadequate' young sex offenders; and Glen Parva hospital does likewise on its therapeutic community wards.

But just as the Cleveland Enquiry makes clear the importance of a multidisciplinary approach in helping the victims, so a multidisciplinary approach is desirable in the treatment of the offenders.

If more is to be done to treat sex offenders in prison, the Home Office will need to give guidance, particularly to those establishments holding large numbers of sex offenders on (prison) Rule 43. This will need to include recommendations for assessment by probation officers, psychologists, chaplains, teachers, physical education instructors, medical officers, psychiatrists, and prison officers. There will also be a need to establish an assessment board to work out treatment programmes, and a review board to assess progress. Such recommendations are expensive of staff time, and so beyond the present policy of humane containment for sex offenders; but they might be achievable within existing resources. A recently set up committee is in fact touching on this very area.

An alternative suggestion is the establishment of a separate secure centre, funded jointly by the Home Office and the Department of Health, for the treatment of sex offenders. The cost of this would be high, but might satisfy the continuing public pressure that more is done. However, it must be remembered that not all sex offenders are motivated to change their behaviour patterns, and consequently cannot be treated.

Drug abusers

Whereas the treatment of the effects of drug abuse is initially a medical matter, the phenomenon is social and the long-term treatment must again be multidisciplinary. The prison medical directorate has initiated a through-care scheme which is now being developed in establishments. The scheme involves close cooperation between medical officers and probation officers. Some medical officers are now members of National Health Service District Drug Advisory Committees, and in addition drug abuse therapists are visiting prisons to offer counselling.

CHANGES AND ACTION REQUIRED

The following are suggestions for action and change:

- There is an urgent need to find ways of keeping the mentally ill out of the prisons; and of making provisions for them other than in the local prisons and remand centres. Many who come into custody are some of the most unattractive and undesirable members of our society. Notwithstanding, they are human beings in need of care, and must be considered when community care provision is allocated. If the mental hospitals cannot admit them, then perhaps psychiatric bail hostels should be provided.
- Within the remand system the present medical facilities cannot meet the demand. If the mentally ill cannot be diverted from the prisons, then alternative accommodation will need to be made available by displacing the healthy. The Home Secretary is considering urban remand centres and private remand facilities. If accepted these might indirectly improve the lot of the mentally abnormal within the penal system.
- More appropriate facilities for the treatment/asylum of the sentenced mentally disordered offenders are beginning to emerge. Current research should help to further identify the need and target more appropriately the facilities.

7 Special unit, C wing, HMP Parkhurst

SUSAN EVERSHED

INTRODUCTION

In a converted half of a traditional wing of the Victorian prison, Parkhurst, there exists a new and innovative special unit designed to take a maximum of 22 adult male prisoners. The unit is part of a Prison Department initiative for dealing with prisoners who present control problems. It is designed to take disruptive prisoners who have proved intractable to ordinary prison management, and who are seen as mentally abnormal. The unit aims to contain prisoners in an humane manner, to manage them effectively by minimizing their problem behaviour, and perhaps effect longer-term changes in their attitudes, behaviour, and mental state.

The unit opened on 30 December 1985 as a direct result of a review by the Control Review Committee which published a series of recommendations to improve the management of prisoners serving long sentences (Control Review Committee, 1984). In their report, the Committee noted that in the long-term prison system there is a group of prisoners who present serious control problems for prison management. This was thought to be a small group, certainly less than 10% of the whole, but a group which posed problems out of proportion to its numbers. The Committee divided this small group into three smaller groups: the disruptive, the subversive, and the mentally abnormal, although they recognized that this breakdown was simplistic and that the subgroups were clearly neither exhaustive nor mutually exclusive. Among the recommendations proposed for managing these prisoners was one to establish a number of special units operating a variety of regimens.

The Committee noted that 'for some kinds of mentally disturbed prisoner a revitalized Parkhurst C wing and a developed Grendon regimen would have much to offer' (see Chapter 8 for further discussion of Grendon.) The original C wing at Parkhurst operated between 1970 and 1979. It was closed in 1979 in order to accommodate prisoners from the main prison after a disturbance. The unit provided a facility which was halfway between normal prison location and prison hospital for a group of about 35 difficult and disturbed men. The test for admission was that the prisoner had a psychiatric diagnosis and had demonstrated disturbed behaviour of a kind which could not be managed in an ordinary prison regimen. The behaviour included violence towards staff, inmates or property; attempted suicide, self-mutilation or regular hunger strikes;

mental illness; chronic sick-reporting; and repeated disciplinary offences. The Committee were impressed by the regard which the C wing unit had commanded in the prison service and the powerful support for it outside the service. The Committee went on '. . . we believe that a facility of this kind had a very valuable role to play in containing disturbed prisoners . . . We therefore recommend that every effort should be made to re-establish such a facility as soon as possible.'

A further recommendation was for outside academics to participate in the planning and evaluation of new developments of this kind. This led to the establishment of the Research and Advisory Group on the Long-Term Prison System. This group produced a report in 1987 (Research and Advisory Group on the Long Term Prison System, 1987) which, following the Control Review Committee initiative, recommended the establishment of 'a range of special units, each characterized by differing kinds of specialist assistance'. One of these units, the first to be established, was to be in C wing at Parkhurst and was to include specialist psychiatric assistance, together with specialist psychological assistance in the form of counselling and social learning therapy programmes; a moderate degree of structure; a high degree of staff involvement with prisoners; and opportunities for prisoners to find ways of modifying their own problem behaviour. But there was to be no inmate participation in the running of the unit. It was clearly designed, therefore, to selectively take inmates presenting control problems who had mental disorder or who were strongly suspected of having mental disorder. It would have to deal with prisoners who were not thought to qualify for NHS or Special hospitals, but who often attract the label 'borderline personality disorder' because of transient psychoses. Prison reports about them would include comments such as 'bizarre', 'disturbed', 'psychopathic tendencies' or 'abnormal personality'.

THE UNIT OPENS

In November 1984, a junior governor was posted to Parkhurst prison and given the task of opening the new unit by the end of 1985. In the style of the old C wing, he was to work with a multidisciplinary management team consisting of a medical officer, a psychologist, and hospital chief officer. Development of the unit was to be overseen by the principal medical officer at Parkhurst prison hospital (who had also been involved in the previous C wing) and the Control Review Committee implementation team at head office.

One of the first tasks to be undertaken by this group was to agree upon a set of aims for the unit. Clearly one of the aims had to reflect the recommendation that the unit should help to relieve the long-term prison system by containing men who presented a problem of control because of their mental abnormality. At the same time the new unit was to be based on the old C wing and thus the aims had to indicate the unit's specialist function. After much thought, four aims were identified:

1. To provide a national resource for the management of certain types of disruptive and disturbed prisoners who are at present contained largely in the dispersal system.
2. To achieve a constructive way of managing such prisoners within a discrete unit by individualizing the management of inmates, and by encouraging a high degree of staff involvement.
3. To facilitate observation of inmate behaviour in order that early signs of impending crisis can be identified, and preventative or remedial action taken.
4. To encourage attitude changes and improvements in the mental state, behaviour and social skills of inmates.

(Home Office, 1985)

In addition, a set of selection criteria for prisoners was devised to help governors of institutions in the referral process, and to aid in the allocation of prisoners to the new unit.

The inmate population will comprise prisoners who are currently presenting and have persistently presented at more than one establishment, one or more of the following behaviours in an uncontrolled fashion:

(a) Violence towards staff and/or prisoners;
(b) Repeated offences against discipline;
(c) Damage to property within institutions;
(d) Behaviour that generally and persistently gives cause for concern including behaviour that is dangerous to self and others;

and who have a history or who present symptoms of mental abnormality.

(Home Office, 1985).

The Unit Management Team in devising the selection criteria were keen to take prisoners who had displayed disruptive or difficult behaviour at a number of different establishments so that the likelihood of their settling into normal prison regimen is limited. In addition, the difficult behaviour exhibited by the prisoners was to have been uncontrolled or irrational, stemming from their mental abnormality rather than any preconceived, rational motivation.

INMATE POPULATION

During the first two years of operation, 55 prisoners were referred by their institution governors for consideration for the Special Unit and of these, 29 were selected. A further eight men were also selected to go to the second Special Unit at HMP Lincoln (which takes disruptive prisoners with no indication of mental abnormality) and four more prisoners were withdrawn from consideration by their referring prisons. Thus only 14 men were actually rejected after failing to meet the Unit's selection criteria.

All the men were referred to the Special Units by their governors, who gave details of their specific problem behaviours, and the results of any efforts to control them. Reports from wing officers and managers, and different specialists were included allowing a great deal of information to be made available to the Special Units Selection Committee. The Committee consists of members of the unit management teams, the control review implementation team, the directorates of psychological services and medical services, and those at head office having responsibility for the allocation of Category A and life-sentence prisoners. They select prisoners most appropriate for C wing and Lincoln Unit giving priority to those held in dispersal prisons and long-term prisoners (those serving sentences of more than five years).

Of the 29 men accepted for C wing, 21 were serving life-sentences and all but three were serving sentences greater than five years. They had received these sentences largely for crimes against the person (with 16 having killed, a further seven having violence offences, and two with sex offences). Nineteen of these men were Category A prisoners, deemed as the most dangerous in the system and 12 had been resident in Special Hospitals at some period in their lives, indicating a degree of mental abnormality.

In terms of the problems they were causing within the prison system the average numbers of offences committed by the men was seven per year, whereas the 'normal' prisoner commits just over two per year. Table 7.1 indicates the number of men who had been involved in specific types of disruptive behaviour during the three years prior to referral to the Special Units Selection Committee. One can see that the men had indeed been highly disruptive. Moreover four of the men had actually killed other inmates whilst in prison or Special Hospital, and a further two had so attempted. Four men had taken hostages in prison, three taking inmates (two on more than one occasion) and one taking and attempting to kill a member of staff. Thus, the men were also seen as extremely dangerous and disturbed since, for the majority, these problems were seen as stemming from their mental state. Only two of the men were not described by their prisons' medical officers as suffering from some form of mental abnormality, and the majority (22 men) were seen as psychopathic or personality disordered. More details of the inmate population are given in Evershed, 1988.

Table 7.1 Number of men exhibiting difficult behaviour during the three years prior to referral to C wing special unit

Number of incidents	Violence to staff	Violence to inmates	Damage to property	Self-mutilation
At least 3 (i.e. 1 per year	9	2	5	1

DESCRIPTION OF THE UNIT

The wing itself, built on three floors, is very spacious; although it takes a maximum of 22 inmates there are more than twice that number of cells. To date, however, the top floor has not been used. The extra space in the unit was felt to be important to counteract the effects of containment within such a small unit with a small and fairly static population (in terms of both inmates and staff). Access to other parts of Parkhurst Prison is extremely limited for the inmates since the unit is for the most part self-contained. The unit has workshop and gymnasium facilities of its own and both religious and educational activities are conducted within the wing. The inmates are able to make use of some main prison facilities however: they have access to the main gymnasium for three hours per week; they can use the main prison library and canteen at specific times and their visits from family and friends take place in the main prison visits rooms. However, the aim remains to keep the unit separate from the main prison as far as is possible—a discrete prison within a prison—to encourage the breakdown of hostile attitudes towards prison staff and towards other inmates.

The inmates are encouraged to spend as much time as possible out of their cells mixing with both staff and other inmates. Since the majority have offences for violence and have problems mixing with others, it is felt that for improvements to be made inmates should be encouraged to associate with both staff and prisoners; to develop social behaviour.

The range of activities provided on the unit are wide. The workshop is set up to allow prisoners to try a range of crafts from leatherwork to computerized braille work. By far the most popular activity has been soft- and wooden toy manufacturing for charity. The emphasis, however, is on the inmates making up items individually or in small groups according to their level of skill rather than employing a 'production line' style of working. In terms of education, the unit's teachers have provided a variety of facilities so that men have been able to study almost whatever they chose from remedial English to Greek mythology. Possibly the most popular activity, however, is music with a number of men now learning to play the guitar.

In line with the relaxed atmosphere in the unit the prisoners are able to decline all unit activities, including work. In normal circumstances an inmate would incur a disciplinary report if he refused to work but on C wing this does not happen. However, if he declines all constructive activity he will lose money from his weekly wages.

In general the unit aims to provide a relaxed and safe environment where prisoners who have probably spent a great deal of time segregated from other prisoners can associate more freely with their peers. At the same time it is hoped that their attitude to prison, the staff, and to other inmates might change, and as a result their institutional behaviour improve.

Given the nature of the inmate population it was felt that, in order to maintain a safe environment that allowed the prisoners freedom to associate, a very strict monitoring of prisoners was essential. For this reason, and for the 'treatment' needs of the inmates, a 'personal officers' scheme was introduced.

Every inmate arriving in the unit is assigned to a personal officer (and also to a deputy officer working in the opposite division to the personal officer). It is the responsibility of the personal officer to develop a close knowledge of his inmate, to monitor and record his misbehaviour and his progress, and to build up a relationship with him.

The inmate's first ten weeks on the unit are treated as an 'assessment' period. During this time his personal officer and all of the specialists will assess his needs, his interests, and his strengths and weaknesses. At the end of the period a meeting is held of all concerned (including, where possible, the inmate himself) to draw up an individual 'training plan' for the prisoner. This document will set out the inmate's activities and provide him with a set of targets (based upon the results of the assessment) for the following 15 weeks. The activities and targets may relate to a variety of areas—educational, behavioural, social—depending upon his needs.

Every 15 weeks thereafter progress is reviewed and amendments made to the training programme as appropriate. The ultimate aim is to help the inmate to change sufficiently to be able to cope in normal location in another establishment. The end-result is that every inmate has his own individual plan coordinated and supervised by his Personal Officer.

Following the recommendations of these meetings, the specialists on the wing undertake treatment with the majority of the prisoners. By far the most common type of help given by the probation officer on the wing is counselling for family problems and help to develop coping strategies for imprisonment. The psychologist has undertaken a variety of work with different prisoners, the most common type of help involves the teaching of anger control techniques, social skills training and relaxation training to alleviate tension.

Often the help given to the prisoners by the different specialists has overlapped, but the techniques and the timing of treatment have varied. For the most part the treatment given to the men has been complementary and has usually involved the personal officer in the work to some extent.

The medical officer on the unit is also involved in counselling with the inmates and is in charge of the medication. About three-quarters of the men have been prescribed drugs (usually sedatives) during their stay in the unit although for some this was not on a regular basis. Only 13 men were prescribed drugs other than sedatives, mostly antidepressants and antipsychotics.

Much of the treatment has involved training the inmates in social skills, techniques for controlling anger, and ways of coping with the problems of imprisonment. The general ethos within the unit is one of non-confrontation. Staff are encouraged to use interpersonal skills in dealing with antagonistic behaviour, such as verbal abuse, to use discipline as a last resort, and to employ their skills to prevent difficult situations arising. Hence, formal punishments for disruptive behaviour are relatively rare. Instead, problem behaviour is largely ignored, but prisoners are calmed and counselled, and encouraged to talk through issues of concern. The detailed monitoring on inmate behaviour is crucial to this policy, as is the quality of the relationship between the inmates and their personal officers.

IS IT SUCCESSFUL?

It is almost impossible to provide a simple answer to the question 'Does it work?' C Wing can be seen as successful for a particular individual on the Unit whilst doing little for others. Since the Unit takes men who have been classifed as 'no hopers' it can be argued that any improvement in any individual prisoner means that the Unit is successful.

Also C Wing can be measured in terms of success on at least three different levels as reflected in its aims: the containment of difficult and disturbed prisoners; the effective management of these men; and the facilitation of their long-term change into better adjusted and less problematic prisoners. Whether or not the wing works, one must compare these aims to what has actually occurred on the Unit and what has happened to the prisoners afterwards.

The Unit does appear to have contained a number of highly disturbed and disruptive prisoners, holding them in conditions superior to those in which they were held previously. On average the C wing prisoners spent 36% of their time in segregation in a severely restricted regime, before their arrival on the Unit. During their stay they spent an average of 7% in segregation on a limited regime: a huge reduction.

Only five men have been transferred out of the Unit in less than a 12 month period because they were causing problems on the Unit. However, they were not causing the type of problems for which they were referred to the Unit, rather they were subverting other inmates against the Unit and persuading them not to interact with their Personal Officers, thus putting at risk the whole ethos of the Unit. The remaining 23 men have all spent at least a year on the Unit and thus far seven have been transferred back to other prisons after periods of behaviour on the Unit that were seen to be more stable.

During their stay in the unit, the prisoners' behaviour might be expected to improve if the claims of 'managing prisoners more effectively' are to be upheld. So far the frequency of incidents on the unit has indicated a dramatic improvement in the inmates' behaviour. There have been assaults on inmates, staff and property on the unit, but the figures show that violence to staff has reduced by over 40%, damage to property by over 50% and incidents in general by almost 30%.

Whereas violence to other inmates and self-mutilation have not decreased in frequency, the severity of offences (as in all other cases) has been reduced markedly. In fact, most of the violence demonstrated towards other prisoners amounts to minor scuffles rather than serious attacks.

Only anecdotal evidence has been collected about the few inmates who have 'graduated' from the Unit. One man has so far 'failed' and has returned to the Unit although his behaviour on transfer was much improved compared to his behaviour prior to the Unit. The remaining 6, from reports by their new institutions, all appear to be coping well. One man has even been released from prison on parole and his Probation Officer reports that he has settled back into the community surprisingly well.

This evidence suggests that the majority of prisoners are coping with transfer and are behaving much more appropriately, indicating that longer term changes may well be taking place on the Unit. However with such a small sample of prisoners and after so short a time, no claims for success at this third level are made here. There is underway a longer term research programme which will follow up prisoners who transfer from the Unit to see if any improvements to behaviour, mental state and attitudes are maintained. It will also attempt to discover which type of inmate and problem behaviour respond best to the Unit.

C wing has been criticized, however, not because it is seen to be unsuccessful but because it focuses specifically on those inmates who are problematic for prison governors. The critics question why such a wing should take those prisoners who have, by definition, behaved so badly when other equally disturbed men who have not caused problems in prisons are left in the normal prison system. The response to this argument should not be to close the C wing unit—particularly when it does appear to be fulfilling its function—but rather that more such units should be opened to admit different types of prisoners, and operate different regimens fitted to their needs. This, of course, is still an 'ideal'. For the present, within the limitations on finance and resources, the service, of necessity, places priorities of security and control above treatment. C wing, however, may demonstrate that in some cases the 3 priorities go hand in hand.

REFERENCES

Control Review Committee (1984). *Managing the Long Term Prison System.* London: HMSO.

Evershed S. (1987). Special Unit C Wing, HMP Parkhurst. In *Patterns of Long Term Imprisonment* (Bottoms A. E., Light R., eds.) Aldershot: Gower.

Evershed S. (1988). *Parkhurst Special Unit: The First Two Years.* Internal Report to Home Office.

Gunn J. (1987). *A Psychiatric Study of Intensive C Wing Parkhurst.* Internal Report to Home Office.

Home Office (1985). *Minutes of the C Wing Special Unit Commissioning Meeting* (July 1985) (restricted circulation).

Martin J. P. (1987). *C Wing, HM Prison Parkhurst: Some Aspects of Management.* Internal Report to Home Office.

Research and Advisory Group on the Long-Term Prison System (1987). *Special Units for Long-term Prisoners: Regimes, Management and Research. London: HMSO.*

8 HMP Grendon—the care of acute psychiatric patients: a pragmatic solution

MICHAEL SELBY

INTRODUCTION

The problem of coping with the psychiatric offender in the criminal justice system has been researched extensively and criticized widely. Many commentators and those within the prison service, for example, have concentrated on the unsuitability of the penal system as a placement for such offenders. However, with the closure of many mental hospitals beginning to have an effect on the wider community, a growing number of offenders with psychiatric disorders will (from the American experience) find themselves in trouble with the courts, and, inevitably, be imprisoned. The acute psychiatric unit at HMP Grendon provides an example of positive care for this group of offenders, and offers some optimistic indications that an appropriate regimen can be established. The theme throughout this chapter is the value of the pragmatic approach to solving problems.

Grendon Psychiatric Prison was created on the recommendation of Sir Norwood East and Dr de Hubert in 1939. Their conclusions, published in *The Psychological Treatment of Crime*, formed the basis upon which Grendon started its work in 1962. The objectives for Grendon were outlined in the *British Medical Journal* of 22 September 1962 as:

- The investigation and treatment of mental disorder generally recognised as calling for a psychiatric approach.
- The investigation of the mental condition of offenders whose offences in themselves suggest mental morbidity.
- An exploration of the psychopath and the provision of treatment and management to which they may be responsive.

(Snell, 1962)

THE ROLE OF GRENDON WITHIN THE PRISON SERVICE

After some false starts, the method adopted by the founding medical superintendent, Dr William Gray, was similar to that of the therapeutic community for the treatment of behavioural disorders set up by Dr Maxwell Jones at the Henderson Hospital. In 1978, Gunn and Robertson reported on their evaluation of Grendon's work in *Psychiatric Aspects of Imprisonment* (Gunn *et al.*, 1978) and have since published a 10-year follow-up of men discharged from Grendon in the *British Journal of Psychiatry* (Robertson and Gunn, 1987).

An important phrase from their conclusion is that 'Grendon's role is best regarded as that of a catalyst, acting by giving men who want to change the opportunity of spending their time in prison constructively' (Gunn and Robertson, 1987). A ten-year gap in research at Grendon was followed by a study from the Centre for Criminological Research in Oxford. It was funded by the Home Office, and examined Grendon's therapeutic process. The study will be published in 1990 or 1991.

A significant and unusual aspect of Grendon has been the duration of those in charge. There have been only three directors since its inception. The first two were medical superintendents but, on the death of Dr Raymond Jillett it was decided, after an interregnum year, to place a non-medically qualified prison governor in charge. At the same time, on 29 March 1984 the opportunity was taken to examine Grendon's present position and to give direction for its future in a working party under the chairmanship of the then Director of Prison Medical Services, Dr John Kilgour. This Advisory Committee of the Therapeutic Regime at Grendon (ACTRAG) reported to the Home Secretary on 29 July 1985 (Home Office, 1985). Its conclusions can be summarized briefly: that Grendon had survived was remarkable in itself, because the history of the prison service is littered with defunct initiatives, but in surviving there had been isolation and a process of ossification. So ACTRAG, whilst recommending the continuation of the therapeutic community method, also required an assessment and induction unit to be established, and, most significantly, recommended that the hospital of 28 beds within Grendon should be converted into a rescue unit—the acute psychiatric unit for prisoners who become mentally disturbed. This represented a return to the original objective in the 1930s.

It can, and has, been argued that this acute psychiatric unit (APU) is not only unnecessary but also in conflict with the operation of the Mental Health Act. It retains in the prison system those requiring immediate psychiatric treatment. Furthermore, in providing this kind of facility, Grendon is delaying, if not preventing, the will to find the solution to the problem that this small group of gravely and sometimes grossly disturbed convicted offenders presents. However, in a sense, Grendon not only is at the boundary of the notional divide between prison (punishment) and the Special Hospital (treatment) but is also providing the vital link bridging the two.

Grendon is not only the ideal penal establishment where this experiment could be tried, but arguably the *only* one. The overall regimen at Grendon is characterized by a therapeutic community existing within a prison discipline framework. The philosophies of these two 'institutions' could be considered, theoretically, to be mutually antagonistic but they have not only survived, but prospered, in dynamic tension. One reason is that Grendon has single-mindedly maintained the integrity of the pursuit of this task—which has not been easy. The second is that all staff embody in themselves both treatment and security; care and control; reconcilable in the relationship of the multidisciplinary staff approach with the prisoners and with each other. It is, therefore, possible for a prisoner to state on a television programme, spontaneously, and with only slightly tongue in cheek: 'We don't have grassing here, we call it therapeutic feedback'.

Central to participation in therapy is a commitment to change. Referral is by medical officers from prisons throughout England and Wales. The culture of this community is that of helping each other, as much self-determination as is practicable and observance of a strictly applied 'no violence' 'no drugs' rule.

Inmates have given as a reason for dramatic and sustained improvement in behaviour and attitude that they are allowed to behave naturally. Equally significantly, prison officers respond to the opportunity to exercise the caring aspect of their personalities. The abandonment of traditional antagonisms (causing a culture shock on arrival) and the lowering of the 'machismo' facade by both staff and inmate is beneficial in effecting therapy. In this accepting and guiding community, prisoners are allowed the reality and the dignity of mental illness during a psychotic episode.

The skills acquired within the context of the therapeutic community were invaluable, at all levels, in setting up the APU and throughout its development. Grendon has developed over the last six years—not least in accepting inmates who show a much greater propensity to violence and instability. This follows the decision that its work should be more relevant to the needs of the prison service as a whole and to the recognition that there must be a response to the wider patient need than the therapeutic community method by itself could cater for. Thus, the requirement of at least average intelligence, some articulacy and psychological robustness in order to utilize the therapeutic community form of treatment has limitations for the total prison population. The development of the acute psychiatric unit can be seen in this setting.

Had Grendon Hospital's APU not existed in its present state, those men who had been diagnosed as requiring immediate care due to the nature of their mental disorder would have been incarcerated in various prison hospitals singly or in small groups, subject to the inevitable delay that transfer under Section 47 of the 1983 Mental Health Act entails. During that period, segregation and isolation caused by shortage of staff and lack of availability of proper facilities might have exacerbated the condition and caused distress to both the patient and those looking after him. So, speed of response was the first requirement, and thus within a day or two of request for a bed the transfer to Grendon can be effected. Then, during the one to three months that Section 47 takes to complete, the patient in the APU can be assessed properly and even treated. Indeed, some are ready to return to their normal location before that time.

With regard, therefore, to the propriety of this initiative, it can be shown that it is in the patient's interest to shorten his suffering and that it is also possible to identify the long-term secondary symptoms and plan a programme of alleviation. If it is necessary, and after careful assessment, the patient can be transferred to a Special Hospital using an established network of psychiatric contacts developed by virtue of Grendon's reputation. The overall effect is beneficial. Not only is the prisoner ill for a shorter time, but Grendon has been able to create a centre of excellence with experienced staff, sound facilities, good liaison with outside agencies and adequate career planning.

THE PATIENTS

Patients are all convicted prisoners who are referred to Grendon by medical officers throughout the prisons of England and Wales. The total admitted is sufficient to provide a basis for useful analysis (see Table 8.1). A breakdown of the last 95 patients admitted to the APU up to 1988 is shown in Table 8.2. The primary diagnoses as shown in Table 8.2 may be

Table 8.1 Number of patients admitted to Grendon 1986–1988

Years	Number of patients
1986–7	104
1987–8	125
Total	**229**

Table 8.2 Diagnosis given to the last 95 patients admitted to the APU, up to April 1988

Diagnosis	Number of patients
Schizophrenia	38
Reactive depression	15
Drug-induced psychosis	11
Paranoid psychosis	9
Personality disorder	8
Manic-depressive psychoses	
depressive type	5
manic type	4
organic	2
Mental impairment	3

coupled with secondary diagnoses, such as subnormality or drug or alcohol abuse, which are equally important and may also give rise to social, domestic and prison problems.

THE REGIMEN

The regimen at Grendon is characterized by a coherent treatment philosophy based on the multidisciplinary techniques. It has been successfully utilized by Grendon throughout its history, and has produced a healthy staff attitude.

In charge is a psychiatrist who is a full-time medical officer accountable to the Senior Medical Officer and who determines the medical treatment needs of each patient, and orchestrates the team approach. All the usual psychiatric modalities are used, including psychotropic medication and individual psychotherapy. Daily ward rounds at which the psychiatrist sees all patients are supplemented by weekly case conferences with all staff.

The interpersonal skills utilized by the prison hospital officers—only six of whom have outside nursing qualifications—form a significant matrix for the process of socialization, behaviour modification, the acquisition of confidence in personal contact, and for learning the business of living rather than existing. The hospital officer training is adequate, and is reinforced by on-the-job and supplementary local training. [Hospital officer training comprises a full-time six-month course with resultant skills comparable to state enrolled nurses. It also includes an introduction to psychiatric nursing and attachments to general and psychiatric units in the National Health Service.] In the event there was no increase of staff numbers working in the unit and the overall staff to inmate ratio is less than one to one. At certain times, only four to five staff are actually on duty. This is remarkable bearing in mind the potential for violence in many of the patients.

The regimen provides no time in enforced segregation—in fact, there is no segregation unit. There is limited use of the 'strip cell' (a secluded, unfurnished room) and the positive continuous contact of staff with patient is in contrast to a normal prison regimen which, perforce, requires long periods of isolation and little opportunity for effective prisoner/staff relationships.

Within this framework, the guiding ethos of the regimen is dynamic: to seek, if not a cure, then certainly behaviour improvement from which a positive move elsewhere can be contemplated as part of a treatment plan. The regimen is relaxed in order to provide a stress-free environment where patients can develop their social and educational skills and pursue hobbies such as painting and cookery. This last—survival cookery—is considered to be significant in terms of the inmates' ability to look after themselves on discharge.

Even in this environment some patients find it difficult to cope, but as

Table 8.3 Assaults by patients

	1986–1987	*1987–1988*
On patients	11	3
On staff	9	0

many as possible are encouraged to coax each other to participate and become members of the community. Contact with the outside world— difficult to achieve in prisons—is actively maintained. The 'Drop-In Centre' has many voluntary helpers and prison visitors arrive throughout the day and even prisoners from the other part of the prison visit both socially and to work. The success of fostering this community spirit can be measured in the comparative absence of assaults by a group of inmates who have a history of violence against others, both staff and prisoners, at previous prison establishments (Table 8.3). Indeed, it was found that incidents increased when the roll exceeded 25 indicating that it related to personal space and the quality of the regimen.

USE OF EXISTING RESOURCES

When the problem of setting up the acute psychiatric unit was examined, the rebuilding and alterations required appeared to be both considerable and expensive. Placed centrally in the design, the operating theatre— redundant and unused for several years—presented, seemingly, in-superable obstacles to conversion without a heavy outlay of money. An even greater difficulty was that of staff attitudes: any proposed change is unsettling, and locally there was uncertainty as to Grendon's future. Furthermore, the Directorate of Prison Medical Services had proposed a future increase in qualified nurses in addition to prison officers with hospital officer training. Thus, there was every excuse to delay. But the need remained and was regarded as paramount.

The success of the APU is characterized by the use made of the operating theatre. Its central position was seen as an advantage, and it was converted into a classroom that would be run on the lines of a club. The Education Department funded teacher hours and a teacher was selected— with no formal qualifications that were apparently significant. She had tremendous enthusiasm which infected all who came into contact with her. The result was effective cooperation with the medical staff and hospital officers and volunteers from outside who take part in the classes on an *ad hoc* basis. The task of refurbishing the room became the activity of the 'Drop-In Centre' as it became named. Informality of approach meant that the class, regarded as a club, became used by the patients—who claimed ownership. The emphasis on acquirement of basic social skills—there are frequent informal 'socials' and every excuse for a party—has since been built upon, on an individual need basis.

DISPOSAL

The disposal figures outlined in Table 8.4 indicate that the great majority of patients return to the prison system. The figures confirm the APUs intended role to provide a service to the prison system by enhancing patient care through rapid response, assessment and appropriate treatment. That so few fail to respond to the regimen is indicated by the small proportion who have been sent to the Secure Units and Special Hospitals. Those released into the community present very special problems that are both time-consuming and frustrating. Hospital officer staff are encouraged and trained to participate in more formalized shared working with the probation department. This enables the probation officer to concentrate on the disposal of his men who present such special difficulties. Certainly, those 'inadequate' participants with a history of reactive violence and sexual offences and those who require regular medication present almost insuperable resettlement problems—a subject discussed elsewhere in this book (see Chapter 5).

The APU's achievements are summarized in Table 8.5.

Clearly, the problem of the mentally ill offender patient is likely to increase—certainly in terms of their numbers. The Grendon experiment has been described as an *ad hoc* solution or first-aid patch, preventing a long-term solution. To some extent this could be correct but too many mentally ill offenders in unsuitable penal conditions, awaiting delayed appropriate referral, damaging others and themselves, demonstrate that delay would have been intolerable. The laggardly pace of development of the Regional Secure Units recommended by the Butler Report (Home Office and DHSS, 1975) is only too persuasive an argument for action. Now the uneven pace of the development of the community-based alternatives provides further support for the rightness of Grendon's attitude.

Table 8.4 Disposal of patients at Grendon

Disposal	Percentage of cases	
	1986–1987	*1987–1988*
To prison	78.0	77.6
Release	13.5	17.6
To Special Hospital	3.8	2.4
To Secure Unit	3.8	1.6

Table 8.5 APU statistics April–October 1989

Admissions	84
Discharges	
Other prisons	26
Section 47 Mental Health Act	10
Community	4
Wings within Grendon	41
Deportation	1
Total	**86**
Suicidal gestures/threats	20
Suicides	Nil
Unfurnished rooms used	40 occasions
Assaults	
Inmate-inmate	3 Both period Apr–May
On staff	1 Not summer leave times

The plight of the mentally ill offender simply cannot be wished out of existence. At a deeper level, Grendon's success provides a significant example for the future. It has shown that it is possible to bridge the gaps caused by bureaucratic divisions which have little congruence with patient need. The division of placement between prisons, Special Hospitals, and regional secure units can have haphazard relation to what is necessary for appropriate patient treatment. Grendon demonstrates that putting the patient's needs first, within a seemingly rigid prison structure, can achieve a significant change in the practice of care of the mentally ill offender.

REFERENCES

East W. N., Hubert W. H. de (1939). *The Psychological Treatment of Crime.* London: HMSP.

Gunn J., Robertson G., Dell S., Way C. (1978). *Psychiatric Aspects of Imprisonment.* London: Academic Press.

Home Office (1985). *First Report of the Advisory Committee on the Therapeutic Regime at Grendon.* London: Home Office.

Home Office and Department of Health and Social Security (1975). *Report of the Committee on Mentally Abnormal Offenders* Cmnd 5698. London: HMSO.

Robertson G., Gunn J. (1987). A ten-year follow-up of men discharged from Grendon prison. *British Journal of Psychiatry*, 151, 674–8.

Snell H. K. (1962). HM Prison, Grendon. *British Medical Journal*, 2, 789–92.

9 Thro' cells of madness: the imprisonment of mentally ill people

STEPHEN SHAW and ADAM SAMPSON

INTRODUCTION

The image that the prison system has presented during the 1980s has been one of mayhem, scandal and neglect: woeful overcrowding and decrepitude; industrial relations in a state of semi-permanent warfare; an unstable population of dangerous prisoners increasingly liable to protest or riot; a system rocking from crisis to crisis. But this picture is not wholly accurate. The reality is that most prisons are not overcrowded; most prison staff want to do a better, more humane job; new and better equipped prisons are being built and old ones are being renovated. The image is also simplistic. The prison population is not an homogeneous entity: it includes such disparate groups as mothers with their babies; men who have committed grave crimes against children; those in for a few days for fine default, and those who may never be released (Stern, 1987). More important, perhaps, the impression of a system always on the precipice of disorder draws attention away from what is the everyday experience of custody: the sheer boredom, drudgery and petty indignities of prison—as often as not endured by staff as well as prisoners.

It is the recurrent and unchanging character of imprisonment that is the real evil. It is the continued presence in our gaols of the poor, the homeless, and the inadequate. Above all, it is the imprisonment of mentally ill people which calls into question the whole meaning and purpose of the prison system. Quite simply, there can be nothing which more directly conflicts with the notion of 'justice' than the continued detention in prison of people who everyone agrees should be cared for properly in hospital or in the community at large.

However, the unanimity that mentally ill people have no place in prison is matched by a corresponding inability to achieve this hoped-for objective. It has become a commonplace for sentencers to bemoan the fact that they can see no alternative to imprisoning a mentally disordered offender. Judge Leo Clark has even gone so far as to advise one offender to appeal against sentence:

I have no doubt that the right place for you is in the secure walls of a hospital, but unfortunately no place is available. In the circumstances, there is absolutely no alternative for me but a sentence of imprisonment . . . I hope you will appeal against this sentence because it sometimes happens that facilities are made available that will enable you to be dealt with in a different way. I can only say I hope that happens.

(*The Times*, 8 March 1986).

The urgent need to divert mentally disordered offenders from custody has been echoed from sentencing bench and parliamentary committee, from prison gate and academic lectern. Evidence presented by concerned organizations to the House of Commons Social Services Select Committee on the Prison Medical Service (1985–6) repeatedly stressed that the mentally disordered should not be held in prison. Bodies as different as the British Medical Association, MIND, the Prison Reform Trust, the Prison Officers' Association all argued that transfer of mentally disordered offenders to outside NHS psychiatric facilities should be accelerated.

The Select Committee itself, after describing some appalling scenes which members had witnessed ('. . . in some prisons inmates are being kept in conditions which would not be tolerated for animals' [para. 11]), called for immediate steps to be taken to fund hospital places for those prisoners whose mental illness or severe mental impairment fell within the terms of the Mental Health Act.

The case has also been accepted by government. When the interdepartmental Home Office/DHSS working group was set up in 1986 'to consider the problems presented by mentally disordered offenders in the prison system', it took as its first aim that of 'minimising the numbers of such prisoners' (Home Office and DHSS, 1987).

Yet our prisons continue to be used to contain offenders who are severely disturbed. This is despite the fact that many of these prisoners cause grave management problems. Often they experience the very worst and least civilized conditions that our prisons can provide; on the catalogue of suicides and self-inflicted injuries indicate. Although it seems that all authorities deprecate the presence of mentally ill people in the prison system—and despite the existence in the community or in hospitals of places better suited to their needs—attempts to ensure their removal seem to have failed.

HISTORY

Michael Ignatieff, writing about Pentonville in the 1840s, quotes a doctor's report which suggests that things have not changed much over the last 150 years:

Convict DF 4920: Five and a half months after admission, he was observed to be depressed in spirit and strange in his manner and conversation. He seemed oppressed by vague fears and apprehensions of impending evil which increased towards night.

(Ignatieff, 1989, p. 9)

This is not the only account. Elizabeth Fry, visiting a woman in Newgate on the eve of her execution in March 1817, found:

Besides this poor young woman, there are also six men to be hanged, one of whom has a wife near her confinement, also condemned, and seven young children. Since the awful report came down, he has become quite mad, from horror of mind. A strait waistcoat could not keep him within bounds: he has just bitten the turnkey; I saw the man come out with his hand bleeding, as I passed the cell.

(Fry, 1847)

The nineteenth century methods of coping with the issue of mentally disordered offenders in the prisons were not so dissimilar from today's as some might suppose. Ignatieff tells us that between five and fifteen mentally disturbed offenders were transferred from Pentonville to asylums every year. But judicial diversion from custody was strictly limited, based on an assessment of unfitness to plead and the McNaughton Rules of 1843. These Rules only excluded from criminal responsibility those whose mental abnormality resulted in them not knowing what they were doing or that it was wrong. The Rules did not acknowledge that someone might very well know what s/he was doing, but not be able to control her- or himself (Gostin, 1977, pp. 188–9). Contrast that with the Code Napoléon which as far back as 1810 excused all those suffering from madness (Hart, 1968, p. 189).

English law has come late to a recognition of the need to divert the mentally disturbed from prison by judicial means. However, there was a flurry of legislation in the late 1950s and early 1960s. The concept of diminished responsibility introduced in the 1957 Homicide Act and the 1959 Mental Health Act removed the necessity of proving a causal link between the mental disorder of the offender and the offence as a precondition for making a hospital order (Gostin, 1977, p. 7). Further amendment was made in 1964 under the Criminal Procedure (Insanity) Act.

The landmark, Butler Committee report (1975), sought to revise the somewhat piecemeal nature of the existing legislation, proposing a series of steps designed to prevent the mentally disordered from being placed in prison inappropriately. The report was welcomed by the Government, and money was made available to the regional health authorities for the establishment of the proposed Regional Secure Units (RSUs). It never got there. Twenty million pounds were diverted away for other uses. Some of it was used to fund pay awards for senior staff. According to evidence presented by the Prison Reform Trust to the Social Services Committee, some even went to pay VAT to the Exchequer (Parliamentary All Party Penal Affairs Group, 1980; Kilroy Silk, 1983; Benn, 1983). While appropriate provision is now coming on stream, there remain gaps—particularly so far as unconvicted people are concerned. This is having its effect: there is evidence that 'the courts have limited the psychiatric remands for the less seriously disordered defendants to correspond to the limited services and care available' (Salem 1983, p. 33).

Much of the thrust of the Butler Committee's recommendations was embodied in the 1983 Mental Health Act, and more money was found to begin the process of putting into place the system of RSUs that was envisaged by the Butler Committee. The working of the 1983 Act was reviewed by the Interdepartmental Working Group of Home Office and DHSS Officials on Mentally Disturbed Offenders in the Prison System in England and Wales, which reported in May 1987.

The report of the Working Group is a document of stunning complacency in view of the nature and extent of the problem. As we have seen, the report of the Social Services Committee into the Prison Medical Service, published the previous year, severely criticized the treatment of the mentally disturbed in some prisons. It also made wide-ranging recommendations for legislative and administrative change. It recommended, among other things, that Crown Immunity be removed from prison hospitals; that the 1983 Mental Health Act be revised to allow the two functions of remand to hospital for report or treatment to operate simultaneously; and that prisoners be allowed the legal right of access to a second opinion other than that of the prison medical officer.

In contrast, the Working Group report eschewed any significant criticism and, denying the need for any changes to the existing legal framework, roundly declared:

The group considered that, whilst at some future point amendment to the Mental Health Act 1983 (MHA) might be justified ... there was not at present an adequate case for legislative change.

(Home Office and DHSS, 1987, p. 1)

Instead, the report made only sixteen recommendations, all of an administrative nature, and all of which were accepted by the Government (*Hansard* 26 May 1989, c. 258). There are occasions when the Government accepts all the recommendations of such a committee because the arguments contained therein, however unpalatable, are unanswerable. There are also occasions when the recommendations of such a committee are acceptable because they are not likely to have much effect. This was not one of the former occasions.

NUMBERS

The Working Group report embodies current government policy. It is argued that the problem of the mentally disordered offender in the prison system can be dealt with by administrative means within the current legislation. Ministers have claimed that the provision for such offenders has been gradually improving, (*Hansard*, 16 July 1986, c. 1150). This argument is based on figures that purport to show a gradual decrease in the number of such offenders in prison. The figures quoted in the 1987 Annual Report of the Prison Service show a steady if unspectacular decline in the number of prisoners thought detainable under the 1983 Mental Health Act, from 769 in June 1977 to 251 in September 1985. By 31 March 1988, the figure had fallen to 235. This decline is all the more impressive given that it takes place against the background of a rapidly rising total prison population.

These figures are matched by a commensurate increase in the number of prisoners who are being transferred from prison to psychiatric or Special Hospitals under Sections 47 and 48 of the 1983 Mental Health Act. According to the published prison statistics the number whose transfer was recommended rose from 140 in 1983 to 206 in 1988, and transfer directions were actually issued on 183 in the latter year compared with 110 in the former.

But these statistics are somewhat misleading. To begin with, the figures given of the number of mentally ill prisoners include only those prisoners whom prison medical staff believe would be detainable under the 1983 Mental Health Act. The Home Office figures therefore reflect merely the number of prisoners whose condition would warrant that they should be detained 'in the interest of their own health and safety or with a view to the protection of others' (Mental Health Act 1983 Section 1(2)). They do not include those prisoners who are clearly suffering from a form of mental illness, but who would not be detainable under the Act (Ross and Bingley, 1985).

Secondly, the statistics are based entirely upon the returns submitted by prison medical staff as to the mental status of the prisoners concerned. Only one-third of all full-time prison medical officers possess any psychiatric qualification, let alone any recent training (Home Office and DHSS, 1987, p. 17). It is therefore questionable how far figures compiled by prison medical officers can be trusted, since they will vary according to each individual's idea of mental illness.

Moreover, the figures may reflect only the number of prisoners that medical officers consider it may be possible to transfer to local NHS facilities. If medical officers know that certain categories of prisoner will always be rejected by the local psychiatric or secure facilities, they may not bother to classify them officially as mentally disturbed.

The result of these distortions can be seen in figures cited by Ross and Bingley. They studied the returns made by prison doctors to the Home

Office in 1984. They found that while Wymott, a prison with no psychiatric wing, had 14 offenders classified as mentally disturbed, Grendon Underwood, a specialist psychiatric prison, appeared to have only four. Equally, Kingston, a small prison for offenders with a life sentence, appeared to hold twice as many mentally disordered prisoners as Maidstone, which contains a specialist unit for sex offenders (Ross and Bingley, 1985, p. 61).

Similar considerations apply to the figures for the transfer of sentenced prisoners under Sections 47 and 48. The strong and growing correlation between the number of prisoners classified as mentally disturbed and the number transferred to NHS facilities may reflect a real improvement in the response of both the prison service and the NHS to the problem. The Home Office has noted, for example, that of the 170 prisoners in respect of whom transfer reports were made in 1985, only eight transfers failed for lack of a suitable bed (Home Office, 1987, p. 11). Equally likely, however, is that the figures simply reflect an increase in the ability of the prison medical officers to second-guess the NHS consultants whose consent will be needed before a transfer takes place. Those mentally disturbed prisoners they know will be acceptable, they classify and transfer; those they know will be unacceptable, they try to contain within the prison system.

In the light of these problems, it is very difficult to estimate the number of mentally disordered offenders in prison. The sole recommendation of the Home Office/DHSS report that called for immediate action resulted in the commissioning of a detailed survey of the mental health profile of the prisoner population to be carried out by Professor John Gunn at the Institute of Psychiatry. This survey is due to report by 31 October 1990, and as yet there are no indications as to the findings. However, even with a sample of 2000 prisoners being studied, it will be difficult to draw any significant conclusions about the mental problems of important minority groups within the prison system—in particular, black and female prisoners. It is of vital importance that separate studies of the incidence of mental disturbance among these groups are undertaken in the near future.

The Institute of Psychiatry study will not be the first survey of the extent of mental disturbance among prisoners. In a review of such surveys, Coid quotes another study by Gunn into the psychiatric profile of adult prisoners in the South-East Region carried out in 1980. In this, Gunn concludes that 22 per cent of the prisoners had personality disorders, 13 per cent were alcoholics, 9 per cent were neurotics, 3 per cent were drug-dependent, 1 per cent had affective disorders, and 1 per cent were schizophrenic. Washbrook in 1977 looked at Winson Green Prison and found that 9.2 per cent were in need of psychiatric care (Coid, 1984, p. 79). A 'snapshot' of the prison population organized by the Home Office in 1985 found that 1500 male prisoners were suffering from some degree of mental disorder, of whom 250 were actually mentally ill (Social Services Committee, 1986, para. 62).

Such research is clearly of vital importance in tackling the problem of mentally disturbed people in prison. However, judgements about psychiatric disturbance, even when made in ideal clinical circumstances, are notoriously contentious. To come to any undisputed conclusion about the mental state of an individual in the prison environment is extremely difficult. Prison is a grossly abnormal setting, and it is hardly surprising if one finds evidence of grossly abnormal behaviour therein. Indeed, given such a setting, it is not entirely fatuous to suggest that it is those prisoners who exhibit entirely normal behaviour whose mental state could be called into question.

Strategies adopted by prisoners to deal with their imprisonment can be reinterpreted in prison as evidence of mental disturbance. Suicide attempts, violence, persistent challenging of authority, drug-taking, distress, listlessness and complete disinterest—all these can be interpreted as evidence of psychiatric disorder. All can be seen with equal validity as normal, or at least understandable, behaviour in an abnormal context.

PRISON MEDICAL STAFF

If the problem of judging what behaviour in prison can be deemed to be truly 'normal' and what should be taken as evidence of mental disturbance, is a considerable difficulty to researchers, it renders the task of the Prison Medical Service almost impossible. The Home Office has put great store by the improvements in the training and recruitment of the prison medical officers and the hospital officers and it may be that the proportion of medical officers with psychiatric qualifications has actually increased significantly from the figure of below one-third cited by the Home Office/DHSS Working Party in 1987.

However, the value of these qualifications is questionable. As Dr Julian Candy, a psychiatrist and former member of the Parole Board, has written:

Prospective PMOs should not be failed psychiatrists but competent GPs ... I had ten years experience as a NHS consultant psychiatrist before I joined the Parole Board. After a few months, my impressions of prison psychiatry ... reminded me of the practice of the specialty when I first entered it, nearly 20 years ago.

(Candy, 1985, p. 18)

Although there is no doubt that the morale of the Prison Medical Service has greatly improved over recent years, prison medical officers still work very much in isolation from each other and from the psychiatric and medical mainstream. They are denied the sort of continual peer scrutiny enjoyed by NHS practitioners and may lose touch with changes in practice and theory.

Most of the day-to-day care of mentally disturbed prisoners is undertaken not by the medical officer, who spends only on average $1\frac{1}{2}$ full-time hours each week in actual medical care (Smith, 1984, p. 53), but by hospital officers who receive only brief training. The Prison Officers' Association itself has called the training of hospital officers 'nothing more than an extended first-aid course' and the Royal College of Nursing has said that 'in view of the large number of inmates who require medical and psychiatric treatment while serving prison sentences, the type and amount of training for prison hospital officers is grossly inadequate' (Shaw, 1985, p. 4).

Despite the fact that only one-twelfth of hospital officers have any sort of psychiatric training (Home Office and DHSS, 1987, p. 17), their role in the care of the mentally disturbed prisoner is crucial.

STRESS

There is evidence that the behaviour of Black people and women in the prison system is perceived differently by prison staff from that of the majority of prisoners. There is a greater likelihood that both women and Black people will be defined as disruptive, and both groups feature more frequently in the prison disciplinary system (Home Office, 1989).

No account of mental illness amongst Black prisoners, for example, could ignore the endemic racism of the prison system. Most prison officers volunteer pejorative characterizations of Black prisoners (Gender and Players, 1989). Similarly, Black prisoners are perceived by prison staff as more of a control problem than their White counterparts (McDermott, 1990).

Women prisoners, too, face special problems. The physical conditions in some women's prisons are among the worst in the entire prison system (both Holloway and Durham have come in for recent strong criticism) (Casale, 1989; Lester and Taylor, 1989). In addition, women in prison face particular problems relating to public attitudes towards female crime, to separation from children and to location far from friends and family (Padel and Stevenson, 1988).

However, women and Black people are not the only groups whose experience of imprisonment is particularly stressful. Prisoners on remand are often held in the most overcrowded prisons in the system, experience the most restrictive regimens, and face the pressure of impending trial. It is perhaps not surprising therefore that remand prisoners have far higher rates of suicide than most sentenced groups (Home Office, 1984a).

In our view, the rate of mental disturbance in prisons may well be connected with the nature of prison itself and the conditions in which many prisoners have to exist; the emotional turmoil of imprisonment: fear, sense of failure, isolation and loneliness; the claustrophobia of being locked in a single cell for 23 hours a day with two strangers and just a chamber pot each for sanitation; the sheer, grinding boredom and frustration at the petty restrictions that dog the days. The experience is described by Sharon, one of the women interviewed by Padel and Stevenson:

It's really hard to explain what it feels like to be locked in a cell . . . You sit there, then you stand up and walk to one end of your cell, which isn't very far, stand there for a while, then you walk back, look out the window, and all the thoughts go through your mind—I could be out there, your children, friends, what you'd be doing if you was out there. It's really depressing and you've got to stop thinking about it, 'cause if you don't then the emotions will come and you start crying, and you sort of think to yourself, 'No I've got to stop thinking, I've got to do something.' So you have your wash, and when you've had your wash you do a bit of your clothes washing, like your knickers and your bra, then you tidy up your cell. You've done it a thousand times already, but you do it again, just for something to do. Then you start reading a book, but you can't get into it, so you get up and tidy your cell again, and you read the book again, tidy your cell again, you know, just to keep your mind occupied, 'cause if you don't . . . I can't put it into words.

(Padel and Stephenson, 1988, p. 104–5).

The relationship between prison conditions and the incidence of ill-health among prisoners was well demonstrated by the effects of the prison officers' industrial action in 1979 and 1980. As the Home Office later reported in the 1980 Annual Report of the Prison Department:

Medical officers in several establishments reported that the incidence of inmates requesting to see the medical officer fell during the period of industrial action. This was attributed to a lessening of tension as a result of the reduction in overcrowding coupled with an increase in free association due to the closure of workshops.

(para. 210)

THE WAY AHEAD

If our analysis is correct, then there is an important link between prison conditions and mental disturbance. To reduce the number of mentally disordered people in prison, there must be a radical improvement in prison conditions. Prison regimens should be improved, programmes of prison refurbishment accelerated, and better links between prisons and the world outside established. However, the step that more than any other would lead to a radical improvement in prison conditions is a reduction in the overall prison population.

Writing in 1984, before the prison population had reached current levels, Dr Richard Smith concluded:

After spending 18 months investigating prison health care I believe that there is ample scope for improving both the health of prisoners and the quality of the prison medical service. The single change that would probably do most to improve both would be to reduce drastically the number of prisoners.

(Smith, 1984, p. 170)

Steps to reduce the size of the prison population should encompass measures designed to specifically reduce the numbers of mentally disordered offenders being received into custody. One of the major growth areas in the prison population has been in the number of offenders remanded into custody. To reduce the size of this population would require the creation of a system of bail hostels, including hostels designed to specifically house mentally disordered offenders, and a redrafting of the Bail Act to make it more difficult for magistrates and judges to remand offenders into custody. The latter could also include a strengthening of the power of the magistrates to remand offenders on bail to psychiatric hospitals for treatment and the preparation of reports.

Measures would also be needed to reduce the sentenced prison population. Steps could be taken to limit the powers of the sentencers. There is growing support for the idea of a 'sentencing council' to establish guidelines for the courts and ensure more consistent practice (Ashworth, 1983). A sentencing council might have as one of its briefs the formulation of precise criteria about in what circumstances mentally disordered offenders should be given non-custodial sentences, and whether there are indeed any circumstances in which a mentally disordered offender should be sentenced to prison.

Nevertheless, while we believe there is massive scope for a reduction in the prison population (the UK outstrips every other EEC country in its use of imprisonment), we do not envisage a situation in which there would be no mentally disordered offenders in prison. Some offenders with 'untreatable' mental conditions, for whom non-custodial options have been tried repeatedly and have failed repeatedly, will almost inevitably end up in prison. Some prisoners, no matter how humane the conditions, will develop mental illness in prison. Prisons will have to deal with mentally disordered prisoners for many years to come.

Prisons must now undertake the changes necessary to deal with such prisoners. In our view, there needs to be a change in the organization of prison health care. The Prison Medical Service has shown itself to be less than exemplary in providing the care and expertise needed by mentally disordered prisoners and, indeed, by ordinary prisoner–patients. Although some prisons enjoy regular sessions run by outside NHS consultant psychiatrists, this access is often haphazard. Prisoners, alone of the citizens of this country, are denied the right to NHS treatment. They would be given this right by the abolition of the separate Prison Medical Service and the assumption of the responsibility for prisoner health care by the NHS.

Such a move would have important advantages for prisons in the constant battles to persuade outside psychiatric and Special Hospitals to accept the transfer of prisoners both before and after sentence. Despite the Home Office's claims about the ease of making transfers to outside institutions, there are prisoners who are refused transfer by Special Hospitals and Secure Units (Coid, 1988). The closer liaison between prison and outside institution possible if both are staffed by NHS doctors would help to ease the decision-making process. It would also help in the formulation of plans for prisoners' release back into the community, as the Home Office has itself recognized (Home Office and DHSS, 1987, p. 2).

Of course, such advantages are predicated on the assumption that sufficient beds to deal with the transfer needs of prisons are available in Secure Units and Special Hospitals. We are also aware that the Special Hospitals themselves may be used as dumping-grounds. As Larry Gostin has argued 'the demand for secure beds may continuously increase to meet available supply' (Gostin, 1977, p. 142).

For those prisoners who cannot be transferred to outside NHS facilities, the Home Office has planned the setting up of regional units within the prison system to specialize in the handling of mentally disordered prisoners and prisoners who present control problems (Home Office, 1984b). Each of these units will operate a different regime. To date, only three units have been opened (at Hull, Lincoln and Parkhurst) and only the unit at Parkhurst is designed to provide specific facilities for prisoners with psychiatric problems (see Chapter 7).

The units are intended to complement the existing specialist provision within the prison system: Grendon, Glen Parva, Feltham, Wormwood Scrubs Hospital Annexe, and Holloway C1 Unit, which are mandated to provide regimes specially adapted for prisoners who would be unable to cope with placement on a normal location or who otherwise would benefit from a therapeutic atmosphere. Clearly, if the units improve the treatment of the mentally disordered in our prisons, they are very much to be welcomed. If they match the achievement of Grendon (see Chapter 8), the Barlinnie Special Unit in Scotland, and the Wormwood Scrubs Annexe in concentrating expertise, motivating staff and prisoners alike, and providing genuinely relaxed and therapeutic regimes, they will be institutions of which the Home Office can be justly proud.

But their success is not inevitable. The conditions in Holloway C1 Wing led to a public outcry and the wing is being completely rebuilt. The Wormwood Scrubs Annexe has come under increasing pressure and the senior probation officer has recently claimed that the regime has broken down entirely (*The Independent*, 13 September 1989). The Home Office has to back the units with a genuine commitment to provide adequate funds, trained and motivated staff, and a willingness to allow the units to establish relaxed and innovative regimes. Careful thought must be given to the question of how prisoners are assigned to units, so that referrals are appropriate, prisoners allowed to choose whether or not they are referred, and so that they do not become part of an informal prison disciplinary system.

These units do not exist in a vacuum; they are part of a wider prison system. The pressures on them are the same as the pressures on other prisons, other wings. Reform of the way the prison system treats mentally disordered offenders cannot be achieved in the absence of a fundamental reform of the prison system itself. Racism and limited provision for women prisoners coexist with over-representation of Black people and women in prison hospitals and suicide statistics. The shortcomings of the whole prison medical service result in inferior health care for all prisoners.

The solutions to the problem of the mentally disordered in prison are the solutions to the problem of the state of our prisons. We propose the following:

1. Reduction in the prison population, by diversion, by provision in the community, by legislation, by limiting the powers of the sentencers.
2. Abolition of the prison medical service and transfer of the care of prisoners to the NHS.
3. Provision of better staff training and the establishment more relaxed regimes.
4. Provision for prisoners with legitimate methods of expressing legitimate grievances.

These are not fanciful notions, but rational solutions. Unless they are accepted as such by the Government, there is every likelihood that in 150 years' time our successors will still be wrestling with the problem as our forebears were 150 years ago.

REFERENCES

Ashworth A. (1983). The case for sentencing reform. In *A Prison System for the 80s and Beyond*. London: NACRO.

Benn M. (1985). Jail or hospital—nobody wants them. *New Statesman*, 25 October 1985.

Candy J. (1985). The relationship of the Prison Medical Service to the National Health Service. In *Prison Medicine: Ideas on Health Care in Penal Establishments*. London: Prison Reform Trust.

Casale S. (1989). *Women Inside: the Experience of Women Remand Prisoners in Holloway*. London: Civil Liberties Trust.

Coid J. (1984). How many psychiatric patients in prison? *British Journal of Psychiatry*, **145**, 78–86.

Coid J. (1988). Mentally abnormal prisoners on remand: (i) rejected or accepted by the NHS. *British Medical Journal*, **296**, 1779–82.

Fry E. (1847). *A Memoir of the Life of Elizabeth Fry Edited by her Two Daughters.* London.

Gender E., Player E. (1989). *Race Relations in Prison.* Oxford: Clarendon Press.

Gostin L. (1977). *A Human Condition: The Law Relating to Mentally Abnormal Offenders: Observations, Analysis and Proposals for Reform.* Vol. 2. London: MIND.

Hart H. L. A. (1968). *Punishment and Responsibility: Essays on the Philosophy of Law.* Oxford: Clarendon Press.

Home Office (annual). *Prison Statistics.* London: HMSO.

Home Office (annual). *Reports on the Work of the Prison Department.* London: HMSO.

Home Office (1984a). *Report of the Chief Inspector of Prisons: A Thematic Review of Suicides in Prison.* London: HMSO.

Home Office (1984b). *Report of the Control Review Committee: Managing the Long-Term Prison System.* London: HMSO.

Home Office (1989). *Report of the Chief Inspector of Prisons on HMYOI and Remand Centre Feltham.* London: HMSO.

Home Office and Department of Health and Social Security (1975). *Report of the Committee on Mentally Abnormal Offenders* (The Butler Report) Cmnd. 6244. London: HMSO.

Home Office and Department of Health and Social Security (1987). *Interdepartmental Working Group of Home Office and DHSS Officials on Mentally Disturbed Offenders in the Prison System in England and Wales: Report.* London: HMSO.

Ignatieff M. (1989). *A Just Measure of Pain: The Penitentiary in the Industrial Revolution 1750–1850.* Harmondsworth: Penguin Books Ltd.

Kilroy Silk R. (1983). Scandal of the missing millions. *Sunday Times,* 1 May.

Lee B. (1983). *World Medicine,* 6 August.

Lester A., Taylor P. J. (1989). *Women in Prison: 'H' Wing HM Prison Durham.* Report prepared for Women in Prison, Prison Reform Trust, Howard League for Penal Reform and The National Council for Civil Liberties, London.

Padel U., Stevenson P. (1988). *Insiders: Women's Experience of Prison.* London: Virago.

Ross J., Bingley W. (1985). Mentally abnormal offenders and prison medicine. *Prison Medicine.*

Salem S. (1983). Psychiatric remands: the courts' perspective and alternative models. *Home Office Research Bulletin,* **16.**

Shaw S. (1985). The case for change in prison medicine. *Prison Medicine.*

Smith R. (1984). *Prison Health Care.* London: British Medical Association.

Social Services Select Committee (1986). *Prison Medical Service: Report,* Vol I, *Minutes of Evidence,* Vol II, HC Paper 72. London: HMSO.

Stern V. (1987). *Bricks of Shame: Britain's Prisons.* Harmondsworth: Penguin Books.

Parliamentary All Party Penal Affairs Group (1980). *Too Many Prisoners.* London: Barry Rose.

Section 4
The Mentally Disordered Offender in the Hospital

10 *A case for hospital treatment*

DIANA M. DICKENS

INTRODUCTION

The term 'mentally disordered offender' used in this chapter refers to any person compulsorily admitted to hospital under Part V of the 1959 Mental Health Act, Part III of the 1983 Mental Health Act or under the 1964 Criminal Procedure (Insanity) Act. Those mentally abnormal offenders detained on Hospital Orders of the Mental Health Act may be detained in four categories (either one or more): mental illness, psychopathic disorder, mental impairment, and severe mental impairment. It is, however, most unusual for someone with severe mental impairment to commit the type of offence that will bring them before the courts and, if this is the case, they can usually be considered to be functioning at the level of mental impairment; therefore, for the purposes of this chapter three groups of offender will be considered: those with mental illness, psychopathic disorder, and mental impairment.

Offenders may be admitted to hospitals under the following Sections of the 1983 Mental Health Act:

Section 35: Remand to hospital for a report.
Section 36: Remand to hospital for treatment.
Section 37: The power to make a hospital or guardianship order.
Section 38: Interim hospital order.
Section 41: Restriction order.
Section 47: Removal to hospital of persons serving sentence of imprisonment, etc.
Section 48: Removal to hospital of other prisoners.

Patients admitted under a Section 41—restriction order—form a very important group in management terms as the patient may only be discharged by the Home Secretary on medical recommendation or a Mental Health Review Tribunal. Also the patient may not be given leave of absence, be transferred to another hospital or be discharged without the agreement of the Home Secretary.

STATISTICS

The number of patients admitted to hospital under hospital orders who are

not subject to restriction upon discharge was 709 in 1986, and those under a restriction order was 327.

When the groups of restricted and non-restricted patients are analysed by category of detention interesting differences arise (see Table 10.1). Whereas the percentages for impairment and severe impairment are approximately the same, there is a higher proportion of the mentally ill in the group of non-restricted patients than in the restricted group. The reverse is the case for psychopathy.

If the hospital population of restricted patients as a whole is surveyed (as opposed to the number of admissions) in 1986 only 63 per cent are mentally ill whereas 24 per cent were psychopathically disordered and 13 per cent mentally impaired. This discrepancy arises as mentally ill patients tend to be discharged sooner than other patients. The implication of this would seem to be that, in general, psychopathy and mental impairment carry a far worse prognosis than mental illness.

It is interesting to note that the number of admissions with restriction order has fluctuated, but has risen over the decade from an average of 230 in the late 1970s to over 300 in 1986. The rise occurred in admissions to hospitals other than the three Special Hospitals (this is almost certainly due to the increase in number of Regional Secure Unit (RSU) places, which for the purposes of this chapter are included as hospital places). Less than half these offenders were admitted to the three Special Hospitals—44 per cent in 1986. The proportion of female admissions was 14 per cent.

HOSPITAL PROVISION

The object of a Hospital Order is that a patient may receive treatment for his mental disorder along the lines provided by conventional psychiatry. However, because all the patients within the group are offenders, it may be necessary for many of them to receive their psychiatric treatment in conditions of some security. It is particularly important to note that in all hospital settings ranging from the Special Hospitals to local hospitals, offender and non-offender patients are treated side by side—the treatment

Table 10.1 Patients admitted to hospital in 1986 by type of mental disorder*

	Non-restricted (%)	Restricted (%)
Mental illness	631 (89)	245 (74.9)
Psychopathic disorder	41 (5.8)	63 (19.3)
Mental impairment	31 (4.5)	17 (5.2)
Severe mental impairment	6 (0.8)	2 (0.6)
Total	709	327

*Extrapolated from various tables in *The Home Office Statistical Bulletin*, 1988.

perspective being considered to be <u>primarily</u> that of their <u>mental disorder</u> rather than whether or not they are offenders. Depending on the type of offence committed, varying degrees of security may be necessary and a hospital setting is provided which gives the most appropriate degree of security. Although psychiatric care may be provided in ordinary NHS psychiatric facilities, RSUs or Special Hospitals, the degree of security offered by these may, in many cases, overlap. For example, Ashworth East (Special Hospital) has no perimeter fence whereas some of the RSUs may have fairly sophisticated levels of security, including a secure perimeter.

SPECIAL HOSPITALS

The three Special Hospitals in England and Wales are for patients detained under the 1983 Mental Health Act who 'in the opinion of the Secretary of State, require treatment under conditions of special security on account of their dangerous, violent or criminal propensities' (Mental Health Act, 1959 s97(1)). 'Until July 1989, the hospitals were managed directly by the Department of Health through local Hospital Management Teams with the advice and guidance of Local Boards. Within the Department, the Secretary of State's functions under the Act were executed by a Special Hospital Service Board. From July 1989, the Special Hospital Service is supervised operationally by a Special Hospital Service Authority (SHA). This SHA exercises its management responsibilities through General Managers at hospital level and is accountable to the Secretary of State, represented by appropriate machinery within the Department of Health working closely with the Home Office.' (Department of Health, 1989). (For further discussion of the management of Special Hospitals, see Chapter 12 by Clifford Graham).

Current arrangements for provision of the Special Hospitals Service have gradually evolved over many years. It now has a bed capacity of 1710, spread through the three hospitals. This has reduced gradually from over 2200 in 1967.

Broadmoor Hospital, Crowthorne, Berkshire. The oldest of the three hospitals and was opened in 1863. It has 510 beds (395 male and 113 female patients), and takes mainly mentally ill and psychopathically disordered patients from the south and western areas. It is presently undergoing extensive rebuilding.

Rampton Hospital, Retford, Nottinghamshire. Opened in 1912 to take mentally impaired patients as Broadmoor was overcapacity. It takes all types of mentally disordered patients, with departments for mentally ill and mentally impaired patients, and has a total of 560 beds (433 male and 128 female patients). Its catchment area is the Midlands and eastern areas, plus the south and western areas for mentally impaired patients. The hospital has a programme of extensive modernization underway.

Ashworth Hospital (formed by the amalgamation of Park Lane and Moss Side Hospitals). Ashworth South and East (Moss Side Hospital) Maghull, Liverpool. Has been used for mentally disordered patients since 1930. It has 295 beds (201 male and 75 female patients) and draws its patients mainly from the nothern areas of England. It specializes in low-dependency patients and adolescents, but recently has been taking increasing numbers of mentally ill patients.

Ashworth North (Park Lane Hospital), Maghull, Liverpool. Built on a site adjacent to Moss Side Hospital, and formally opened in 1984. It has 360 beds for males only. Its catchment area is again the North of England, with a higher mix of mentally ill and psychopathically disordered patients.

Patients from Wales are admitted to whichever hospital is more convenient to their home address, bearing in mind each hospital's specialization. Scotland and Northern Ireland have separate legislation, and their own 'state hospital'. Transfers are effected between the two hospital systems where necessary.

Although historically the catchment areas of the Special Hospitals have been ill-defined, each hospital now has a clearly defined catchment area both for mental illness and mental handicap services. Under normal circumstances, a hospital will only admit from its own catchment area, but in cases of special sensitivity or where there is a specialized need served by one particular hospital exceptions may be made. It is felt that in due course a full range of facilities for both the mentally ill and the mentally handicapped should be offered on all Special Hospital sites.

The security provided by the Special Hospitals is considerable and has two main components. The first is physical and consists of perimeter security (in most cases) and a sophisticated key system. The majority of patients are cared for with the facility of single lockable rooms. The second relates to high levels of trained staff and the deployment of these staff in the manner that will encourage the provision of security. For example, there are high levels of agreed minimum staffing. It should be noted that the object of security is to ensure two things: 1. that patients who are dangerous to the public are prevented from absconding and, 2. that patients who are violent and assaultative should be managed in conditions which cause minimum injury and damage to both staff and fellow patients. Although the majority of Special Hospital patients are cared for in individual locked rooms, they are only placed in these rooms at night-time and when severely disturbed. During the daytime, patients are not contained in their individual rooms and lead a day which as near as possible approximates to a normal daily routine.

One of the problems posed in the Special Hospitals is the achievement of a satisfactory balance between the need for treatment and the needs of security. This can be a difficult task, particularly in the light of the politically sensitive nature of some of the patients within these hospitals.

Many patients within the Special Hospitals are on restriction orders which can again complicate management, both during inpatient stay and in connection with rehabilitation. Traditionally, patients were only admitted to a Special Hospital with the agreement of the Department of Health — the decision being made in light of the patient's dangerousness and his need for special security. However, now each hospital has its own local admissions panel with the same criteria for admission.

As far as discharges are concerned, these still rely on a series of very complex factors, for example, the ability and willingness of other facilities to accept the patient, Home Office and SHSA approval for planned moves and, quite importantly, the actual desire of the patient to leave the hospital and be rehabilitated. The average length of stay is about seven years.

REGIONAL SECURE UNITS

It was promulgated in the Butler (Home Office and Department of Health and Social Security, 1975) and Glancy (Department of Health and Social Security, 1984) Reports that units should be developed at a regional basis for the treatment of mentally disordered patients (both offenders and non-offenders) in conditions of some security. It was also envisaged that the units should care for the mentally ill, psychopaths and patients with some degree of mental impairment. The target figure for provision of Secure Unit places was based on the figure of 20 places per 1 000 000 population and since this time various regions have made plans and set up such units.

The number of beds derived in this way varies from region to region, ranging from 104 beds in the West Midlands to 36 for East Anglia.

The first RSU was opened in 1980 and steadily the number has increased throughout the regions since then. The target of beds based on the figure of 20 per 1 000 000 population is 927 commissioned beds, and at the present time there are 676 beds available. The majority of these are for mental illness, although a Special Unit (Borocourt, Berkshire) has been set up for mental impairment. Other regions have also found it necessary to provide for this group, although this has not been done in units designated as RSUs. Although the regional development of Secure Units can be seen as an inpatient facility, all units aim to run a regional forensic service which consists of outpatients and other forms of community support, such as the community nursing service and Social Work Service. These regional services are essential to support the patient following discharge and, on occasions, by good preventative practice, to prevent the admission of a patient.

Different regions have developed different strategies in the provision of these beds, for example, the West Midlands has developed all its beds in one unit (the Raeside Clinic, Birmingham), target figure 100 beds, although in addition it has a small facility of 8 beds as an Interim Secure Unit for mental impairment.

Another pattern of service is that of South-East Thames where there is a central unit of 30 beds at the Bethlem Royal Hospital with smaller units of 15 beds spread throughout the region. Although Glancy originally felt that these RSUs should cater for patients with a degree of mental impairment, in practice, this has not been found to be very successful and several regions are now looking at a separate provision for these patients.

Admission to Secure Units is controlled by the consultant and the team within the unit, and the patients are discharged to whatever facility seems the most appropriate. Secure Units provide a high level of care and treatment at a multidisciplinary level. Some are self-contained, but many have been built on the sites of existing hospitals and on occasions they use the facilities of these hospitals as back-up.

One of the inherent features of Secure Units is that patients are not accepted where it is felt that they have chronic problems which will not respond to treatment within two years. This is to avoid the silting up of Secure Units and, with some functioning with 20–30 beds, this would appear to be an important policy. On the other hand it does mean that some patients, where management at this level of security is appropriate, are excluded and remain in Special Hospitals. This time scale is inappropriate for mental impairment as these patients in general require longer periods of rehabilitation, resocialization, and so on.

Levels of security within Secure Units are variable; the majority have a secure perimeter and control the issue of keys. Most have single room accommodation for all patients but, on the whole, it is not practice to use the patients' bedroom as a seclusion facility; separate seclusion is usually provided.

LOCAL HOSPITALS

Some mentally disordered offenders (particularly those only on a Section 37 and not a restriction order) may be cared for appropriately in local hospitals. The provision is very variable ranging from a locked ward to completely open management. This type of provision may also be used for the rehabilitation of patients who have been cared for in greater degrees of security.

The present problems as regards this type of provision are that: 1. in the case of mental impairment, the mental handicap hospitals are closing down rapidly and have long ago ceased to take patients functioning at the mildly mentally handicapped level of intelligence; 2. in the case of psychiatric illness, hospitals are ceasing to have locked wards and are also in a programme of fairly extensive run-down. Admissions and discharges to local hospitals are determined by the consultant and clinical team there.

The three types of hospital facility should provide a continuum of both treatment and security. In an ideal situation it is vitally important that patients can move freely from one facility to another according to their immediate needs in both these respects. There are a number of reasons which prevent this ideal being achieved; the most important one being the actual availability of suitable beds, particularly in Secure Units and in local hospitals.

THE PATIENTS

Mental illness

The majority of the mentally ill within the hospital service for mentally disordered offenders are schizophrenics although a few patients with manic–depressive psychosis may be represented. Having taken into account the appropriate drug therapy for the patient (and electroconvulsive therapy (ECT) if indicated) treatment strategies for this group can be expanded as outlined below.

Where patients are seriously disturbed and violent, special measures, such as seclusion, may be necessary. It should be emphasized that in all hospital settings patients lead a daily life which is based on a normal routine, that is, they leave their rooms before breakfast and return to them late evening. Unless seriously disturbed, they do not remain in the rooms during the day.

In mentally ill patients the offence behaviour is usually symptomatic of the underlying mental illness and, therefore, to some extent, the progress of the mental illness acts prognosticatively for the danger of the patient. On the whole, the schizophrenic patient needs a fairly well ordered existence but one that can take into account the symptomatology of his illness (for example, if a patient is seriously retarded and withdrawn it is pointless to attempt to coerce him into a preordained programme of activities or work). These patients are often seriously deluded and may become violent as a result of their delusions. One of the important methods of treatment with the schizophrenic is an attempt for him to become accustomed to living and relating to other people in a normal and appropriate manner. In this area, high staff levels and the ability of staff to have time to sit and talk to patients and build up relationships is very important. Many of the schizophrenics have disordered personalities and may be low on social skills and possibly educational skills; it is important that for the rehabilitation of this group of patients they should be able to be socially competent, not only in daily living skills but also in interactive skills.

As far as the hospital service is concerned, the main problems posed by the mentally ill patient is that of the chronic patient who cannot be rehabilitated into the community and needs a caring environment, perhaps with a degree of security on an indefinite basis. The dilemma for many of these patients is that they do not need the sophisticated security of the Special hospital and they are not appropriate for RSUs because their length of stay inevitably is going to be permanent or semipermanent, rather than the short term 18 months to two years set up by the Secure Units. Yet despite this the patient perhaps needs a degree of security and asylum. The majority of mental illness hospitals no longer have locked wards and may well be closing.

It should be realized that the concept of a unit with security does not necessarily imply merely a physical barrier: many units run very successfully without locked doors, relying entirely on staffing numbers and observation.

Psychopaths

This group of patients usually requires little in the way of drug treatment. The problem is to create an environment which will teach patients to adapt their behaviour to that which is socially acceptable both in the day-to-day living environment and also in areas of specific disturbance (for example, aggression control and sexual behaviour). Most wards in hospitals which deal with psychopaths have a regimen whereby the effect of the patient's behaviour is very much relayed back to him, particularly with regard to inconvenience and distress which it might cause to other members of the unit. Some units may adopt a very behavioural approach to this group of patients—that based on the reinforcement of good behaviour. Alternatively, regimens based on that of the therapeutic community may be chosen where psychotherapy may be used as well as general milieu treatment. It is important that specific behaviour problems such as substance abuse, aggression control and problems of sexuality can be dealt with in individual groups aimed at these particular areas.

The problem for the hospital system with these patients is that in a certain proportion it becomes certain that they are not 'treatable'—they have shown over a period of time that they have not responded to treatment. The dilemma here is that of the hospital perhaps being left with potentially dangerous people whom it is not appropriate to detain on the grounds of psychopathy as they are deemed untreatable.

Although patients who are mentally ill and psychopathic can be treated in mixed units, where there are sufficient facilities to separate them, this is often done. The ward environment and routine for each group of patients can be very different; for example, the hallmark of dealing with a group of mentally ill patients may be that of flexibility of approach, whereas with psychopaths, because of the problem of manipulation, a cohesive and very structured approach may be more appropriate.

Mental impairment

These patients are mentally handicapped and as such require management strategies different from those patients of normal intelligence. Many of their problems may be due to delayed maturity, social inadequacy and learning difficulties. These problems need to be addressed along with those of the underlying illness—be it of a psychopathic tendency or a mental illness. On the whole, although originally envisaged that this group should be cared for in RSUs with patients of normal intelligence, the general consensus is that the mix is not appropriate and that special units for patients with mental impairment should be set up. This group as a whole do not present specific management problems within the hospital setting but the question of discharge is very difficult. Many mental illness services will not deal with the mentally impaired. RSUs for mental illness do not accept this group and many of the mental handicap hospitals who have coped with them traditionally do not now deal with patients who are only mildly mentally handicapped. Discharge into the community can be problematic as it is far less likely that these patients will find employment and, on the whole, they do not have the necessary personal resources to cope easily with an unstructured life of unemployment and perhaps relative poverty.

Index offence

In the above description, no mention has been made of specific index offences. On the whole these do not bear any direct relation to the underlying pathology although there are some correlations; for example, the incidence of sex offenders is higher in the group of mental impairment than in other groups. As might be expected, there is a difference in incidents of index offences between restricted and non–restricted patients (see Table 10.2).

Table 10.2 Persons made subject to hospital orders by type of offence in 1986*

Offence	Restricted (%)	Non-restricted (%)
Violence against the person:		
homicide	19.8	1.0
other	35.4	31.0
Sexual offences	9.7	4.5
Burglary	4.8	7.4
Robbery	7.8	1.3
Theft	4.6	15.3
Fraud	1.2	2.7
Arson	11.3	6.7
Damage to property	2.4	4.8
Summary offences	1.0	23.0
Other indictable offences	2.2	2.1

*Extrapolated from various tables in *The Home Office Statistical Bulletin*, 1988.
Reproduced with the permission of the Controller of HMSO.

If the total hospital population is surveyed for restricted patients, the figure for homicide rises to 27 per cent, sexual offences to 13 per cent and arson to 14 per cent. As might be expected, this emphasizes not only the considered dangerousness of these categories by their increased length of stay, but also a reluctance to discharge them. This is reinforced by the much lower representation of these categories in unrestricted patients. It should be emphasized that in the treatment setting of the hospital, the mental disorder of the patient is of the prime concern and not the index offence. Also, there may be a constellation of offending and disturbed behaviour which needs addressing as well as this offence. However, having said this, when it comes to the management of the patient, particularly in conditions of security, the index offence has to be taken into account because of its relationship with the dangerousness of the patient.

One of the core problems of the management of the mentally disordered offender is the assessment of the dangerousness and the effect this has on the appropriate placement of the patient, especially in the light of security needs.

REHABILITATION

The ultimate aim of all hospital treatment is to rehabilitate the patient as quickly as possible, so that he can be discharged or transferred to a unit with a lesser degree of security when his dangerousness no longer warrants high security.

In the case of the Special Hospitals, other units are often wary of taking their patients because it is not easy to test the likelihood of recurrence of their offence behaviour while in the Special Hospital. Many different ways have been looked at to overcome this. For example, at Ashworth Hospital there is an integrated rehabilitation unit, and at Rampton there is a very active Community Nursing Service and a Rehabilitation Area. In addition, there is a hostel run by Turning Point (a voluntary organization specializing in the management of substance abusers) in Nottingham. It is managed jointly with Rampton and takes patients from all Special Hospitals to rehabilitate them in conditions of lesser security. The preferred route for discharge of restricted patients is a unit of reasonable security such as a Secure Unit.

In 1986, 263 patients (restricted) were discharged from hospital, of which 42 per cent were conditionally discharged into the community. An additional 10 per cent of all discharges were into the community mainly as a result of absolute discharge.

CHANGES OR IMPROVEMENTS WHICH MIGHT BE ENVISAGED IN THE SERVICE

It is hoped that in the very near future the Special Hospitals will develop a well-defined catchment area. This would enable closer links to be set up with local hospitals, RSUs, social service departments and prisons. An ideal situation would be that each Special Hospital site offers a full range of facilities for patients, including treatment of the mentally handicapped. In practice, to adopt this approach Park Lane would have to take mentally ill women and Broadmoor would have to start taking the mentally handicapped. Until this state of affairs is reached, it would seem reasonable that separate mental handicap and mental illness services are developed in the Special Hospitals. This would enable the catchment areas for these services to be discrete.

Although before June 1989 admissions were dealt with by a Central Admissions Panel at the Department of Health, from this date local admissions panels were set up. Therefore, admissions are agreed at a local level by an admission panel, usually consisting of a Director of Medical Services (Chairman) and representatives of nursing, social work, psychology and administration. Normally, each hospital only admits patients who originate from their own catchment area, but sensitive or contentious cases are reviewed centrally by the health authority. These closer local links might also help to speed up the discharge and rehabilitation of patients. It is envisaged that the specialist services within each hospital will still be offered on a nationwide basis—for example, the Ashworth unit for young psychopaths, and work with deaf patients at Rampton. With a clearly defined catchment area for each hospital, that Special Hospital would be expected to deal with all cases from that catchment area. However, there may be certain exceptions to this—for example, where the patient is particularly difficult or politically sensitive, or where there are specific reasons where it is inadvisable for the patient to be cared for in the proximity of where the offence was committed.

With the hospital system there is an urgent necessity for the provision of chronic beds, particularly for the chronic psychotic patient who is in need of a sheltered and possibly secure environment, indefinitely. At the moment this need is not being met by the RSUs, and local hospitals do not often provide facilities that have some degree of containment. If these facilities were developed it would help to ensure that only patients who required the special security of a Special Hospital would be contained within them. It is also important that rehabilitation programmes are carried through from the beginning of the patient's stay in the hospital. If this is the case then it is hoped that chronic institutionalized behaviour might become less.

There is also a need for provision of units for the mentally impaired. It is suggested that these should be at a level of security roughly comparable with the RSU system. There are three such units in existence at the moment, the one at Leavesden Hospital, Hertfordshire, having been run for the longest period of time. When the operation of these units is examined carefully it is obvious that they are meeting a very specific need for the treatment and rehabilitation of this type of patient.

RESEARCH

It is obviously important that basic research into causation, treatment and management of psychiatric conditions should have relevance to the containment of the mentally disordered offender within the hospital setting. Leaving aside research into, for example, mental illness in general, one of the greatest areas of needed research is in the evaluation of services. For example, from surveys from admissions to Special Hospitals and outcome studies, a clearer idea might emerge as to prognosticative features.

Equally important, is research into the estimation of dangerousness. Whilst it is recognized that the assessment of dangerousness is one of the most important equations within the overall management of hospital patients, it is equally recognized that there is no reliable objective way in which this can be assessed.

Yet another area of interest would be the outcome of those patients where Special Hospital admission had been requested but was refused. This might, for example, identify patients who find themselves in prison or unsatisfactorily cared for in other ways and might identify lack of appropriate facilities.

CONCLUSION

The point should be made that when mentally abnormal offenders fit clearly within the hospital provision their placement may not be problematic. On the other hand, when there is doubt about the appropriate service there may be difficulty in placing patients, with the feeling that the eventual placement may be inappropriate. Examples of these patients are: first, the mentally abnormal offender who it may be difficult to allocate to either prison or hospital as the most appropriate placement; second, the psychopath who is deemed not to be treatable. Finally, there is the mentally impaired offender who is not acceptable for a Secure Unit and yet for whom there is no alternative accommodation.

Although this chapter has dealt with the hospital provision for the mentally disordered offender, it must be emphasized that this is not a self-contained provision and should integrate and liaise with other services very closely—such as the prison services and social service departments. These links should facilitate not only the appropriate placement of the patient in the first instance, but also the most effective and expeditious rehabilitation which is most closely geared to the needs of the patient.

REFERENCES

Department of Health (1989). *Special Hospitals Service Authority Operational Brief.* London: HMSO.

Department of Health and Social Security (1984). *The Revised Report of the Working Party on Security in NHS Psychiatric Hospitals* London: HMSO (para 33; Ch 4–8).

Health Advisory Service and Social Services Inspectorate (1988). *Report on Broadmoor Hospital.*

Gostin L., ed. (1985). *Secure Provision—A Review of Special Services for the Mentally Ill and Mentally Handicapped in England and Wales.* London: Tavistock.

Home Office (1988). *Statistical Bulletin* (Issue 28/88, 4 October 1988, ISSN 0143 6384). London: HMSO.

Home Office and Department of Health and Social Security (1986). *Offenders Suffering from Psychopathic Disorder.* London: HMSO.

Home Office and Department of Health and Social Security (1975). *Report of the Committee on Mentally Abnormal Offenders* (The Butler Report) Cmnd 6244. London: HMSO.

Royal College of Psychiatrists (1983). *Report on the Future of the Special Hospitals.* London: Royal College of Psychiatrists.

Royal College of Psychiatrists (1980). *Report of the Review of Rampton Hospital.* London: Royal College of Psychiatrists.

11 The mentally disordered offender in hospital: the role of the Home Office

ROBERT BAXTER

INTRODUCTION

Since the beginning of the nineteenth century the Home Secretary has been involved in the management of mentally disordered persons who have committed serious offences. This goes back to Hadfield's case in 1800. The court found him not guilty by reason of insanity of an attempt to kill King George III, and made it clear that he should be detained in order to protect the public. In Lord Chief Justice Kenyon's view:

people of both sexes and of all ages may, in an unfortunate frantic hour, fall a sacrifice to this man, who is not under the guidance of sound reason; and therefore it is absolutely necessary for the safety of society that he should be properly disposed of, all mercy and humanity being shown to this most unfortunate creature.

(Walker, 1988)

Shortly afterwards, in the same year, an Act 'for the safe custody of insane persons charged with offences' was passed by Parliament, making statutory provision for the special verdict of not guilty by reason of insanity and requiring the court to order the detention of the accused, following such a verdict, in strict custody until His Majesty's pleasure was known (40 Geo. III. 1800, c. 94).

This represents the origins of the present day concept of the hospital order and restriction order. In Hadfield's case the court's recommendation of mercy and humanity was a reflection of their view that asylum in Bethlem Hospital was more appropriate than imprisonment. Under the 1800 Act, it became the Home Secretary's practice to order detention in Bethlem Hospital, where a special wing was built after the recommendation of a House of Commons' select committee in 1807. This was replaced in 1863 by Broadmoor and, briefly, also by Rampton between 1912 and 1918. The purpose of these institutions was to detain disordered offenders in secure conditions so that they would not pose a risk to others, and to provide them with treatment and care under medical supervision with the aim, where possible, of eventually returning them to the community.

During the nineteenth and the first half of the twentieth centuries the law developed in a piecemeal fashion. From the Home Office's point of view its principal features were that any accused person who was found not-guilty by reason of insanity or unfit to plead was ordered to be detained indefinitely in Broadmoor or, in some less serious cases, in a local mental hospital, to be released when the Home Secretary was satisfied that he was no longer a danger to others. They were joined in Broadmoor by prisoners who had been convicted and sentenced to imprisonment, but who required treatment for mental illness during the course of their sentences. These provisions related essentially to people suffering from mental illness. The Home Secretary did not have any similar responsibilities in relation to the mentally handicapped detained under the Mental Deficiency Acts.

Two important reforms were undertaken in the late 1950s. The first was the introduction of the defence of diminished responsibility in the 1957 Homicide Act. Until then the insanity provisions of the criminal law had been the only way of avoiding a mandatory death sentence in murder cases. Shortly afterwards, the 1959 Mental Health Act gave courts the power to make hospital orders following conviction of a criminal offence. Almost immediately conviction of manslaughter on the grounds of diminished responsibility followed by a hospital order replaced the insanity provisions as the principal route for offenders to be sent to hospital—accompanied in most cases by restriction orders, which placed their discharge in the hands of the Home Secretary.

The 1959 Act was the product of the work of the Royal Commission on the law relating to mental illness and mental deficiency—the Percy Commission—and was a major act of codification (Royal Commission, 1957). In practical terms, it left the powers of the Home Secretary unchanged, except to alter the terminology and to extend them to offenders suffering from subnormality, severe subnormality, and psychopathic disorder made subject to hospital and restriction orders. As a consequence of the 1959 Act, it was open to a court, after convicting a person of an offence which carried a penalty of imprisonment, to make a hospital order if it was satisfied on medical advice that the offender was suffering from mental disorder. If the court felt it was necessary for the protection of the public, it could also make a restriction order lasting for either a fixed or an indefinite period. The justification for the restriction order was provided by the Percy Commission. It observed:

There is a strong case for trying to ensure that patients with dangerous tendencies for whom ordinary penal measures are inappropriate or insufficient ... are not discharged prematurely if they are sent for medical treatment in hospital in place of imprisonment, and for detaining some of them for longer periods than other criminals ... We think it desirable that the discharge of patients admitted following court proceedings who are known to be dangerous should be controlled by a central authority who would have special regard to the protection of the public.

(Royal Commission, 1957)

This is the essential reason for the Home Secretary's involvement with mentally disordered offenders. In cases where the courts have convicted a person of an imprisonable offence, but have chosen to send him to hospital for treatment, they have been able, under the 1959 Act, and now under the 1983 Act, to make a restriction order where they believe this is necessary for the protection of the public from serious harm. Section 41 of the 1983 Act requires a court to hear oral evidence from a medical practitioner before making a restriction order, but the decision as to whether to make it rests with the court alone in the light of its views on the question of public protection. This provides that the patient may not be granted leave of absence, or transferred to another hospital without the consent of the Home Secretary. His discharge is also subject to the Home Secretary's agreement except that—and this was an important modification made under the 1983 Mental Health Act—Mental Health Review Tribunals now also have a power to discharge restricted patients.

In the overall national picture of care of the mentally disordered offender, restricted patients form a tiny minority. In England and Wales there are about 100 000 mentally disordered patients admitted to hospital under informal procedures. There are less than 7000 detained patients, and of these only about 1700 are subject to restriction orders. About two-thirds of restricted patients are detained in Special Hospitals, the rest being in Regional Secure Units (RSUs) and local hospitals. About a further 500 are conditionally discharged in the community, usually subject to compulsory medical and social supervision and may be recalled to hospital by the Home Secretary for further treatment. Around two-thirds of restricted patients suffer from mental illness, and a further quarter from psychopathic disorder. For the most part they have been convicted of serious offences of violence. About 27 per cent have been convicted of homicide and a further 35 per cent of other acts of violence. About 13 per cent have been convicted of sexual offences, and 14 per cent of arson. (These figures have been extrapolated from a variety of Department of Health and Home Office publications.)

Although the majority of restricted patients acquire their status as a result of a court decision following conviction of an offence, there are two other routes. The 1964 Criminal Procedure (Insanity) Act makes provision for people charged with offences who are found unfit to plead or not-guilty by reason of insanity. Before the 1957 Homicide Act and the 1959 Mental Health Act, these findings were the principal means by which the courts could send offenders to hospital. Since the late 1950s it has declined greatly in significance. In the 1980s no more than three or four persons each year have been found not-guilty by reason of insanity, and about 15 each year found unfit to plead. In either case the automatic court order following such findings is the detention of the defendant as a restricted patient in a hospital designated by the Home Secretary. He will, of course, have the same right as a restricted patient detained under the Mental Health Act to apply to a Mental Health Review Tribunal for his discharge.

The third route to the status of restricted patients is followed by prisoners who are transferred to hospital either while serving a sentence of imprisonment or while on remand. The provisions of section 47 of the 1983 Mental Health Act relate to sentenced prisoners suffering from mental illness, mental impairment, severe mental impairment, or psychopathic disorder. Section 48 relates to remand (and civil) prisoners who are suffering from mental illness or severe mental impairment and in urgent need of treatment, and section 49 authorizes the Home Secretary to impose restrictions on prisoners transferred under Sections 47 and 48 while detained in hospital—about 200 such transfers from prison to hospital take place each year. The second of these sections may apply to prisoners who are mentally disordered when they come into the prison system on remand and require urgent treatment in hospital. In such cases the principal objective is to provide them with treatment and return them to prison as quickly as possible so that they can stand trial. Prisoners may become mentally disordered, or suffer a relapse after initial successful treatment, while serving a period of imprisonment and require hospital treatment. This may be designed to treat a specific condition which will permit the patient's return to prison on the advice of a doctor or a Mental Health Review Tribunal to continue serving his sentence. In some cases, however, it is clear that on mental health grounds the patient should not be returned to prison as this would lead to a relapse, and that his return to the community should be from hospital. The Home Secretary's freedom of action is itself limited in these cases because of his duty to ensure the court's sentence is carried out. For this reason, prisoners who have been transferred to hospital are considered for rehabilitative leave in the community on a similar basis to those detained in prison. In the case of those serving determinate sentences this means, broadly speaking, one-third of their sentence when they will reach their parole eligibility date. After that point, rehabilitation, including trial leave in the community, can proceed subject to considerations of public safety. Any restriction direction which has been imposed under Section 49 will expire on what would have been the patient's earliest date of release had he remained in prison.

Life sentence prisoners are detained for the period of custody necessary to satisfy the requirements of retribution and deterrence. This is fixed by the Home Office in consultation with the judiciary and in due course offenders will be released on life licence under the provisions of the 1967 Criminal Justice Act on the advice of the Parole Board. There is, however, an exception. Occasionally offenders receive life sentences inappropriately: they may have been disordered at the time of their trial but have insisted on pleading guilty to a charge of murder; or, no hospital might have been willing to offer a place. In either case the court would have been obliged to sentence them to life imprisonment. Offenders who fall into this group are not numerous, but they will be transferred to hospital when a suitable bed does become available and then, with the agreement of the judiciary, treated as though they had been made subject to a hospital and restriction order. If their mental health improves so that their return to the community becomes possible, they will be conditionally discharged under the provisions of the Mental Health Act rather than released on life licence.

In 1988, 82 unsentenced prisoners were transferred to hospital. The average length of their stay in hospital was approximately 2½ months. One hundred and eighteen sentenced prisoners were transferred (including 20 serving life sentences) and 38 were returned to prison. Fifty sentenced prisoners were released into the community direct from hospital or were in hospital when the restriction direction expired on their earliest date of release from their sentence.

Although the Home Secretary has control over the movements of restricted patients which may bring them into contact with the public—leave, transfer to another hospital, or discharge—the patients themselves are detained and treated in hospitals which are managed by the Special Hospitals Service Authority (SHSA) or by the National Health Service (NHS). Consequently, the Home Secretary is not concerned with the medical treatment a patient receives nor with his day to day management. These are professional matters and responsibility for them rests with the hospital's professional staff—the doctors, nurses, psychologists and others involved in the patient's treatment. The only point at which the Home Office will become involved is if the management of the patient involves his leaving the hospital. As this could pose a risk to the public, the Home Secretary's consent is required.

The Home Office's concern with the protection of the public does not mean that this is seen as being opposed to the need to provide patients with whatever treatment is possible, and to work towards their rehabilitation. From the earliest days the Home Office has recognized the importance of humane treatment under medical supervision with the aim of discharging those patients whose mental condition permits it. There are three main practical aspects to the Home Office's work, relating to admissions, detention, and discharge.

ADMISSIONS

Most of the work in arranging hospital admissions is undertaken by the prison medical service. People who are charged with serious offences and are thought to be mentally disordered are likely to be remanded in custody by the courts. The prison medical officer will provide a report to the court and, where he believes a hospital order is desirable, will ask either a local hospital, an RSU, or the SHSA if a Special Hospital place is sought, to send a doctor to examine the prisoner and consider making a place available. Once this is arranged, reports are submitted to the court which, after conviction, may make a hospital order and a restriction order if it wishes. After the patient is received in hospital the Home Office will then write to the hospital, send a copy of the police report on his offence, and ask for regular reports on his progress.

The arrangements for transferring prisoners to hospital are similar in that the initiative is taken by the prison medical officer in identifying the need for transfer and in approaching a local hospital, RSU or the SHSA. Difficulties are sometimes experienced in arranging the transfer of mentally disordered prisoners because of variations in the level of hospital provision in different parts of the country, pressure on beds in Special Hospitals and RSU, and the reluctance of some local psychiatric hospitals to accept prisoners. However, at present the overall position is better than it has been for some time. Once a place is made available and the Home Office is satisfied that it provides sufficient security for the protection of the public a transfer direction is made by the Home Office, together with a restriction direction (unless the prisoner is very close to his earliest date of release). After the patient's arrival in hospital, the Home Office will send a copy of the police report on his offence and ask for regular medical reports. Different admission arrangements are made in cases which are dealt with under the 1964 Criminal Procedure (Insanity) Act. After a defendant is found unfit to plead or found not-guilty by reason of insanity the court is required to order his admission to such hospital as the Home Secretary may specify. In such cases the Home Office is responsible for directing the patient's admission to a hospital. This will be done after consultations with the hospital managers.

DETENTION

Where a patient is subject to a restriction order without limit of time, the authority for his detention does not need to be renewed and cannot expire. The responsible medical officer is required to provide periodic reports—at present annual—to the Home Office on the patient's condition and progress. Restricted patients may apply once a year to Mental Health Review Tribunals for their discharge from hospital, and the Home Secretary is required to refer to a Tribunal the case of any detained restricted patient which has not been considered by a Tribunal within the previous three years. When Tribunals consider the case of a restricted patient they receive from the Home Office a statement outlining the offences which caused the patient to be admitted to hospital or prison and setting out its view on any proposal his doctor may have put to the Tribunal to transfer him to a different hospital or to discharge him.

Patients who are detained in Special Hospitals may be discharged directly into the community, although transfer to an RSU or to a local hospital is more usual. Where transfer to conditions of lesser security is thought right by a patient's doctor, the Home Office considers his recommendation from the point of view of public safety. The Home Secretary will give his consent only if he is satisfied that it will not give rise to any unacceptable risk and, after the patient has been transferred, the Home Office watches his progress closely to see if he settles well in his new environment. Once it is satisfied that he has, the Home Office will be willing to agree to reasonable leave arrangements that may be proposed by the responsible medical officer. These are likely to vary, depending on the type of hospital. While escorted leave and group outings take place from Special Hospitals, unescorted leave is rare. Patients at RSUs are normally expected to be given gradually increasing freedom, working through escorted leave, short periods of unescorted leave, to longer periods which may in some cases involve overnight or weekend absences, or regular absences to attend a training course or take up a job. Responsibility for arranging a transfer, including finding a hospital place, rests with the hospital managers and the patient's doctor.

Proposals for transfer or discharge must be approached with caution. The Home Office cannot forget why it is that a patient is detained in hospital—what it was that led the court to send him there and why the court judged a restriction order necessary—and in considering any proposal to give him greater freedom it must examine and assess the risks of further serious offences being committed. No decision can be entirely without risk, but it must be minimized as far as possible and nothing which could be foreseen must be overlooked.

The Home Office recognizes that a patient sent to hospital under Sections 37 and 41 of the 1983 Act is detained for treatment. Its view on the length of detention in any particular case depends on the progress it believes the patient has made and the degree of risk his transfer or discharge might pose to the public. This may lead to criticism of being overcautious. Assessing a patient's mental condition and trying to determine the degree of risk he would present to the outside world is not easy, and there is always likely to be a degree of risk in deciding to transfer a patient to conditions of lesser security or to discharge him. There is, however, no alternative to erring on the side of caution because the consequences of a mistake can be very serious. In considering proposals which are put to the Home Office, its concern is to establish whether there is an adequate understanding of how the patient came to commit the offence which led to his detention in hospital, whether there is some definite reason to suppose he has changed while in hospital and is unlikely to commit further serious offences and, if discharge is proposed, whether the patient has a realistic conception of his future life in the community and a sensible approach to his plans for the resumption of normal life.

ADVISORY BOARD ON RESTRICTED PATIENTS

In particularly difficult cases, the Home Secretary will seek the views of the Advisory Board on Restricted Patients on any proposal to discharge a restricted patient or transfer him to a less secure hospital. The board is a non-statutory body whose origins go back to the tragic case of Graham Young and the Aarvold Report (Home Office and Department of Heath and Social Security, 1973). This is a salutory reminder of how much can be at stake in seeking to treat and rehabilitate some of the patients detained subject to restriction orders. Young was conditionally discharged from Broadmoor in February 1971, and in June 1972 was convicted of murder and other serious offences committed by poisoning between the time of his discharge and his arrest in November 1971. A committee set up under the chairmanship of Sir Carl Aarvold recognized a small proportion of restricted patients in whose case the risk of serious reoffending was particularly difficult to predict and where special care was therefore required in the assessment of proposals for transfer or discharge. The committee recommended that such proposals should be considered by a special advisory board before the Home Secretary gave his consent to them.

The Board which was set up took a slightly different form from that proposed by the committee, and it has since changed a little. It is now chaired by a senior lawyer and consists of a second legally qualified member, two forensic psychiatrists, senior members of the probation service and social services, and two members with special experience of the criminal justice system. It is open to a patient's responsible medical officer as well as to the Home Office to to raise the question of whether a case could be referred to the Advisory Board, and this sometimes happens. More normally, a case will be referred to the Board on the decision of the Minister at the point when proposals are put to the Home Office for a restricted patient to be transferred or discharged. There are no formal guidelines for identifying which individual cases require special assessment. The cases put to the Board are usually ones in which there is considered to be a continuing risk of the patient harming other persons, together with some uncertainty which makes it particularly difficult to predict the likelihood of reoffending. The number of proposals which are referred to the Board has remained relatively constant in recent years at about 50 each year.

The Board's consideration of each case is based on comprehensive reports about the patient's background and progress in hospital, and on an interview with him by one of the Board members, who will provide the Board with a report of this. Although in many cases the Board is able to endorse the proposal which has been put to it, where it feels unable to provide its endorsement the Home Office will try to offer advice on the matters on which it and the Board still need to be satisfied.

MENTAL HEALTH REVIEW TRIBUNALS

Restricted patients have a right, at periodic intervals set out in Section 70 of the 1983 Mental Health Act, to apply to a Tribunal for their discharge. The Home Secretary is required by Section 71 of the Act to refer to a Tribunal the case of any restricted patient detained in hospital whose case has not been considered by a Tribunal within the previous three years. Under the provisions of Section 73 of the Act a Tribunal has the power to direct the conditional discharge of a restricted patient detained subject to a hospital order under Section 37 if it is satisfied that one of two statutory criteria are met: 1. that the patient is not suffering from a form of mental disorder which makes it inappropriate for him to be liable to be detained in hospital for medical treatment, or 2. that it is not necessary for the health or safety of the patient or for the protection of other persons that he should receive such treatment. It may also discharge a patient absolutely if it is satisfied that it is not appropriate for him to remain liable to be recalled to hospital for further treatment. These powers do not apply in respect of prisoners who have been transferred to hospital and are subject to restriction directions under Section 49. These patients will normally be returned to prison if a Tribunal believes they no longer require to be detained in hospital.

The powers conferred on Tribunals represent a significant change from the arrangements established under the 1959 Mental Health Act. This is a consequence of the judgment of the European Court of Human Rights in the case of *X v. the United Kingdom*, 1981. It provides the restricted patient with an opportunity to apply to a Tribunal to have the merits of his detention reviewed. However, the Home Secretary's power to discharge remain as before, and in the normal course of events a responsible Medical Officer who believes his patient is ready for discharge will make a recommendation to the Home Office, whether or not the patient has applied for a Tribunal hearing.

When a Tribunal considers an application by a restricted patient the Home Office will be given the opportunity to comment on it and, if it believes there would be an unacceptable risk to the safety of the public, the Home Office will oppose the patient's application for discharge, if necessary seeking to be represented at the Tribunal hearing either by an official or by Treasury Counsel.

If a Tribunal decides to discharge a patient conditionally it may order the discharge to be deferred until satisfactory after-care arrangements have been made. The Tribunal may set out any condition it thinks fit. After discharge the patient's progress is monitored by the Home Office in the same way as that of a patient conditionally discharged by the Home Secretary, and the Home Secretary may vary (or remove) conditions imposed by a Tribunal. The power of recall to hospital remains vested exclusively in the Home Secretary.

MENTAL HEALTH ACT COMMISSION

The Mental Health Act Commission is concerned exclusively with patients who are detained under the Mental Health Act. As restricted patients represent perhaps a quarter of all detained patients, it might seem surprising that there is little contact between the Commission and the Home Office on a day to day basis. However, the Commission's remit does not include a power to review the decisions of the courts to make or not to make hospital orders, or the Home Secretary's exercise of his powers of discharge, consent to leave and transfer, or recall. Nor does the Commission have an express statutory role towards mentally disordered prisoners. Nevertheless, the Commission's role in the oversight of mental health care does give it a legitimate interest in these areas. It has not fought shy of addressing issues of concern, and in particular apparent delays by the Home Office in deciding on proposals for individual restricted patients' transfer or discharge, with approaches at Ministerial or official level or more generally in its biennial reports. The Home Office is anxious to maintain cooperative relations with the Commission and is content, wherever possible, to provide information and comment both on individual cases and on wider issues.

ANNUAL REPORTS

The Percy Commission (Royal Commission, 1957) in proposing the current arrangements for mentally disordered offenders to be treated in hospital, but for their transfer and discharge to be under the control of the Home Secretary, sought to ensure that the rehabilitation aims of the hospitals would be shared with the Home Office as a safeguard for the safety of the public. It is only natural in such circumstances that those involved with the rehabilitation of patients who have committed serious offences will wish to move cautiously. There is, however, a duty to ensure that patients are not denied their right to rehabilitation. It was this consideration which led the Butler Committee to recommend in 1975 the introduction of statutory annual reports to the Home Secretary (Home Office and Department of Health and Social Security, 1975). They saw that detention under a restriction order, which was usually without limit of time, carried with it the danger that the period of detention might be longer than was strictly necessary. They proposed that regular reports should be made to the Home Office by the responsible medical officer both to provide a satisfactory account of the patient's mental condition and his continuing need for detention, and to help to relieve the problems which might arise between hospital doctors and the Home Office through inadequate communication. The annual reports provide a valuable source of information, particularly about patients who do not apply regularly for

Tribunal hearings, and ensure that in the absence of such hearings the patient's case is reviewed each year. Contact with the hospitals is also reinforced by a regular programme of visits by Home Office staff, as well as by a growing number of visits by hospital staff to the Home Office.

CONDITIONAL DISCHARGE

Once a restricted patient reaches the point where the hospital staff believe he no longer requires treatment in hospital and the Home Office agrees that he can return to the community without unacceptable risk to the public, he will be conditionally discharged by the Home Secretary. The conditions are invariably that the patient will reside at a specified address, which may be a hostel, family home, lodgings, etc., and will cooperate with medical supervision from his doctor, and with social supervision by a social worker or probation officer. The purpose is to help the patient to re-establish himself and to guard against a breakdown in his mental health or antisocial behaviour which may require recall to hospital for further treatment. The choice of accommodation will depend partly on what is available and partly on what is acceptable. In some cases it is clearly desirable that the patient should live in a carefully structured environment which some hostels can provide, while in others greater independence may be desirable. The range of facilities varies around the country, and a welcome example of recent developments is the establishment in Liverpool of groups of flats to which patients can be discharged from the local RSU. These provide good quality accommodation, privacy for the patients and an opportunity to manage their own affairs, while at the same time receiving close supervision from the staff of the hospital with whom they remain in contact through visits from a community nurse. The flats in Liverpool were set up with financial support from the Liverpool Housing Trust, are managed by MIND and have clinical support from the Mersey Regional Forensic Psychiatry Service. (See too Chapter 14 by James Higgins.)

In other parts of the country, suitable accommodation may be more difficult to find. In all cases, however, the features of conditional discharge remain the same: the Home Office wishes to know where the patient is living and that his home in the community is satisfactory. It also wishes to be sure that he sees his doctor regularly so that he receives whatever medication is thought necessary and a check can be made on his mental health, and that he sees his social worker or probation officer regularly so that he is aware of how the patient is living and coping. Their regular reports enable the Home Office to monitor the patient's progress and satisfy itself about his stability and successful rehabilitation. Wherever possible the social supervisor helps to find work for the patient. This may be difficult because of the patient's institutionalization, residual mental disorder, or lack of necessary work skills. Where jobs cannot be found, alternatives are sought, such as attendance at training courses, day centres, 'drop-in centres' run by a hospital, or at the hospital itself as a day patient if this is desirable.

The objectives of these arrangements are to minimize the risk of further offending by providing the patient with a structured life after leaving hospital, by giving him what help is possible, and by keeping an eye on him to watch for any signs of a breakdown. If further hospital treatment appears necessary he can be recalled by the Home Office—31 patients were recalled in 1988. His return to hospital may be brief if that is all that is necessary, for example, to adjust his medication. It may be more prolonged if it has become apparent that discharge was premature and the patient continues to pose a risk to others. Under normal circumstances, while a patient is conditionally discharged, the Home Office will receive reports on him quarterly from his doctor and social supervisor, sometimes half-yearly if, after a number of years, he has made good progress and gives rise to no cause for concern. Usually after a period of about five years, successful rehabilitation, an absolute discharge will be considered on the recommendation of his supervisors, though this may sometimes be done after about two years when the patient's offending history is less serious. More difficult or troubling cases may take longer.

CONCLUSION

The arrangements which have been developed for the detention and treatment of mentally disordered offenders and for their rehabilitation into the community are designed above all to protect the public and to minimize the risks involved by ensuring that hospitals can provide treatment in conditions of sufficient security, and that discharge follows careful consideration and provides effective supervision and support. It is not perfect—as no system which depends on human judgement can be. The Home Office recognizes not only that everything reasonably possible must be done to guard against the risk of further offending, but also that patients should be returned to the community as soon as this can be done safely. It is a difficult balance which was eloquently described in the Aarvold Report:

The making of recommendations and decisions about the discharge and continuing care of mentally disordered offenders entails, fundamentally, the assessment and prediction, by one group of human beings, of the probable future behaviour of another. Prescribed procedures can offer real safeguards against the chance of human error going undetected, but we do not believe that in this sort of situation there can be an absolute guarantee of infallibility. Indeed, there might be a risk that the adoption of over-elaborate procedures could reduce the quality of judgments made, by weakening the sense of personal responsibility which those who care for these unfortunate individuals bring to their tasks. The complete elimination of any risk to the public could only be achieved by continuing to detain these patients perhaps indefinitely, long after many of them had recovered from their mental disorder, and for periods in excess of any term of imprisonment they might have served as sentences for their offences. We are sure that in our society this would be seen as an inhumane avoidance of the responsibility for making a proper judgment in each case.

Aarvold Report, 1973

This view remains valid and reflects the Home Office role in its dealings with mentally disordered offenders. © Crown copyright 1991. Published with the permission of the Controller of HMSO.

REFERENCES

Home Office and Department of Health and Social Security (1975). *Report of the Committee on Mentally Abnormal Offenders* (The Butler Report) Cmnd 6244. London: HMSO, para. 7.25, 14.25 and 57.

Home Office and Department of Health and Social Security (1973). *Report of the Review of Procedures for the Discharge and Supervision of Psychiatric Patients Subject to Special Restrictions* (The Aarvold Report) Cmnd 5191. London: HMSO.

Royal Commission (1957). *Report on Law Relating to Mental Illness and Mental Deficiency 1954–1957* Cmnd 169. London: HMSO, para. 518.

Walker N. (1968). Hadfield and others. In *Crime and Insanity in England*. Edinburgh: Edinburgh University Press.

12 *A Department of Health Perspective*

CLIFFORD GRAHAM

INTRODUCTION

The Department of Health has a responsibility to ensure that a comprehensive range of hospital, community health and social services are available to meet the needs of mentally disordered offenders. In discharging that responsibility, full account has to be taken of the requirements of the criminal justice system, and of the wider public safety considerations. Those factors inevitably, and properly, condition the pattern and organization of such services. But they remain an integral part of the overall network of psychiatric provision, and are planned and provided in keeping with the development of services for mentally disordered people generally. The term 'mental disorder' encompasses a wide range of by no means mutually exclusive psychiatric conditions, and the treatment, care and support needs of mentally disordered people (be they offenders or not) are correspondingly diverse and complex. The overriding aim, therefore, is to match as closely as possible the services that are provided to the needs of the individual recipient, at the right time, and in the right setting.

As stated previously (in Chapter 11), it is the Government's policy that in all appropriate cases mentally disordered offenders should be kept out of, or transferred from, prison establishments. The difficulties associated with the full and effective implementation of this policy are discussed elsewhere. The intention here is to focus on the services that are provided outside the penal system, and in which the Department of Health has a direct interest. But it is fully recognized that the ability of the health service, in particular, to respond to the needs of the courts, and of the prison service, has had, and will continue to have, a significant impact on where, when and how mentally disordered offenders are able to be diverted from the penal system, and enter the appropriate National Health Service (NHS) or other, non-custodial, facility.

Health service provision for the mentally disordered offender has its origins in the parallel, but largely separate, development of the Special Hospitals Service, and of other locally and regionally based psychiatric services within the NHS. This, in turn, reflects the dual nature of the past role of the Department of Health in this field. Under the 1977 National Health Service Act, the Secretary of State is required to provide 'a comprehensive health service' through a network of health authorities. But to date, and for largely historical reasons, the Department has retained a direct central management responsibility for the four Special Hospitals that constitute the national Special Hospitals Service. (This arrangement came to an end with the setting up of a central Special Health Authority for the Special Hospitals Service on 1 July 1989—see below.) The Department's involvement in the development of mental health services generally has followed a more usual pattern. Ministers determine broad policy aims; agree service objectives with regional health authorities; and monitor, and review, performance in the achievement of those objectives. Although, therefore, the Department on behalf of Ministers, can and does influence, guide and shape the way in which health authorities put into effect the intentions and wishes of the Government, it does not normally do so in any directive or managerial sense. Rather, it does so by a process of consultation, persuasion and encouragement—in which, of course, the availability and deployment of funding plays a significant part! This is particularly the case in the administration of something as complex as the NHS. The separate development of the Special Hospitals Service, and the fact that Special Hospitals' provision is made on a national basis—rather than falling within the ambit of regional health authorities—has resulted, to some extent at least, in an inappropriate fragmentation of what should be a closely interrelated, and complementary, range of services. That said, the full spectrum of psychiatric services, including the Special Hospitals, are available to treat and care for offenders with mental health problems.

For most psychiatric patients requiring hospital admission, it should be possible to arrange for this to happen locally. But for the relatively very small number of patients requiring treatment and care in a secure setting—and a significant proportion of mentally disordered offenders fall within this category—it is necessary to ensure that a comprehensive service is available by working out a more complex pattern of hospital responsibility. The pattern of services that has evolved provides for a concentration of secure facilities at the Special Hospitals, and Regional Secure Units. But it is important to recognize that the needs of the mentally disordered offender range much wider and that, in many instances, they can most appropriately be met in a local psychiatric hospital.

SPECIAL HOSPITALS

The Special Hospitals Service is provided in response to a statutory duty placed on the Secretary of State for Health by Section 4 of the 1977 National Health Service Act 'to provide and maintain establishments [in this Act referred to as Special Hospitals] for persons subject to detention . . . who, in his opinion, require treatment under conditions of special security on account of their dangerous, violent or criminal propensities'. The courts and the prison service are the major 'consumers' of this service.

Overall, about 80 per cent of all Special Hospital patients—there are currently some 1700—are detained on the order of the courts or following transfer from prison, and well over 60 per cent of the Special Hospital population is subject to special restrictions deriving from mental health legislation. The four Special Hospitals also cater for a high proportion of *all* those mentally disordered offenders identified as needing hospital care: about 850 are made subject to hospital orders each year, of which 15 per cent are admitted to a Special Hospital; and of the 200 or so transferred annually from prisons to hospitals, about 35 per cent go to Special Hospital. The Special Hospitals provide the highest level of security available within the hospital system, and it is intended that only the most 'dangerous' patients who require treatment in these conditions are admitted. This is reflected in the fact that about one quarter of court and prison transfer applications are not thought appropriate and, indeed, why the majority of disordered offenders judged to be in need of hospital care receive it elsewhere. There is little or no evidence to suggest that, given the remit of the Special Hospitals as at present defined, there are any serious difficulties in arranging for the admission of those mentally disordered offenders who are judged to be appropriate for this kind of facility—the question of availability of a bed, for example, should not arise.

The arrangements for the admission of patients, including the criteria that are applied in individual cases, are currently being reviewed as part of a series of important changes in the management and operation of the Special Hospitals. These developments, linked as they are to redefined Ministerial objectives for the service, are aimed at building on what is already a very valuable resource—not only in terms of the large number of secure places that it provides, but also because of the professional expertise, specialist skill, and commitment of the well-over 3000 staff that it employs.

The Special Hospitals aim to provide, in a secure environment, a suitable therapeutic regimen for each patient, under the clinical management of consultant-led multidisciplinary teams. Over the last decade or so, and in response to widespread and informed criticism, the hospitals have been largely successful in moving towards the provision of a clinically orientated service, with a greater emphasis on treatment and rehabilitation. (Previously there had been a tendency to concentrate mainly on meeting custodial requirements.) These advances have been made possible by a substantial build-up in resources, the outcome of a sustained Departmental policy of according a high priority to the needs of the Special Hospitals. Between 1980/81 and 1988/89, revenue spending increased from £28 million to £67.2 million (or well over 30 per cent in real terms), and the number of staff increased from 2380 to 3200 (or 35 per cent). Over the same period the numbers of patients fell, from over 1980 to 1720 and the increase in unit cost, from just under £14 400 to over £35 600 was, therefore, even more significant (over 50 per cent in real terms).

The Government is committed to the further development of services for Special Hospital patients. Ministers have indicated their intention to promulgate a new statement of national policy that, together with the planned programme of changes in management and organization, will open up the Special Hospitals to new ideas and fresh thinking. The primary aim, consistent with the ever present need to ensure public safety, will be to minimize the existing geographical, professional and service isolation of the hospitals. This will be done by strengthening the present vital links with the wider spectrum of psychiatric services, the community health and social services and with the Prison Medical Service and the courts. To this end, the Government has identified six basic objectives that will provide a strategic framework within which future policies will be formulated, and the business of the service conducted. These are to:

1. Ensure the continuing safety of the public
2. Ensure the provision of appropriate treatment for patients
3. Ensure a good quality of life for patients and staff
4. Develop the hospitals as centres of excellence for the training of staff in all disciplines, in forensic and other branches of psychiatry and psychiatric care and treatment
5. Develop closer working relationships with NHS local and regional psychiatric services
6. Promote research in fields related to forensic psychiatry.

The Department has been greatly assisted in taking forward this process of change by the 1988 report on Broadmoor Hospital by the Health Advisory Service and Social Services Inspectorate (HAS/SSI(88)SHI). The report recognized much existing good practice but also pointed firmly to the need for major change in a number of important areas. Many of its recommendations have implications for the Special Hospitals Service as a whole and detailed plans for their implementation have been drawn up, and are being acted on, at all of the hospitals, and within the Department.

All this is taking place in parallel with the establishment of the new central Special Health Authority, and the introduction of general management within the hospitals. From October 1989, the Department of Health relinquished its operational management responsibilities for the service, and these were assumed by the new Authority. As well as addressing the needs of the criminal justice system, and Authority will review the size and organization as a whole, and in the light of the continuing debate on the balance that needs to be struck between therapy and security, will seek to set—and achieve—clearly defined service objectives, particularly in relation to the quality of treatment and care. These moves will serve to reinforce the 'hospital' nature of the service, and will bring it into a closer, and more consistent, relationship with the NHS in general. At the same time, the new arrangements will provide an improved environment in which roles and relationships, and lines of accountability, are more clearly defined, and in which better informed decisions can be taken on key issues—including those that involve the day to day lives of patients, and the use of resources.

It must be emphasized that a patient should only remain in a Special Hospital for so long as it is necessary for treatment to be provided in conditions of utmost security. When the clinical team responsible for the patient's care is satisfied that discharge or—in the case of a convicted prisoner—return to prison is appropriate, or that further treatment should be provided in a less restricted environment, arrangements are put in hand to effect the transfer as speedily as possible. The average annual number of departures (including non-offenders) over the last five years is 165. But in the case of a patient subject to restrictions, the Home Secretary's consent is required before a move can take place. In some instances this has resulted in delaying the transfer, and difficulties may also arise, and delays occur, in identifying a suitable, alternative hospital bed or community placement. Ministers are aware of these problems, and have taken steps to speed up the process of discharge and transfer, by personally drawing to the attention of each Regional Health Authority chairman those cases that are proving 'difficult to place', and also by ensuring that cases are processed as efficiently as possible within central departments.

REGIONAL SECURE UNITS

The range of secure provision for mentally disordered people (including offenders) extends from the Special Hospitals to facilities provided by the Regional Health Authorities, the main focus being a network of Regional Secure Units (RSUs). Arrangements vary from region to region, but, in broad terms RSUs provide treatment and care in 'medium' secure conditions—that is they are rather less stringent than those that apply in a Special Hospital, but more than can usually be found in a local setting. RSU provision has been developed, since the early 1980s, in response initially to an urgent need identified by the Butler Committee and others, for an intermediate form of secure facility. (See also Chapters 10 and 13.) At that time, the Special Hospitals were grossly overcrowded and a serious 'gap' in service provision had emerged—which may well have contributed to the overcrowding—that was linked to the policy of the progressive development of community-based psychiatric services, and the implementation of 'open door' hospital service policies. Also running down of large psychiatric hospitals had removed most of the local 'locked ward' type secure provision. With one exception (and work on that is well in hand) every Regional Health Authority now has a secure unit and many also have interim secure facilities. The RSUs are intended to take patients who present severely disruptive behaviour, who are mentally ill or psychopathic, and who require treatment in the short term, not usually exceeding 18 months to two years.

Although the total number of places currently available—518—is still substantially less than that recommended by the 1975 Butler Committee (2000) (Home Office and Department of Health and Social Security (DHSS), 1975) and the Department's own original 1976 assessment of requirement (1000) (DHSS, 1976), the regions seem to regard the present level of provision as adequate—but, it must be stressed, in relation only to those specific groups of mentally ill, short-stay patients for which the RSUs have been expressly provided. (The needs of other, longer-stay groups are discussed below.) Even allowing for their very different roles, the fact that RSUs also provide considerably fewer beds than the Special Hospitals Service has given rise to a questioning of the present balance between the various levels of secure provision. Special Hospitals are rightly considered to cater only for the *most* dangerous patients, and could be described as forming the top slice of a pyramid of interrelated secure facilities.

The development of 'medium' secure facilities clearly demonstrates the complex nature of the Department's involvement in the process of health services planning, organization and delivery. Acting promptly on the Butler findings, the Department promulgated a clear policy that aimed, specifically, to generate the growth of RSU provision and—as an indication of the importance attached to it—made available substantial funding to enable the regional health authorities to put that policy into effect. The reaction was mixed—in some regions encouraging, in others disappointing. Overall, the RSU programme has taken far longer to implement than had originally been anticipated and even now there would appear to be considerable scope for the further provision of regionally based secure facilities (although not necessarily with the RSU focus). This is something that the Department is discussing further with the Regional Health Authorities, and will also be of interest to the new Special Hospitals Service Authority.

No hard and fast information is available centrally about the extent to which RSUs cater for mentally disordered offenders. It is estimated that the pattern resembles quite closely that of the Special Hospitals, with more than 60 per cent of patients being referred from the criminal justice system. This figure is thought to include a fairly high proportion, perhaps about one third, of mentally disordered offenders treated at, and transferred from, the Special Hospitals and who are en route to local NHS hospitals or to discharge to the community. The working arrangements between the RSUs and Special Hospitals are of particular interest to the Department—there may well be scope for some improvement in the ease and speed with which patients can be transferred between these two types of facility. (See Molly Meacher's (Chapter 13) comments on this.)

REGIONAL FORENSIC SERVICES

Closely associated with the build-up of the RSU network has been the development of regional forensic services. This has enabled, with the appointment of consultants in forensic psychiatry, a more co-ordinated and structured approach in the NHS response to meeting the needs of the mentally disordered offender. But forensic psychiatry is still very much a new speciality, and the majority of hospital orders for the seriously mentally ill result in the patient being admitted to local hospitals, under the care of a local consultant psychiatrist. In the majority of these cases—they are very small in number, as compared with the psychiatric hospital population overall—the offences are relatively minor, and the patient can be cared for without recourse to elaborate security arrangements. There are, nevertheless, wide variations in the number of 'secure' beds in mental handicap and mental illness hospitals at district level, and in the ability and/or willingness of local hospitals to accept referrals from the courts, and transfers from the prison service. There is an equally wide variation in the way in which hospitals are organized to meet the needs of these patients. In some cases, hospitals specifically set aside a ward to deal with the more disruptive patients and offer higher than average staff/patient ratios. To foster this approach, the Department and health authorities are encouraging the creation of consultant posts for consultants with a specific interest in forensic psychiatry.

THE MENTALLY DISORDERED STILL WITHIN THE PENAL SYSTEM

There has been considerable debate over a number of years, not least within the Department of Health and the Home Office, about the extent to which services are planned, organized and delivered to meet effectively the health care needs of mentally disordered offenders. Much concern has been expressed about the numbers of such offenders who remain within some form of specialized therapeutic facilities (whether or not they are detainable under the Mental Health Act), and at any one time there are between 250–300 seriously disordered offenders who are considered to be detainable in hospitals. (This estimate is based on information derived from the regular returns made by Prison Medical Officers to the Home Office.) There is a widely held view that there exists an urgent need to provide some form of 'sanctuary' for 'patients' who are not covered by the provisions of the 1983 Mental Health Act, and for whom existing hospital and community services are inappropriate. And there is a clear need to develop more effective referral mechanisms between the courts and Prison Medical Service, and the whole range of health and social services outside the criminal justice system.

The Department of Health and the Home Office have co-terminus responsibilities in this regard, and they are currently working together towards the implementation of recommendations of the 1987 report of an Interdepartmental Working Group on Mentally Disturbed Offenders in the Prison System (Home Office and DHSS, 1987). The report provides a strategy to guide the work of both Departments, and has identified a series of practical and achievable measures that can be taken, particularly in relation to improving ease of access to health and social services, to ensure that full use is made of existing provision.

In the case of the Department of Health, the report calls for the continued promotion of the development of comprehensive secure provision, including facilities for those chronically mentally ill and mentally impaired patients not appropriate for treatment in an RSU. In tandem with the Home Office, the Department will also continue to seek ways of improving co-ordination and communication between those involved in developing policies for, and providing services to, offenders with mental health problems.

SOME OF THE PROBLEMS

There has been a great deal of speculation about a possible link between mentally disordered offenders within the prison system and the phased closure of large, single specialty, psychiatric hospitals as a consequence of the policy of creating locally based services to provide better, alternative facilities. There is widespread agreement that, for the vast majority of psychiatric patients, this policy represents a move towards the provision of a more appropriate, and responsive, service. But Ministers have acknowledged that some patients may be discharged without due attention being given to their future needs within the community, and that other patients may continue to need some form of hospital care or community haven—the 'sanctuary' concept referred to above—sometimes in a secure environment. At present there is a lack of systematic information to assess the extent of the problem of the unmet needs of people within the penal system, or in the community, who may be slipping through the health service net. Therefore, work has been urgently put in hand within the Department to bring together information held by health authorities and the Social Services Inspectorate, together with research findings and the views of, and information from, voluntary agencies.

There is also a lack of comprehensive, objective and quantifiable information about the extent to which the present levels and patterns of NHS psychiatric services actually reflect, and provide a sensitive and flexible response to, the widely differing needs of mentally disordered patients (including offenders), one between another and, in individual cases, at different times. As well as the possible gaps in services referred to above, there is evidence to suggest that significant numbers of patients are being treated and cared for in inappropriate settings, and that more needs to be done to ease the flow of patients between the various facilities—the Special Hospitals, RSUs, local hospitals, the community and the Prison Medical Service. In this context, the two Departments are collaborating in the development of two research projects: 1. the health requirements of the prison and remand centre population, and 2. the treatment and security requirements of the special hospitals patient population. In addition, the Department of Health has just started a follow–up study of the subsequent criminal and psychiatric hospital admission records of all patients discharged from Special Hospitals from 1972 to 1992.

More generally, Department of Health and Home Office Ministers have launched a full review of the health and social services provided for mentally disordered offenders (and others requiring similar services) in England. A Steering Committee has been set up, drawn from both departments, and from the health and social services, the Special Hospitals Service Authority and the criminal justice system. The purpose of the review is to determine whether changes are needed in the current level, pattern or operation of services and how such changes might be promoted. The review will take account of, *inter alia*, the new arrangements for management and delivery of hospital and community care; the implications for NHS forensic psychiatry of action arising from the Efficiency Scrutiny of the Prison Medical Service, published in October 1990, and any relevant recommendations of the Inquiry of Lord Justice Woolf into the disturbances in early 1990 at HM Prison Manchester and other prison establishments. The review will also look at present arrangements for funding service developments and their possible improvement and will take account of the findings of any relevant research. The review is due to be completed by mid-1992 and regular progress reports are to be made to Ministers.

CONCLUSION

In concluding this brief review of the role of the Department of Health, it is appropriate to acknowledge the vital and dynamic contribution that is made by—to use a well worn but, in this instance, an accurately all-embracing phrase—'non-Governmental agencies' in the evolutionary development of mental health policies. As part of the process of policy formulation, there is always a need for an objective and informed alternative perspective, and for an independent source of new ideas—and even, indeed, for constructive and considered criticism!

RELEVANT PUBLICATIONS AND REFERENCES

APHA (1979). *Setting Priorities for Health Policies in England: Some Pointers for International Comparison.* New York.
APHA (1979). *The Comparative Costs of Health Care, Given Inside and Outside Hospital:* A European View. New York.

APHA (1987). International Comparisons in Health Care—The UK Example. New Orleans.

Council of Europe (1979). *Comparative Costs of Health Care given inside and outside Hospitals: Consequences of Taking Action.* Strasbourg.

Council of Europe (1980). *Comparative Costs of Health Care Given Inside and Outside Hospitals: Report of a Select Committee of Experts.* Strasbourg.

DHSS (1974). Revised Report of the Working Party on Security in NHS Psychiatric Hospitals (unpublished).

DHSS (1976). *The NHS Planning System.* London: HMSO.

DHSS (1976). *Priorities for the Health and Personal Social Services in England.* London: HMSO.

DHSS (1976). *Sharing Resources for Health in England.* London: HMSO.

DHSS (1977). *The National Health Service Act.* London: HMSO.

DHSS (1977). *Priorities in the Health and Social Services: The Way Forward.* London: HMSO.

DHSS (1979). *Review of Health Capital—a Discussion Document on the Role of Capital in the Provision of Health Services.* London: HMSO.

DHSS (1980). *Activities in Support of Health Care Exports: Rayner Scrutiny Report.* London: HMSO.

DHSS (1980). *Drug Products Licensing Systems.* London: HMSO.

DHSS (1983). *NHS Management Inquiry* (Griffiths Report). London: HMSO.

DHSS (1984). *Implementation of the NHS Management Inquiry Report*—HC (84)13. London: HMSO.

DHSS (1986). *In Praise of the Civil Service; Some Reflections of a Long-Service Bureaucrat.* London: HMSO.

DHSS (1987). *Listen to the individual Person: the Best Way to Improve the Planning, Management and Delivery of the Social Services for the Benefit of Government and the Consumer.* London: HMSO.

DHSS (1988). *Special Hospitals Service: Past, Present and Future—Rampton Hospital.* London: HMSO.

DHSS (1988). *Special Hospital Patient Statistics.* London: HMSO.

DHSS (19??). *Supply Estimates for the Department of Health, and in the Health and Social Services Appropriation Accounts.* London: HMSO.

DHSS (1974 and 1975). *Report of the Committee on Mentlly Disordered Offenders, with the Interim Report.* Cmnds 5698 and 6244. London: HMSO.

Disability Alliance Conference (November 1977). *Joint Planning and Joint Funding: A Challenge for Health and Personal Social Services.*

Estes Park Institute (1988). *Anglo/American Comparisons in Health Care.* Williamsburg, USA.

European Health Management Association (1988). *National Health Service Management Issues of Importance Internationally.* Oxford.

HO (Biennial). Statistics relating to 'restricted' patients. London: HMSO.

HO and DHSS (1974). *Revised Report of the Working Party on Security in NHS Psychiatric Hospitals.* (Unpublished).

HODH (1987). *The Inter-Departmental Working Group of Home Office and DHSS Officers on Mentally Disturbed Offenders in the Prison System in England and Wales.* London: HMSO.

Society for Social Medicine (1978). *Research and Policy Making: The Policy Maker's Perspective.* Edinburgh.

World Health Organization (1979). *Health Outcome Measurement: Summary of Available and Usable Measures.* Copenhagen.

WHO/IEA (1977). *Measurement of Levels of Health—Priority Setting.* Poland: Nieborow.

WHO and PAHO (1978). *Sharing Resources for Health in England and Through a Decentralized Planning Process.* New Orleans.

13 *Provision for the mentally disordered offender in hospital: suggestions for action and research—a Mental Health Act commissioner's viewpoint*

MOLLY MEACHER

The issues affecting patients in each of the three main forms of hospital provision for mentally abnormal offenders: Special Hospitals, Regional Secure Units, or local psychiatric hospitals will be discussed with some proposals for action and research.

SPECIAL HOSPITALS

The three Special Hospitals—Broadmoor, Rampton, and Ashworth—cater for people subject to detention 'who in the opinion of the Secretary of State for Social Services require treatment under conditions of special security on account of their dangerous, violent or criminal propensities' (1977 National Health Service Act).

The facilities available are, in many ways, exceptionally good. There is a higher staff/patient ratio than in most psychiatric hospitals and a wide range of occupational and educational opportunities. Special Hospital staff have considerable expertise and do not in general lack compassion. The problems for patients in the Special Hospitals stem to some extent from the attempt to provide maximum security conditions in hospitals built in the Victorian era and with a national catchment area.

While in a Special Hospital there are perhaps three central issues for the patient: how soon he/she can be transferred; the links with his family and community; and his treatment in the widest sense of the term. These three issues will be examined briefly.

Transfer delays

The detention in a Special Hospital of people not requiring maximum security is a matter of serious concern. Patients in these hospitals are subjected to a degree of security and restriction of freedom which is indefensible if it is unnecessary (see also Chapter 10).

The Butler Committee in 1975 reported delays of more than six months in Home Office decisions in 7 per cent of cases of restricted patients where tribunals had recommended discharge. The Committee stressed in their recommendations 'that all consultations should be carried out with the greatest sense of urgency' [p. 282 para. 120] in order that delays in transfer of patients are no longer than necessary (Home Office and Department of Health and Social Security (DHSS), 1975).

The length of delays has worsened considerably since that time. In July 1984 for example, more than 20 per cent of the Moss Side population were awaiting transfer. Seven had been waiting for 2–3 years and three for 3–4 years since transfer had been recommended by their Responsible Medical Officer (RMO). The Mental Health Act Commission (MHAC) examined the cases of two groups of patients in Rampton hospital during the period January 1986 to March 1987. The first group of 37 patients were subject to a three-year delay following a transfer recommendation by their RMO and a further 30 patients had been awaiting transfer for more than two years. The study revealed a widespread lack of urgency on the part of those dealing with transfer recommendations. It is commonplace for months to elapse before RMO letters are replied to, whether by the Department of Health, Home Office, Health Authority or National Health Service (NHS) consultant (MHAC Biennial Report 1985–87, p. 37 section 12.2).

Resistance and delays in assessing patients' suitability for transfer on the part of the proposed receiving hospitals are also common.

Referral of an increasing number of cases to the Advisory Board on Restricted Patients (or Aarvold Board, as it is popularly known) appears to have played a part in worsening the delay record. The Advisory Board was established as a result of the recommendations of a committee chaired by Sir Carl Aarvold in 1973 (for further discussion see Chapter 11). The Board was to provide the Home Secretary with advice on any proposal for substantially relaxing control over any restricted patient who had been identified *by his RMO* as requiring special care in assessment. The Aarvold Committee also recommended that the Home Secretary be able to consult the Board on any case on which he felt special anxiety (Home Office and DHSS, 1973). In making the latter recommendation the Aarvold Committee expressed the hope that this would only occur in exceptional circumstances where the patient had not been identified previously by the RMO as requiring special care in assessment.

The current position is that delays often occur in the process of deciding whether a reference to the Board is appropriate. The MHAC has the impression, though this has been difficult to prove, that the Board's advice is being sought on an increasing number of occasions. Between 1 January 1983 and 31 December 1986, for example, the Board considered the cases of 118 patients for the first time.

The Rampton study quoted the case of a consultant in a hospital in the relevant catchment area who had visited and assessed a patient and confirmed the view of the RMO that the patient could appropriately be placed in a local hospital, but then declined to accept the patient on the grounds of inadequate facilities.

Another version of this problem occurs where the patient is assessed by the potential receiving institution as needing more security than can be provided in a local hospital but not so much security as would be provided in a Regional Secure Unit. Patients in this situation can remain in a Special Hospital unnecessarily for, literally, years.

The selection of patients for transfer

Much has been written over the years on the difficult task of assessing dangerousness. Sadly, however, the process of assessment remains far from perfect. Susanne Dell in her study of the transfer of Special Hospital patients concluded that 'a patient's chance of being recommended for transfer could depend less on him than on his doctor' (Dell, 1980). Dell quotes as an example a patient described by his consultant on a tribunal report as paranoid and dangerous, fit neither for discharge nor for transfer. He was subsequently allocated to another doctor who, within 18 months of this description, was successfully organizing his transfer, reporting that he had presented no management problems *within the last five years*. No change in the patient's mental condition or behaviour accounted for this turn of events. I am familiar with a patient who has experienced the reverse effects of a change of RMO. Having anticipated a transfer under his previous RMO the patient remains in Broadmoor with no prospect of transfer for the foreseeable future.

A second finding of the Dell study is the relevance of a high turnover of consultants to the patient's chances of transfer. It takes time to get to know a patient well enough to form a view as to his suitability for release. A constant change of doctors will reduce the number of transfer recommendations.

Recommended action identified for debate in the MHAC Biennial Report, 1987

This was:

1. That the Departments of State involved be made subject to a time limit within which a decision must be reached.
2. Where a decision will depend upon the advice of the Advisory Board this should take place at the beginning rather than at the end of the process. The Board, too, should be required to conclude its deliberations within a limited period.
3. That a firm proposal for leave or transfer be forwarded by the RMO to

the Department of Health and Home Office at the same time. The MHAC recommend that 90 days is a reasonable time limit within which both Departments of State should have arrived at a decision.

4. Where a delay occurs as a result of the unwillingness or inability of the local health authority to provide sufficient facilities, that authority might be required to pay the cost of the patient's care elsewhere. This could act as an incentive to health authorities to provide facilities. At present there is no effective sanction for non-provision.

5. Consideration should be given to the establishment of regional conciliation panels including consultant psychiatrists and other professionals to resolve disputes involving either demarcation of responsibility for a particular patient or questions of clinical judgment.

6. Consideration should be given to establishing a procedure analogous to that provided for in Section 39 of the 1983 Mental Health Act whereby the Chairman of the Regional Health Authority or his/her representative would be required to advise the Secretary of State of the reasons why a bed cannot be found for the patient in question.

Links between Special Hospital patients and their families and communities

The Special Hospitals draw their patients from the whole of England and Wales; most relatives face very long journeys that make frequent visits impossible. Many patients do not have family contact at all. For others, visits by relatives are few and far between.

For these reasons, and also due to the exceptionally restricted life of patients in the Special Hospitals, escorted leave is extremely important. It is, for many, the only opportunity to maintain contact with the outside world. It is an essential part of the rehabilitation process. Escorted leave provides a more adequate opportunity than in-hospital experiences for assessing the feelings and conduct of patients when interacting with members of the opposite sex; when given access to a public house; when out shopping. Sufficient escorted leave experiences are crucial to provide the case team, the Department of Health, Home Office, Advisory Board and Mental Health Review Tribunal (MHRT) with the information they need to make a well informed decision about the patient's suitability for extended leave, transfer or discharge.

All escorted leave is dependent upon the availability of nurses. Due to understaffing and the understandable requirement to have a minimum number of nurses at the hospital site for reasons of security and safety, escorted leave for anything other than emergencies or compassionate leave has been extremely limited. Evidence from Park Lane Special Hospital, for example, suggests that in 1986 escorted leave would be available on average once every two years for social reasons, rehabilitation, assessment purposes and compassionate leave. Commissioners are aware of cases where the Home Office, local hospital or MHRT have taken the view that insufficient

escorted leave visits have been undertaken to enable a thorough assessment to be made. It is perhaps worth noting that at Rampton Hospital requests for escorted leave for compassionate, social or rehabilitative purposes are normally met.

Treatment in the Special Hospitals

An important area for research would be the treatment regimens in Special Hospitals. The majority of patients in Broadmoor, for example, spend their days on occupations which, though important, have little to do with treatment. How much time is in fact spent on social skills' development; group or individual analysis; behaviour modification or work skills' development? Patients with personality disorders may receive no medication. To what extent are those patients receiving any 'treatment' over and above that of patients with similar personality disorders who have been referred to prison? There are few wards upon which individualized rehabilitation goals are set in consultation with the patient, and followed through on the ward, in the educational, occupational or social environment.

Integration of the sexes at Broadmoor is minimal. Staff are strongly resistant to the introduction of a mixed pre-discharge ward; and only very limited progress has been made in the workshop areas. Ashworth, on the other hand, opened a mixed ward about two years ago. Rampton, too, has accepted the value of integration in the rehabilitation process.

As far as physical treatments are concerned, since the passing of the 1983 Mental Health Act the emphasis has been upon the protection of patients. Part IV of the 1983 Act represents an innovation in mental health legislation in that it introduces a statutory system requiring the consent of the patient *and* a favourable second opinion before certain treatments for mental disorder can be administered. Section 57 of the Act will be discussed towards the end of this chapter. Of more relevance to mentally disordered offenders in the Special Hospitals is Section 58. This comes into effect before the administration of electroconvulsive therapy (ECT) at any time, or the administration of medicines for mental disorder after three months since the first occasion in the period of detention when medicines were administered.

Before giving ECT, and before continuing medication beyond the three month period, the RMO must be in a position to certify that the patient is capable of understanding the nature, purpose and likely effects of the treatment and is consenting to this. If the patient is either incapable of giving a valid consent or is capable but is refusing to accept the treatment, then a second opinion must be sought. Before giving his consent a MHAC-appointed second-opinion doctor must consult a nurse and another person (neither a nurse nor a doctor) who has been professionally concerned in the patient's treatment. He must then certify, as appropriate, that:

1. The patient is capable of giving valid consent and has consented; or
2. Although the patient is incapable of giving a valid consent, the treatment ought to be given, having regard to the likelihood that it will alleviate or prevent deterioration in the patient's condition; or
3. Although the patient is capable of giving valid consent and refuses to do so, the treatment ought to be given, having regard to the likelihood that it will alleviate or prevent deterioration in his/her condition.

Mentally disordered offenders have perhaps gained most from these safeguards:

- They should now know what medication they are being given and why;
- If the system works properly an RMO, having obtained the patient's consent for a given dose of medicine, cannot increase this or switch to a different category of drugs without the consent of the patient or a second opinion;
- If the patient at any time after the initial three months of detention feels he is being given excessive doses of medication the visiting commissioners will recommend that a second opinion be sought;
- If a patient wants consideration to be given to alternative treatments to ECT or drugs, the second-opinion doctor must discuss this with at least one non-medical and non-nursing professional. In the special hospitals, the opportunity for multidisciplinary involvement in treatment plans has been difficult to achieve but is very important.

The Commission has found strong resistance to these safeguards from a small number of consultants, particularly in the Special Hospitals. Regular visits to all Special Hospital wards by Commissioners provides an opportunity to check medical records, consent forms and patient complaints.

Research into compliance with Section 58, patient attitudes to the procedures, and the effects of the Section on treatment plans would be helpful.

REGIONAL AND INTERIM SECURE UNITS

Following the publication of the interim Butler report in 1974 the then DHSS asked Regional Health Authorities to establish Regional Secure Units (RSUs) as a matter of priority. Initially they were to provide 20 beds for each one million of the population, increasing to 40 beds per million population if there was sufficient demand and if resources were available. The Department estimated that 929 beds would be needed to meet the Glancy report's recommendations (Glancy and DHSS, 1974). Currently, the number of beds available in regional or interim Secure Units is in the region of 500 (see also the discussion in Chapter 10).

Resource limitations

The first problem for patients in respect of RSUs is the difficulty of getting into them. A research study in 1985/6 found that lack of resources was 'by far the most important factor leading to refusal to admit' (Offen and Taylor, 1985). Two hurdles have to be overcome before achieving a place on the official referral list. If too many names are already on the list some consultants will refuse to add others if suitable patients need transfers or admission. Secondly, Special Hospital staff and prison officer colleagues refer only a minority of potentially suitable patients because a particular unit is known to be unlikely to admit the patients. In the research study, of those who successfully cleared the first two hurdles, half of those who failed to be admitted were turned down due to under resourcing in one guise or another. For example, no bed may be available or may be likely to become so for some time; or the nursing level may be too low to support the beds notionally available. Offen and Taylor estimate that nearly half of the patients referred for admission to Secure Units will not be accepted (Offen and Taylor, 1985).

Inconsistency and irrationality of RSU policies and practice

RSU consultants are in an exceptionally powerful position in relation to the local hospitals in their region and indeed in relation to the Special Hospitals. Consultants come begging to them for a bed and it is very much a matter for the RSU consultant to choose which patients he elects to admit. In general, they prefer to take patients directly from the Courts rather than from the Special Hospitals. The results can be wholly unjustifiable. For example, the case of a young man whose wife had left him and lived across the road from his home. She entertained her lover every night until one night her husband could take it no longer. He stabbed his wife and threw himself onto a railway line. He lost both legs but lived. He was admitted as an informal patient to an RSU, though he did not require the secure conditions of the unit. At the other end of the scale is a Special Hospital patient who was accepted by an RSU on condition that his local hospital would accept him when he was ready for transfer. The local hospital took three years to agree to this arrangement. The RSU then claimed to have a waiting time of 1–2 years before admission could be arranged. In all, this patient will wait for 4–5 years for transfer to an RSU from the time when his RMO and the Home Office agreed he no longer needed the high security facilities of the Special Hospital.

A contributory factor in the RSU tendency to take people direct from the Court is the preference of solicitors for an assessment from a forensic psychiatrist from an RSU rather than one from a consultant in a local psychiatric hospital. The best interests of the patient appear to take second place though it is arguable that any consultant psychiatrist will have sufficient experience of potentially violent patients to be in a position to make an assessment of dangerousness.

The admissions policy of RSUs is not uniform, however. Some RSU consultants regard a court history as a condition of admission. Others do not. When about 10 per cent of Special Hospital patients are detained under Section 3 of the Mental Health Act (and have thus not been admitted through the courts) it is difficult to justify the former view.

Another major inconsistency relates to difficult-to-manage patients. Some RSUs take a proportion of such patients over a 2–3-year period in an endeavour to achieve sufficient improvement to enable them to settle in a less restrictive environment. Others play an important role in outreach work, spending time in local psychiatric hospitals training and supervising staff in the nursing of difficult to manage patients. The original RSU brief did not envisage this approach but there is no doubt that the concentration of skills amongst RSU staff can be used to great benefit in this way.

On the question of security, it might be supposed that the security requirements of an RSU would be less than those of the Special Hospitals. In some cases this is not the practice. An extreme example of excessive concern with security is an RSU where a visiting consultant psychiatrist was required to hand over his personal keys to the staff before entering. It is common to find less internal freedom of movement in RSUs than in Special Hospitals despite high external walls.

RSU as an essential stepping stone from Special Hospital back to the community

One of the reasons for excessive transfer delays from Special Hospitals is the lack of RSU facilities or the refusal of RSU consultants to admit suitable patients combined with the growing tendency on the part of the Home Office to regard the RSU as the required next step after a Special Hospital placement. Not surprisingly local psychiatric hospitals are supporting this trend.

A more flexible approach would be desirable. Where continued secure conditions are necessary the appropriate RSU should have an obligation to accept a Special Hospital patient assessed as ready for transfer as soon as a bed becomes available, and certainly in preference to a person referred by the courts where secure conditions are not essential. On the other hand, a Special Hospital patient needing skilled rehabilitation and unlikely to abscond or to be a danger if he did so, would be more approriately placed in a local psychiatric hospital. RSUs do not have rehabilitation skills comparable with those of a psychiatric hospital, and frequently have very limited or non-existent work opportunities.

Recommended action

Mentally abnormal offenders in general would benefit from the preparation of clear guidelines for solicitors, RSU consultants, local hospital and Special Hospital personnel as to suitable admissions to RSUs and a re-examination of the number of places required in secure conditions on the basis of those guidelines.

The Butler Committee was clear about the boundaries to the role of the RSUs: 'We do not suggest that all patients in the Special Hospitals should be transferred to the Secure Units as a stage towards eventual discharge: on the contrary this would be both undesirable and unnecessary.' Butler goes on to say: 'We hope . . . that the psychiatric hospitals and psychiatric units in general hospitals will play their part in the continued treatment and rehabilitation of offender patients not requiring secure conditions' (Home Office and DHSS, 1975, p. 6, para. 4.29).

LOCAL PSYCHIATRIC HOSPITALS

The open–door policy has undoubtedly been of overwhelming value to the great majority of patients who can enjoy their freedom while receiving treatment in local psychiatric hospitals. Treatment on an open ward affords the patient a degree of dignity; it helps to ensure that every effort is made to occupy patients in a constructive way; that staff treat patients with care and courtesy; and that attention is paid to the wellbeing of patients at all times. Both staff and patients report a marked improvement in staff–patient relationships when doors are unlocked.

The implications of the open–door policy for mentally disordered offenders, however, have been detrimental. Staff in local psychiatric hospitals have lost their commitment to caring for difficult or disruptive patients. Larry Gostin reports that a visiting consultant psychiatrist at a local prison wrote: 'Our principal problem remains the difficulty of obtaining beds in mental hospitals for those suffering from psychiatric diseases. At present the major problem is schizophrenics in prison where there is little scope for their social rehabilitation' (Gostin, 1986, p. 38). As we have already noted, patients remain in Special Hospitals for months or years after they are ready for transfer because local hospitals refuse to offer them a bed.

A study in Camberwell showed a need for security for 13 per 100 000 population, or some 6500 beds per 50 million people (Wykes *et al.*, 1982). The number of beds actually available in secure conditions falls very far short of that target. The Special Hospitals currently cater for just over 1500 patients and RSUs and Interim Secure Units now provide for about 500 patients—in total about one third of the beds needed according to the Camberwell study. In 1983, the regional returns showed about 900 further beds in lockable wards or special care facilities. In all, the NHS and DHSS provide a total of about 3000 secure beds or less than half the number needed.

The local psychiatric hospitals must play a central role in the provision of secure facilities not only for offenders who are not regarded as sufficiently dangerous to justify a bed in an RSU but also for the larger number of difficult-to-manage patients who have never been through the courts. Every local psychiatric hospital or group of hospitals should include an intensive care unit with a high staff/patient ratio and which could be locked if necessary. Patients who may at times or in some circumstances be dangerous could then be placed locally with ready access to their families and communities. They would avoid the stigma of placement in a Secure Unit—whether a Special Hospital or RSU—and could spend some of their time in open conditions when appropriate.

Such units would provide a greater degree of supervision and control than the rest of the hospital. However, with a high staff/patient ratio and emphasis on the quality of staff and special training the units would have a considerable therapeutic potential. A good example was the interim secure unit at Friern Hospital. A patient recently pleaded with visiting Mental Health Act Commissioners to persuade the staff to allow him to remain in the secure unit rather than be transferred back to an open ward! The South East Thames Regional Health Authority is planning a central regional Secure Unit with four smaller secure clinics in other part of the region. An important feature of such services is that there should be easy movement in and out of the intensive care or secure ward.

ISSUES AFFECTING MENTALLY DISORDERED OFFENDERS ACROSS THE HOSPITAL SERVICES

Hormone implants and Section 57 of the 1983 Mental Health Act

Under the 1959 Mental Health Act it was assumed that if patients were compulsorily detained in hospital for treatment, their consent was not necessary before treatment could be given. For many treatments for up to three months this remains the case. However, in 1983, because of concern about oestrogen implants and their serious side-effects, regulations included these treatments within Section 57 of the Mental Health Act. The safeguards of Section 57 of the 1983 Mental Health Act come into play if a psychiatrist wishes to use a hormone implant. That Section requires that before administering a hormone implant it must be the opinion of a MHAC-appointed doctor that it should be administered *having regard to the likelihood that it will either improve, or prevent deterioration in the patient's condition.* The Commission doctor must also confirm that the patient can understand the nature, purpose and likely effects of the proposed treatment and has consented to it.

To date, the Commission is aware of a very small number of such implants. However, we understand that they could become an alternative to a prison sentence in a growing number of sex offence cases. A novel treatment, zoladex (Goserelin) developed for elderly cancer patients has recently been given by an injectable implant to younger men with sexual disorders. In a court case, *R. v. Mental Health Act Commission (ex parte*

Witham, 1988), the implant was ruled as not falling within Section 57 of the Mental Health Act because Goserelin is a hormone analogue, and because the mode of administration was judged as not surgical.

Research is urgently needed into the long-term implications for the patient of hormone implants to control the male sex drive. It is also arguable that the Secretary of State should use his powers under the 1983 Act to extend the list of treatments falling within the Section 57 to include hormone analogues given by injectable implant.

Access of patients to Mental Health Review Tribunals

The length of the hospital treatment order was reduced by half in the 1983 Mental Health Act. Instead of one year in the first instance followed by a further year and successive periods of two years, the periods are now six months, six months and one year, respectively. Access to MHRTs has by this means been doubled—at least in theory. Patients admitted for treatment have access to a Tribunal once during each period of detention and the halving of their periods of course doubles these occasions. A further innovation of the 1983 Act has been the provision that appeal to a Tribunal is now available in the first 14 days of admission for assessment under Section 2 (a 28 day order). More radical still is the automatic referral to a Tribunal hearing of all cases where the patient has not sought a hearing for a period of three years. As a result of these changes the total number of applications to Tribunals rose from 1329 in 1982 to 3445 in 1984 (MHAC Biennial Report, 1983–1985, p. 28).

A major reform of Tribunal powers in the 1983 Act enables Tribunals to determine whether patients subject to restriction orders should be discharged. Previously Tribunals could only advise the Home Secretary on the matter. (For further discussion of Tribunals, see Chapter 11.)

Delays in arranging Mental Health Review Tribunal hearings

Although precise figures are difficult to obtain, the length of delays for 125 Special Hospital patients for whom no hearing date had yet been set included the figures shown in Table 13.1.

Table 13.1 Mental Health Review Tribunal delays for 125 Special Hospital patients

Length of delay (months)	No. of cases	Length of delay (months)	No. of cases
4–5	14	8–9	5
5–6	8	9–10	3
6–7	22	>10	12
7–8	2	>1 year	7

Extracted from the Second Biennial Report 1985–87 of the Mental Health Act Commission. Reproduced with the permission of the Controller of HMSO.

The main reason for the delays would appear to be a shortage of Tribunal staff to cope with the vastly increased number of hearings since 1983. The requirement on Tribunal staff to ensure a Tribunal hearing within seven days of the application for Section 2 patients who ask for one has been beneficial to those concerned but has been at the expense of patients detained under Section 3 or under hospital orders or transfer directions.

Recommended action by the MHAC Biennial Report, 1985–1987 (p. 59)

This outlines that:

1. Tribunal offices be given sufficient staff to carry out their functions promptly.
2. Consideration should be given to fixing a hearing date on receipt of the application rather than waiting for all the reports to be received. This may be justified even if such an arrangement would lead to an increase in the number of adjournments.

(MHAC Biennial Report, 1985–1987, p. 59, Section 18.3.)

CONCLUDING NOTE

The issues discussed here merit urgent action with a view to improving the service for mentally disordered offenders. One of the overwhelming concerns for this particular patient group must be the incarceration of people for many years in unsuitable environments, even when all the professionals involved agree that a less restrictive alternative would be more appropriate.

On our visits to Special Hospitals, RSUs and local psychiatric hospitals, Commissioners draw attention to the points raised in this chapter. There is a growing awareness that a gap in the health service has emerged as RSUs and local psychiatric hospitals have defined their own priorities, without sufficient consultation with each other and in the absence of satisfactory regional hospital plans which could ensure full cover for this as well as other patient groups.

Some responsibility for the situation lies at each level of the service; some Special Hospital consultants are unduly cautious; the Home Office and Advisory Board contribute to interminable delays in reaching decisions; some RSU consultants are inflexible or irrational in their admission policies; and, above all, local psychiatric hospitals increasingly turn their backs on the mentally disordered offender. In the meantime private sector facilities for mentally disordered offenders flourish. In the longer term, the NHS is in danger of losing the skills as well as the facilities to cater for people needing a degree of security or special care. Private enterprises will then be able to name their price to health authorities who will have no option but to pay for whatever care is offered.

As more beds close in the old psychiatric hospitals, Regional Health Authorities can offer less and less facilities for this patient group.

REFERENCES

Dell S. (1980). Transfer of Special Hospital patients to the NHS. *British Journal of Psychiatry*, **136**, 222–34.

Glancy J. E. and Department of Health and Social Security (1974). *Report of the Departmental Working Party on Security in NHS Psychiatric Hospitals.* London: HMSO.

Gostin L. (1986). *Institutions Observed*. Oxford: Oxford University Press, p. 94.

Home Office and Department of Health and Social Security (1973). *Report of the Review of Procedures for the Discharge and Supervision of Psychiatric Patients Subject to Special Restrictions* (The Aarvold Report) Cmnd 5191. London: HMSO.

Home Office and Department of Health and Social Security (1975). *Report of the Committee on Mentally Abnormal Offenders* (The Butler Report) Cmnd 6244. London: HMSO.

Mental Health Act Commission (1985). *Biennial Report 1983–1985*. London: HMSO.

Mental Health Act Commission (1987). *Biennial Report 1985–87*. London: HMSO.

Offen C., Taylor P. J. (1985). Violence and resources: factors determining admission to an Interim Secure Unit. *Medical Science and the Law*, **25** (3), 165–171.

Wykes T., Creer C., Start E. (1982). Needs and the deployment of services. *Psychological Medicine*, Monograph supplement 2 part 1, 41–55.

Section 5
The Mentally Disordered Offender in the Community

14 *The mentally disordered offender in the community*

JAMES HIGGINS

INTRODUCTION

Ideally, the mentally disordered offender in the community should be treated no differently from the non-offending psychiatric patient. He should have identical access to the full range of local psychiatric services. However, this is not often the case. Many psychiatrists, together with their colleagues of other disciplines, lack interest or confidence in the assessment and treatment of offenders. The reasons for this may be many: inadequate training and consequent unease with medicolegal issues; preoccupation with offending behaviour no matter how slight or common at the expense of acceptance of psychiatric disability which requires treatment; a difficulty in coming to terms with the possibly conflicting notions of control and treatment; or even a simple dislike or disapproval of offenders as a whole, or of a particular type, no matter the psychiatric pathology.

On the other hand, some mentally disordered offenders do present particular problems in assessment and management. Pre-trial medicolegal issues may be complex, even obscure. There may be markedly conflicting views on diagnosis, level of dangerousness and eventual disposal. Special expertise and experience may be required. Treatment in the community may require nice decisions on the balance between the freedom of the patient and his right to accept or refuse treatment and supervision, and the protection of the public. The public's expectation, mediated by the Home Office or some other statutory agency, is that treatment and supervision will be enthusiastic, intrusive and given for as long as is necessary.

General psychiatric services frequently disclaim facilities for offender patients thus often condemning them to inappropriate sentences of imprisonment, protracted periods in secure psychiatric hospitals or even abandonment to a disorganized, unsupported and untreated life in the community. Such results have become more prominent as the locus of care of the psychiatric patient has moved from the large custodial mental hospital to relatively brief periods of inpatient care in district general hospitals and outpatient care in such settings as day hospitals and day centres. Current proposals for 'Care in the Community' will take this one step further. Long-term residential care is expected to be provided at home or by a range of accommodation provided by the social services, the voluntary agencies or privately. Nursing will be provided by peripatetic community psychiatric nurses with extensive case loads, supported by short-term admission to the local psychiatric unit only when urgently necessary. Undoubtedly, such a scheme will prove beneficial to the majority of those who, in the past, became long-stay patients in hospital for want of effective treatment and rehabilitation. However, with the current range of psychiatric treatments there will still remain a small proportion— though a considerable number nevertheless—of younger seriously mentally ill individuals whose illness does not respond well to treatment, whose level of distress and behavioural disturbance is high and whose insight will not permit them to fit easily into the system proposed. In the interests of the majority, they will be extruded and then disbarred from future entry into the system. They will, however, not go away: they will remain ill and disturbed, they will concern the public, they will be brought to the notice of the police, then the courts, then the penal system, and then the forensic psychiatry inpatient and community services. The days of the separate specialist parallel forensic psychiatry service will have arrived (Gunn, 1977).

In 1964, the Gwynn report recommended posts of consultant forensic psychiatrist in each of the National Health Service (NHS) regions in England and Wales to promote the development of assessment and treatment services for the mentally disordered offender (Home Office, 1964). These posts were jointly appointed and funded by the NHS and the Home Office, and the consultant was to work in the facilities of both. The impetus behind these proposals was a lack of psychiatric expertise in prisons and a lack of forensic expertise in general psychiatry. The posts were not invariably successful: an NHS consultant did not fit easily into the Prison Medical Service line management and hierarchical structure; a forensic psychiatrist insisting on inpatient and outpatient facilities for his patient group was rarely welcomed by his colleagues in the NHS, who, in the late 1960s and early 1970s, were bent on an open-door policy in hospitals and therefore did not want the return of patients for whom they no longer intended to provide secure facilities. Eventually, only seven of the intended 14 posts were instituted. However, these few consultants, for want of secure inpatient beds, set about the development of outpatient assessment and treatment facilities within their regions, forming particularly close links with their local probation services who, alone, warmly welcomed them. These embryonic regional forensic psychiatry services virtually consisted of a single consultant with the occasional psychiatric trainee. The emphasis was much more on assessment than treatment and the patients taken on for treatment tended to be personality disordered rather than mentally ill, the treatment offered more psychotherapy of an individual or group nature, depending on the training and interest of the consultant forensic psychiatrist.

The reports of the Glancy Committee in 1974 and the Butler Committee in 1975 did more than just highlight the plight of the difficult to place non-offending psychiatric patient and the mentally abnormal offender. Both recommended the provision of Regional Secure Units intended to provide not only in-patient assessment and treatment but to stimulate teaching and research (Department of Health and Social Security (DHSS), 1974 and Home Office and DHSS, 1975). Even more importantly, large sums of money were to be earmarked for forensic psychiatry and there was considerable political pressure, not all of it successful, to ensure that the money was spent properly. The Regional Secure Unit programme was slow to develop and after 15 years it is still not complete (Snowden, 1985). The hesitant start was, however, not entirely disadvantageous. In three of the regions which had already appointed a joint consultant forensic psychiatrist (Wessex, North Western and Mersey) small Interim Secure Units were quickly opened. Despite their limitations these provided most valuable information on the types of patients who would require admission, how they could be managed in an innovative way, how these units could and could not relate to existing psychiatric facilities and, above all, what facilities, what staff and what network of relationships were required to ensure the relatively rapid throughput of even quite difficult patients and to keep them safely and comfortably in the community (Higgins, 1981). What was required varied from region to region. Important variables were the orientation of the original consultant, the degree of cooperation of his medical and other colleagues, geographical considerations, and just good fortune. The experience of these three units changed the emphasis of the proposed developments from a narrow Regional Secure Unit programme, with a single regional unit with an almost exclusively inpatient orientation, to the concept of more elaborate regional forensic psychiatry services, consisting of a Regional Secure Unit or units but with an equal if not greater emphasis on the supporting infrastructure of community assessment and after-care services.

The extent to which this has been achieved has varied in the three original units and their subsequent developments, and in the other units which have followed them. The literature on Regional Secure Units has dwelt almost exclusively on the inpatient aspects (Treasaden, 1985). What information there is on outpatient work is but description of the numbers, types and source of patients assessed and treated in pre-secure unit days. There is no literature on the more comprehensive regional forensic psychiatry services, dealing not only with outpatient assessment and treatment of mentally disordered offenders who do not require inpatient treatment but also those who have been inpatients and require specialist after-care.

In the Mersey Regional Forensic Psychiatry Service, after-care for discharged patients is perhaps the most extensive in the United Kingdom. The outpatient assessment service, however, is much more typical but with a greater input than usual from a substantial number of forensic clinical psychologists. The work of both of these elements of this service, together with mention of alternative or additional community services elsewhere, will provide the background to this chapter. In the hope of achieving clarity, aspects of patients, personnel and facilities will be considered separately, though it must be appreciated that this is a highly artificial approach to what is a complex interrelated whole.

PATIENTS

Patients seen in the community by forensic psychiatry departments fall into two broad groups. Those who are referred for a pre-trial psychiatric assessment and report by a court or a solicitor, or by another agency involved with offenders (principally the Probation Service). Those arising from psychiatric inpatient facilities such as Secure Units and Special Hospitals (and less frequently directly from prison) who require continuing treatment and support.

Referrals for pre-trial psychiatric assessment

Courts and solicitors readily get to know which psychiatrists in their area are expert in forensic work and are keen to do it. The services of specialist forensic psychiatry departments are usually oversubscribed. All types of offender remanded on bail will be referred. This is not often because there are specific issues of medicolegal importance to be determined, such as whether the individual is under disability, is criminally responsible, or is suitable for a hospital order, but more to provide information on a defendant's psychological state and social circumstances in the hope that this will render the offence more understandable and might lead to an offer of treatment or support in the community as an alternative to a custodial disposal. Certain offender groups predominate: the violent and the sexual. Rarely is frank mental illness found. If a psychiatric formulation is possible, it is more likely to involve complex interactions between the offender's personality and his social circumstances, perhaps complicated by alcohol or other substance abuse, or by intellectual handicap.

The proportion of such offenders actually found to have a psychiatric problem worthy of treatment depends, of course, on the sophistication of the referring agencies. Non-psychiatrists, when faced with behaviour which is difficult to explain, often suspect psychiatric pathology. They often have unrealistic expectations of what can be achieved, even when social and psychological problems are deep-seated and are of long-standing.

Pre-trial assessment is therefore a sifting process. Only a few will be found to warrant specific treatment as an outpatient or even less frequently as an inpatient, though this will vary with the range of interest and expertise of the staff of the forensic psychiatry department. More, however, will be found who might benefit from the interventions of a probation officer, and the offer of ongoing psychiatric advice and support to the probation officer if and when required is the better and more efficient course. In some cases, a collaborative venture of psychiatric treatment as a condition of a probation order will be indicated.

Cases referred by other agencies for advice on management are rather different. Those completely without psychiatric pathology are usually absent. General practitioners, other psychiatrists, probation officers and social workers refer cases which have already proved difficult to help in the hope that the forensic psychiatry department with its interests in sexual and violent psychopathology might be of assistance.

Sadly, some clearly mentally ill individuals are referred just because they have been rejected by their local psychiatric services, having been reclassified as suffering from an untreatable personality disorder. The extent to which such referrals for assessment can be accepted depends on the size and expertise of the department. It is crucial, however, to provide ready access for probation officers, not just to have selected clients seen but to allow an opportunity for discussion of cases giving concern.

Individuals in these two assessment groups may be of any age though young adult men predominate. However, there will be some adolescents, but most regional forensic psychiatry services would not claim particular expertise with this younger age group. This is unfortunate as most offenders are teenagers and there might be opportunities for preventive work but the effectiveness of this must not be overstated. The Douglas Inch Centre in Glasgow has traditionally taken an interest in adolescents, going so far as to provide a highly specialist educational establishment in its outpatient premises and offering drop-in facilities to young offenders seen in the penal setting. Two psychiatrists working at the Institute of Psychiatry do work exclusively with the adolescent offender. In Manchester, the Gardener Unit in Prestwich Hospital, a secure unit for adolescents, provides outpatient assessment and treatment facilities for this group. In general, services specifically for the adolescent offender are very limited. Alcohol already plays an important part in offending and substance abuse seems set to follow it. Forensic psychiatry departments do not usually see the treatment of these problems as their primary role and almost invariably refer relatively uncomplicated cases on to specialist facilities.

Forensic outpatients from psychiatric inpatient facilities

Forensic outpatients coming from psychiatric inpatient facilities and requiring long-term treatment and support are quite a different group. They are predominantly mentally ill, mostly suffering from schizophrenia. To have warranted a hospital order and to have come from a Secure Unit or Special Hospital they have usually committed a serious offence. Many will be subject to a restriction order. Often the patients' mental illness will be complicated by adverse personality characteristics such as sexual deviance or a tendency to violence. They may also have problems with alcohol or be intellectually handicapped. Often a number of these features are present in an individual case. Specific provocative factors to their offending can usually be readily identified and require careful monitoring. Such patients often have a number of agencies involved with them and can pose a great clinical and organizational challenge over a long period of time.

PERSONNEL

The numbers and types of staff in the community forensic psychiatry services vary quite markedly from one region to another. There are a number of reasons for this. Apart from the Douglas Inch Centre in Glasgow, forensic psychiatry services without a secure inpatient unit have never attracted sufficient funds to employ a wide range of staff. In some areas, even when funds were available following the Glancy and Butler reports, a very narrow view was taken of the activity of the Secure Unit, and as a consequence little, if any, provision was made for staff such as community psychiatric nurses, clinical psychologists and social workers who could play a major role in community based work. In others, as such small numbers of these disciplines were planned and funded, the emphasis must be on inpatient work. Some saw that the supporting outpatient services were so crucial that sufficient staff were appointed to meet the inpatient need and to develop community services.

Psychiatrists

Psychiatrists generally tend to do much more outpatient assessment than treatment, dictated principally by the numbers of referrals for court reports. Some, however, may have an interest in particular types of patients for whom they will offer individual or group psychotherapy of a dynamic or, more usually, of a supportive kind. They must, however, play a major part in the management of the discharged mentally ill patient, if only because such supervision is usually a requirement of a conditional discharge.

Clinical psychologists

Clinical psychologists undertake more treatment than assessment, though some are now being recognized as expert witnesses on certain issues and are preparing reports to court. They also have much to offer in the treatment of offenders, with a range of useful assessment and therapeutic techniques: psychodynamic or behavioural approaches for sexual offenders, anger control techniques, counselling, social skills' training programmes. They provide a valuable addition to the psychiatric model for the majority of offenders, even those who suffer from a frank mental illness. Some forensic clinical psychologists have developed particular expertise in the assessment and management of child sexual abuse, assisting not only the victim and the perpetrator but also aiding the police in developing procedures to handle these sensitive and difficult cases.

Forensic community psychiatric nurses

Forensic community psychiatric nursing is a rapidly emerging discipline. It became apparent in the early Interim Secure Units that a considerable proportion of patients could not be discharged via local psychiatric services and followed up by general community psychiatric nurses. A surprisingly high proportion of patients, about 50 per cent, were found on discharge to require unbroken continuity of care by those who had been looking after them as inpatients. For some, their dangerousness resulted not from their mental illness alone but from an interaction of this with sometimes only nuances in their social circumstances and relationships apparent best to those who knew them well. Some would be reluctant to continue taking necessary medication without regular reminders from Secure Unit staff of the consequences to themselves and others. For others, the mixture of criminal and psychiatric elements would raise difficulties which conventional psychiatric services would be unused to and might not want to or be able to cope with. Some just did not want to have to tell their horrific and distressing stories to another set of people and wished to remain with those whom they knew. At a practical level it was found that overstretched general community psychiatric nurses, each with a case load of about 50–100 patients, could only see patients infrequently, often just to dispense medication, providing more a 'fire-fighting' rather than the necessary 'fire-prevention' role. Difficult, potentially dangerous and multiply handicapped forensic psychiatry patients could get lost with sometimes worrying results.

It was therefore felt that the community forensic psychiatric nurse, with a smaller case-load, experienced in the care and supervision of a mentally abnormal offender, able and keen to deal with intricate mixtures of illness, personality and social factors, prepared to adopt a hard-headed, rigorous, intrusive and, if necessary, very firm stance would not just better protect the public but more importantly ensure the continuing wellbeing of the patient. With the early and, in some places, continuing difficulty in obtaining social work support to serve units, forensic community psychiatric nurses have had to expand their role—finding accommodation for patients, supporting their families, liaising with statutory and voluntary social agencies, 'selling' the patients to them, representing the patient in difficulty, and providing recreational activities and even holidays for lonely and isolated patients. In Liverpool, community forensic nurses have also set-up an ever-expanding drop-in-centre and two sets of cluster flats to accommodate quite dependent ex-inpatients. They also provide a 24-hour emergency service and can readmit to hospital any patient in difficulty. The value of such staff cannot be overstated, the volume of work that they do and the type of case load that they carry is remarkable. The drop-out rate of patients is very low indeed, most patients continuing to attend even when there is no further statutory obligation on them to do so.

Forensic social workers

Social work support to Regional Secure Units has been slow to emerge. This has been because local social service departments, and their parent local authorities, have not been inclined to fund scarce social work posts in Regional Secure Units which, by chance, happen to have been built in their catchment area and few of whose patients are their responsibility. The Department of Health, not wanting to set any precedent, will not provide central funds for social workers as they do for all other staff in Regional Secure Units. Social services departments within a Regional Health Authority catchment area are often unwilling to collaborate in providing funds, each claiming that it also has a regional specialist unit for which it must provide. Top slicing of joint funding monies sometimes proves a solution. Some Regional Secure Units, despite much endeavour, have difficulty in appointing and then keeping social work staff in the face of the competing pressures of their local social services departments. Inadequate numbers of social workers has meant that they have had to spend much of their time hard-pressed by demands of inpatients. Their contribution to the care of outpatients has usually been limited to finding accommodation in hostels and local authority or private housing and in ensuring that proper levels of benefit are obtained. The therapeutic role of the forensic social worker in community care is as yet underdeveloped.

Outpatients who have never had inpatient care almost invariably already have a probation officer and many probation officers are the statutory supervising officers of conditionally discharged patients. It will be interesting to see where the dividing lines between forensic social workers, probation officers, and community psychiatric nurses emerge, and what new roles forensic social workers develop. Perhaps some of these will be giving advice to social services departments on how to handle difficult clients and teaching other social workers, particularly approved social workers, on forensic aspects of their work.

Probation officers

Probation officers are an integral part of a community forensic psychiatry team. The most effective role for any forensic psychiatrist is as adviser to his local probation service. He can see individual clients referred at outpatient clinics, or hold such clinics in probation offices. He may visit probation hostels on a regular basis either to see residents or to hold discussions with the staff. He may even provide psychiatric support to specialist units dealing with particularly difficult client groups such as the homeless and rootless recidivist. In return, probation officers will find much material for him to assess and treat. They will liaise with courts on his behalf and they will give access to probation hostels and day training centres and will act as social worker to a forensic psychiatry service, even for patients for whom they have no statutory responsibility. Some forensic psychiatrists, for want of social work support for their Regional Secure Unit, have even managed to obtain this from their local probation service. Most forensic psychiatrists seem happier with probation officers being the supervising officers of a conditionally discharged patient, despite the probation officers' often limited experience and training in psychiatry and lack of direct access to the social services' range of facilities for the mentally ill. Where there are sufficient numbers of conditionally discharged patients in a circumscribed area, it has been found useful that supervising probation officers meet, sometimes together with the supervising consultant, to discuss the issues that arise in the management of these difficult and at times stressful cases.

Besides the recently revised Home Office general guidelines for the supervision of conditionally discharged patients, more specific local codes of practice may be drawn up to meet local needs. The Merseyside Probation Service has always supplied a part-time liaison officer to the local regional forensic psychiatry service to co-ordinate the activities of both services and to organize a regular teaching programme. The liaison officer's role is not to undertake the supervision of any particular client but to ensure that probation departments which will be asked to supervise a conditionally discharged patient are informed as early as possible to ensure involvement in the decisions on discharge and to make the optimal arrangements for return to the community. It cannot be stressed too heavily how important it is for probation officers to see themselves as part of their regional forensic psychiatry service. The benefit to both services is very great and the quality of care to the individual patient/client greatly improved.

Officers of C3 Division of the Home Office

It may seem peculiar to include the officers of C3 Division of the Home Office in the personnel of a community forensic psychiatry service. However, unless efforts are made to set-up good bilateral communications in as personal a style as possible, neither party will be as informed as it should be about the work of the other—all to the detriment of individual patients. In the last ten years, C3 Division staff have been more than willing to visit forensic psychiatry departments to discover what range of community facilities can be offered and have even attended case conferences on particular patients when difficult decisions which would take months to resolve on paper are settled there and then. As other Regional Secure Units and their community services develop, this is an area of activity which should also expand.

FACILITIES

Outpatient facilities

The facilities of community forensic psychiatry services vary very markedly from one region to another. Some have none apart from the provision of outpatient facilities at the Regional Secure Unit or its parent hospital. Some offer day-patient attendance at the Secure Unit. The size of some regions and the way in which their population is distributed has resulted in secure inpatient services which are not centralized—not so much because the inpatient treatment would be handicapped but because discharge and after-care by unit staff would prove very difficult—if not impossible. The most well-developed example of this is the Special Assessment Service in the South-East Thames Region (SASS), where there is a medium-sized central Secure Unit and four peripherally sited smaller units—each in size and function rather like the original Interim Secure Units: each with its own outpatient and support services at a local level. An even more radically decentralized approach is in preparation in the South-West Thames Region. A central Regional Secure Unit is not intended. The regional service is to be provided by seven intensive care units based on existing psychiatric hospitals. The theoretical advantages of this approach are obvious, but in practice it leads to serious dilution of staff, lack of peer group support and stimulation and difficulty in developing a comprehensive specialist service for very small scattered groups of patients. Other regions, by siting their entire regional facilities in peculiar peripheral sites (dictated only by expediency), have found it very difficult to produce extensive community facilities in the centres of population in their regions. As a result, they have had to rely on the assistance of general psychiatry departments in the discharge of patients and have often been seriously handicapped by this.

For many years the Douglas Inch Centre in Glasgow has pioneered a self-contained forensic psychiatry outpatient department, sited not in a hospital but in a private building in the city centre. This as been replicated in Liverpool and now in the North-West Thames region of London. There are considerable advantages in such an arrangement. Being in a city centre the department is closer to the homes of the majority of the clients and the agencies which deal with them. Many individuals referred for assessment for a court report prefer not to have to attend a hospital. Some who are offered treatment seem happier to attend a setting where discretion and confidentiality are easier to maintain. But even more than these, a free-standing outpatient department provides a counterweight to the institutionalizing pressures of the inpatient unit. It allows staff of all disciplines the opportunity of having a base within which and from which they can develop community-based strategies not just for discharged inpatients but also for a wider range of forensic patients.

Housing and accommodation

Finding accommodation for mentally disordered offenders is difficult. Often they are homeless and rootless. Their offending might have taken place within their family, with resultant serious damage to relationships. Their neighbours might resist their return. Their offence category, usually makes other agencies wary of offering them accommodation. Because of their illness and personality characteristics they may be irresponsible, disorganized and difficult to pin down. Finding suitable accommodation is so important—not only for the patient but for the successful functioning of the Secure Unit—that it is not an exaggeration to say that it must be tackled as soon as a patient is admitted, if not even at the time a patient is assessed for admission.

There are a number of ways that finding accommodation can be tackled. The ideal is that the patient remains in, or returns to, his own family, unless emotional involvement with them is a major reason for breakdown in the first place and might cause a breakdown again or there is just too great a risk involved, or it is just 'politically' impossible. Returning a patient home requires a great deal of preparatory work with the family, and the family will need continuing support, often intensive at the outset, but usually declining slowly with time.

Under Section 117 of the 1983 Mental Health Act, social service departments have a duty to supply appropriate aftercare for previously detained patients for as long as is required. However, social service departments rarely possess the facilities to meet this. Limited mental health hostel places are usually heavily oversubscribed and mentally disordered offenders are frequently a low priority, the severity of the index offence giving ample cause for rejection. In any event, hostels, while they may be able to provide the degree of supervision required, are usually unwilling to have a patient remain for a period of more than a year. This is often too short a time for the reintroduction of a very handicapped and institutionalized individual into the community.

The probation service is more used to antisocial behaviour amongst its clients. It is much less reluctant to admit stable, serious offenders to its hostels. However, generally it has reservations about mental disorder, no matter how well treated. For years there has been a national embargo by probation hostels on patients diagnosed as psychopathic, though this is currently under review. Probation hostels also set limits to length of stay, geared to probation orders, with conditions of residence of about one year. Nevertheless, if a probation service has close links with its local forensic psychiatry service it will tend to be helpful in placing mildly mentally disordered offenders—provided reliable continuing support is promised.

Private hostels can also be of value. Some are ready to take a potentially difficult client group perhaps because they are less hindered by the protracted bureaucratic procedures and local politics which can hamper social services departments. They can directly negotiate a satisfactory contract of support with a referring agency. One hostel, in Wallasey, has taken particular interest in mentally disordered offenders because the owner is an ex-Special Hospital nurse. His hostel copes with a group of highly dependent long-stay patients who have spent many years in Special Hospitals and who are not much different from many of the peers they have left behind.

Private accommodation is next best to living with a family. In certain parts of the country this is difficult to obtain or is extremely expensive. Often what can only be obtained is 'hard to let' accommodation of a standard much lower than the patient has been accustomed to in hospital. Attempting to cope with poor housing is sometimes one burden too many, leading to real or not-so-genuine deteriorations and the need for readmission to hospital.

One interesting development is that a forensic service itself can provide the accommodation. This can be done in association with a local housing authority and a voluntary agency such as MIND. In Liverpool there are now two groups of six cluster flats. The residents have their own tenancies and can therefore remain for as long as they wish. Each has a self-contained flat but shares a communal social area. Community nurses visit the group very regularly not only to ensure that the patients remain well but to help resolve any difficulties they cannot cope with. With a proper mixture of patients the able can assist and support the less able, and considerably dependent patients can thus lead a surprisingly productive and independent life in the community. Having patients in a group also makes supervision much more economical. Other schemes are planned in different parts of the region to allow patients from those parts to live nearer their home district. Cluster flats with a resident warden, probably a member of the forensic nursing staff, is under consideration to provide for even more dependent patients.

Daytime activities

A life of unemployment, aimless living and social isolation is bad for morale and bad for mental health. However, intense enforced social contacts can also be counterproductive for the mentally ill. Daytime activities must therefore be tailored to patients' needs and, as importantly, to patients' wants. Social services departments usually run a range of day-centres for psychiatric patients living in the community. There is a wariness of accepting mentally abnormal offenders and a tendency to indulge in overgenerous supervision. Mentally disordered offenders often find such highly structured activities ill-fitting to their less reliable and at times disruptive and delinquent ways, and will stop attending promptly. More flexibility is required of the regional forensic psychiatry service.

In Liverpool, in the basement of the outpatient department the community psychiatric nurses have developed a drop-in-centre. This has proved very popular with patients and staff. Some of the most disorganized and poorly compliant patients attend surprisingly regularly—to get cigarettes and have a smoke, to have a meal cooked by other patients, to meet other ex-patients and go for a drink, to play cards or pool, and to organize group outings and even holidays. By attending the drop-in-centre, they meet the community psychiatric nurses and receive their regular intramuscular medication, often an unspoken price of their attendance. They also meet their supervising probation officer or social worker. These features play an important part in the very low drop-out rate from medication, even in those patients who cannot be compelled to continue taking it. But the drop-in-centre has another and very important function. Recovering patients in the Secure Unit are usually expected to attend it, first escorted by staff but then making the long way there and back on their own. This is a good test of a patient's improvement and it is also very good for morale to meet those who have successfully made the transition to an independent life. Perhaps the attendance of inpatients also reminds ex-patients of their past and ensures greater compliance with treatment! It is intended, shortly, to open this drop-in-centre every day of the week and to expand its activities to make it the focus of the final stages of rehabilitation of all patients in the Secure Unit. Being in the city centre, it offers many more realistic daytime activities than the rather sterile parole in the small village in which the Secure Unit is sited.

DISCUSSION

In describing what forms of treatment and support can be given to mentally disordered offenders in the community, I have drawn heavily on my own experience and on the services within which I work. This is a small, highly specialist service, offering assessment and treatment to a particular group of individuals and its links with other agencies reflect this. It deals with only those mentally ill, psychopathically disordered and mentally handicapped who have committed a serious offence or a serious antisocial act or who seem highly likely to do so. It also offers assistance to other individuals who would not warrant formal psychiatric diagnosis but who behave in a way seriously distressing to themselves and to others—for example sexual offenders.

Gunn described two potential models of forensic psychiatry service: the integrated and the parallel (Gunn, 1977). The integrated is the ideal. Specialist facilities should only care for a patient for as long as absolutely necessary before returning him to his local general psychiatry service. This is less stigmatizing, more economical, promotes comprehensive care in each district and minimizes elitism and isolation in specialist services. This seems to be the style preferred by the Department of Health. The parallel approach is to do the opposite and run these risks because it is necessary for a particular small group of patients, otherwise they will be rejected by general services or, if accepted, will get so lost in the much bigger group that they are neglected because there is the lack of personnel, facilities, and skills to deal with them humanely and safely. In practice, both approaches are possible simultaneously for different types of patient. However, unless an extensive parallel system is developed the mentally disordered offender will continue to get a very raw deal.

The current problem is not that general psychiatry services are jealous of their patients and resentful of a parallel service in their midst; quite the contrary, they cannot off-load patients too quickly—patients whom they have looked after before, albeit in outdated ways and in quite unsuitable premises. General psychiatrists are acquiescing in, or are being forced to accept a style of psychiatric service which, if experience in the USA is a guide, will not provide adequately for the most ill, most disturbed, least compliant group of patients—surely the very group which psychiatric services have a duty to care for. The penal system, the last truly philanthropic agency in the country (in the sense that it must take care of whoever is sent into it), will have to deal with increasingly large numbers of the mentally ill, and it will then fall to inpatient and community forensic psychiatry services to look after them.

The problems for small parallel forensic psychiatry services are all too obvious. In the Mersey Region, the community service already carries more than 80 ex-Secure Unit patients besides those who have arisen from other sources. The blast of 'Care in the Community' has not yet been felt though the largest mental hospital is due to close in less than one years' time and early effects are evident.

There seem to be three alternatives for forensic psychiatry services. First, a further narrowing of criteria for admission and thus survival as super-specialist departments while letting all the fringe patients fend for themselves. Second, continual expansion of regional forensic psychiatric services and widening of their remit. Third, doing nothing. This would mean awaiting scandals and political concern and subsequent committees of enquiry.

CONCLUSION

In global terms it is difficult to say whether the lot of the mentally disordered offender in the community has improved since the publication of the Butler Report. The serious offender who is mentally disordered in terms of the Mental Health Act has benefited from recent developments with the advent of Regional Secure Units and their supporting services. The number of regional consultant forensic psychiatrists has risen from about 10 at the time of the Butler Report to about 60 today. New disciplines of forensic nursing, community nursing, social work and clinical psychology have emerged. On the other hand, other groups have fared less well, with the continuing and increasing rejection of them by general psychiatrists. Facilities for the treatment of alcoholics and drug abusers are limited and are not keeping pace with the expansion of the problem. There is persistent therapeutic pessimism about the treatment of personality disordered individuals, even in an outpatient setting. Poor housing, unemployment and a difficult-to-understand benefits system do little to help the chronically 'inadequate' individual, the petty recidivist offender, the social nuisance.

An extensive parallel service in forensic psychiatry is essential, at least in the present climate. Unless mentally disordered offenders are seen as a special group, with special funding, with strong political pressure behind them, neither Health Authorities nor their public or professional colleagues will see them as an important and deserving group. There is a need for a high profile service offering high quality work and a wide range of assessment and treatment procedures. The importance of teaching cannot be overstated and perhaps only in this way will attitudes of general psychiatry alter.

Finally, research is needed into the development and effectiveness of community forensic psychiatry services, both in economic and human terms. Because of this lack of research this chapter is, perforce, a rather personal and parochial one.

REFERENCES

Department of Health and Social Security (1974). *Report on the Working Party on Security in NHS Psychiatric Hospitals*. London: HMSO.

Gunn J. (1977). Management of the mentally abnormal offender: integrated or parallel. *Proceedings of the Royal Society of Medicine*, 70, 877–80.

Higgins J. (1981). Four years' experience of an Interim Secure Unit. *British Medical Journal*, 282, 889–93.

Home Office (1964). *Report of Working Party on the Organisation of the Prison Medical Service* (The Gwynn Report). London: HMSO.

Home Office and Department of Health and Social Security (1975). *Report of the Committee of Mentally Abnormal Offenders* (The Butler Report) Cmnd 6244. London: HMSO.

Snowden P. R. (1985). A survey of the Regional Secure Unit programme. *British Journal of Psychiatry*, 147, 499–507.

Treasaden I. H. (1985). In: *Secure Provision* (Gostin L., ed.). London: Tavistock Publications.

15 *Time to re-think*

MAGGIE PINDER and HERBERT LAMING

BACKGROUND

It is worth stating at the outset that social services departments, along with many other agencies, deal with a wide spectrum of human behaviour. Although some people behave in a way which is destructive to themselves and others, or is unpredictable, or socially unacceptable, or at times bizarre, they do not necessarily come within the remit of the Mental Health Act and would not be classified as mentally disordered offenders.

As long ago as 1975, the White Paper *Better Services for the Mentally Ill* (HMSO, 1975), requested Regional Health Authorities to plan for the run down of long-stay institutions and for the implementation of comprehensive community-based services for all people who are mentally ill or mentally handicapped.

The Government's 'Care in the Community' initiative was announced in 1981, in the Consultative Document on *Moving Resources for Care in England* (HMSO, 1981). As well as setting out the mechanisms for the transfer of resources from hospital- to community-based care, the document stressed the need for close collaboration between the various agencies responsible for providing health care and social services.

At the same time, reaction against institutional care which, at present, represents a stigmatized and on the whole unacceptable model of care has been steadily growing. However, the move from theoretical debate to the practical implementation of care in the community services remains a slow and fragmented process.

The absence of a coherent strategy for the implementation of a comprehensive system of community mental health care has not halted the process of the discharge of patients from hospitals often without adequate after-care arrangements, nor the resistance to admit to hospital the people who present a difficult management problem.

The trend towards fewer and fewer people being detained in hospital against their will, together with the movement towards the management of people in the community, has resulted in a situation where many psychiatric hospitals have few or no facilities for detaining people who display difficult or dangerous behaviour. This is particularly so in small psychiatric units within district general hospitals. Sometimes these units are placed next to maternity or geriatric units. The view is now widely held that the process of de-institutionalization has led also to the situation whereby the mental health services and the mental health professionals are slowly losing the ability to care for difficult and dangerous people. There are far fewer staff in the mental health services with both the skills and the experience to deal with abnormal offenders. (This is also discussed by Molly Meacher in Chapter 13.)

To provide priority services which are designed to support and treat long-term disability or the problems of antisocial and irrational behaviour in people who have no desire to be treated is difficult, professionally unfashionable, and costly. Hospitals and psychiatric units on district general hospital sites with 'open-door' policies have a particularly low tolerance of people who are deviant or antisocial, and the custodial requirements for the care of difficult or dangerous patients are seen to be at odds with the more therapeutic policies of these units. Staff have, therefore, looked more and more to specialist facilities to care for such people. Psychiatric services are more often geared towards the short-term management of acute illness, and to the provision of services to white, articulate people who are able to respond to treatment, many of whom suffer from neurotic disorders.

As a result of these policies, there is a substantial number of people who need care and treatment in secure accommodation, or who would benefit from intensive care in a local psychiatric hospital, but who are not being offered a service. The abnormal behaviour exhibited by such people often leads to rejection by overburdened families and loss of accommodation, with permanent homelessness as the consequence. These people are sentenced to prison, or are in the community sleeping rough, vulnerable to abuse and a danger to both themselves and others. They are neglected, often living on the fringes of society, with a growing mistrust of statutory agencies. However, it must be acknowledged that many people in these circumstances seem to prefer the deprivations of the community to incarceration in a long-stay hospital.

On the whole, mental health services have consistently declined to treat and support these people, and the reaction to this situation is that the community at large is now asking whether or not the open-door policy has swung too far. So far, in fact, that the social services departments and the District Health Authorities have lost the ability and the willingness to assist people who display difficult and dangerous behaviour. Whilst the standards of care, treatment and quality of life in the large psychiatric hospitals left much to be desired and in many ways were unacceptable, it is now acknowledged that those hospitals were able to tolerate and provide services for a wide range of people, particularly those with quite serious behavioural problems.

In July 1988, the Department of Health quietly issued circular HC (88) 43 to Health Authorities, which sets out guidelines for Health Authority planning for two years from April 1989 (DHSS, 1988). The circular says that the chief aim is to develop, at a local level, a comprehensive psychiatric service in every health district, focusing the catchment areas of traditional mental illness hospitals principally on their own districts. In particular, the developing pattern of services should make provision for the continuing care of people with chronic disabilities. Authorities were further advised to take account of the likely increase in the numbers of elderly mentally ill people and to ensure that enough suitable accommodation was provided for those who could not be cared for at home and to also ensure that the catchment population is provided with adequate numbers of supported community places.

A consequence of this would be to run down and close mental illness hospitals which are not needed as part of the developing pattern of district services, and the closure of mental illness hospitals should be as a consequence of these and other policies, rather than an end in itself.

Regional Health Authorities were advised to ensure that no mentally ill Special Hospital patient awaiting a move to a Regional or District facility waited for more than one year. The stated service objective of circular HC (88) 43 is that by 1991 every district should have a 'care programme' to provide co-ordinated care for people disabled with a chronic mental illness living mainly in the community (DHSS, 1988). To those people who have long criticized community care, this was seen as an admission on the part of the Government that its 'Care in the Community' initiative was not working and that the new guidance—*if properly funded*—might lead to a correct balance between hospital provision and community facilities.

MENTAL DISORDER AND THE 1983 MENTAL HEALTH ACT

Section 35 of the 1983 Mental Health Act allows courts to remand people in hospital for reports on their mental health. However, the courts still seem reluctant to remand people in hospital instead of in custody.

Although Section 36 of the Act allows the Crown Court to remand people for treatment, judges do not have the power to commit a person to hospital. Admission to hospital is at the discretion of the hospital managers only (in practice the responsible consultant psychiatrist).

Therefore, Courts do not have the power of disposal to order that a mentally abnormal offender with an apparent mental illness should be committed to a hospital. If the Regional Health Authority or the District Health Authority have no available beds, the person is likely to end up in prison, or if the offence is minor, be discharged without treatment or support.

In contrast, prisons have no such choice and there is now growing evidence that mentally disordered offenders have been sentenced to terms of imprisonment where judges have been convinced of their need for treatment. The prison and probation services feel that people in this situation should not be dealt with by the control and punishment exercised by criminal proceedings and that people so sentenced suffer further from the prison regimen.

TREATABILITY

The Mental Health Act includes the requirement that compulsory detention is based on the test of treatability. The Act permits compulsory admission and detention where, among other conditions, the treatment will alleviate or prevent a deterioration of a condition.

Personality disorders are deemed 'untreatable' by psychiatrists and the label 'psychopath' is often applied to people who come into repeated conflict with society and present a difficult management problem. Their deviant behaviour may involve arson, vandalism, physically or orally aggressive behaviour, a low level of tolerance of frustration, and often an inability to relate to other people. People labelled as such often end up serving long-term prison sentences or are detained for long periods in Special Hospitals, often, because of the diagnosis, with no treatment. A range of disorders are dealt with in this way. For some people, psychiatric treatment will be unsuitable and the need will be for care and asylum, but both the prison and the current mental health services seem unable to offer effective care for this group of people with special needs.

Most psychiatrists also agree that it is impossible to make a clear division between those people who are 'mad' and those people who are 'bad'. Mentally disordered people do not always lack insight or a sense of responsibility and people serving prison sentences often have great difficulty coping with mood swings and aggressive tendencies. However, the wide division between the penal and the mental health systems remains firmly entrenched, the 'treatable' mentally ill go to hospital for treatment and the 'untreatable' offender goes to prison for punishment.

Most mentally abnormal offenders do not fall within the criteria of the Mental Health Act and must therefore serve out their prison sentence. Most prisons offer no more in the way of treatment and management for these individuals than what is currently available to the community. (For the exception to this rule see the Chapters 7 and 8.)

If there is no clear delineation between 'mad' and 'bad' the question arises as to whether prison medical services should be given the responsibility and the resources to provide a psychiatric service which is designed to meet the particular needs of the mentally abnormal offender. (This report is discussed in Chapter 2.)

Key sections of the 1984 Police and Criminal Evidence Act changed the powers of the police to detain and interrogate arrested suspects at the police station, or those helping police with their inquiries. This was done in such a way that, if implemented in accordance with the code of practice, it should go some way to averting inappropriate court appearances and imprisonments.

Included in the changes is the requirement of the presence of an 'appropriate adult' when certain categories of suspects are being questioned. Particular among these are mentally ill and mentally handicapped people. Both the statute and the code stress that where such a suspect is involved, they should not be interviewed, or asked to sign or provide statements in the absence of an 'appropriate adult' or solicitor. The 'appropriate adult', who should be a relative, guardian, or someone who has experience of dealing with mentally ill or mentally handicapped persons (other than a police employee) is not expected to act simply as an observer. The purpose of his/her presence is, firstly to observe whether or not the interview is being conducted properly and fairly; and, secondly to facilitate communication with the person being interviewed.

Although people with a mental handicap or who are mentally ill are often capable of providing reliable evidence, they may, without knowing it or wishing to do so, be particularly prone in certain circumstances to provide information which is unreliable, misleading or self-incriminating.

The 'appropriate adult' involved is there to see the interview is conducted fairly. Because of the risk of unreliable evidence, it is also important to ensure corroboration of any facts wherever possible. These provisions should prevent mentally ill and mentally handicapped people, particularly those who are self-destructive and admit to serious offences they have not committed, being charged and convicted of committing serious offences purely on the basis of an uncorroborated confession. However, it is the Crown Prosecution Service that makes the final decision as to whether or not a mentally ill and mentally handicapped person who is alleged to have committed an offence will be charged.

The response of the Crown Prosecution Service, and subsequently of the Court may be influenced and constrained by the availability of local and regional resources. If regional facilities have no available beds, or if admission is governed by the criteria of treatability, and if local psychiatric services are unable or unwilling to guarantee security, mentally abnormal offenders will be given custodial sentences in order to ensure the safety of the general public.

Such court proceedings serve to reinforce the public's perception that a large number of offenders are both mentally ill and dangerous and that the only way to ensure that such people will be treated in a secure environment is through the criminal justice system. This is exacerbated further by the involvement of psychiatric opinion in the 'conviction' stage of a trial rather than such opinions being confined to the 'sentence' stage. (Once again, see Chapter 2 for further discussion on this point.)

SERVICES FOR MENTALLY DISORDERED OFFENDERS

Those whose offences are unlikely to incur a prison sentence or detention in a hospital can be extremely disturbing to family, friends, neighbours and the community at large. Such people are constantly being referred to community agencies, all of whom, because of the paucity of appropriate services and lack of co-ordination between community agencies, are unable to put together realistic care plans.

The insufficient provision of appropriate care, treatment and 'asylum' inevitably leads to social breakdown, increasing disability, the emotional breakdown of carers, unacceptable burden on families, and isolation. It leads to the criminalization of certain aspects of abnormal behaviour with misplaced referrals and inappropriate admissions and imprisonments.

Regional Secure Units

Most are agreed that what is required is an efficient, caring, locally based service for mentally abnormal offenders. The then DHSS allocated money for the development of specialist units in preference to local services, but this factor did not assist in the development of a service which would cope with more difficult people (Gostin, 1985). Moreover, not all of the money allocated to regional health authorities was spent on the development of Regional Secure Units (RSUs). Mentally abnormal offenders come into repeated conflict with society; they are generally viewed as dangerous, unrewarding and not open to change. Therefore, it is not surprising that a proportion of this money was filtered to provide services to other care groups, who were viewed by the planners and the general public as more deserving.

Ten years on from the Butler Committee Report (Home Office and Department of Health and Social Security, 1975) which suggested the development of 2000 spaces in RSUs, there are approximately 500 bed spaces. The opening of these has done little to assist the mentally abnormal offender who does not fall within the criteria of the Mental Health Act—who, in other words, is treatable. People who are considered to be unlikely to respond to treatment will be denied access to Secure Units.

Special Hospitals

The secure hospitals tend to be remote and isolated. They select their inmates by their degree of dangerousness, thereby collecting together in one place those people seen as presenting the most risk to the community at large.

They have insufficient contact with the National Health Service and organizationally it is difficult to integrate Special Hospitals into the mainstream of mental health and personal social services. Moreover, the regimen in Special Hospitals is designed to exert strict control over the behaviour of inmates, association with families and friends. Continuing association with the fabric of everyday life, shopping, hobbies and so on, is impossible to maintain. There is no contact with the opposite sex, an absence of domestic responsibilities and a loss of social role and status. Some of the worst effects of long-term detention arise—not from detention itself, but from the loss of relationship with in the outside world. For people so detained, there is no realistic opportunity for rehabilitation until transfer to a locality-based psychiatric service takes place.

Local hospitals

The transfer of patients from Special Hospitals and RSUs is often impeded when the admission policies of local hospitals are such that offenders are not seen as suitable referrals. Without support from local mental health professionals, departments of social services and housing authorities are reluctant to offer hostel accommodation to ex-offenders.

For the people who require psychiatric services on a long-term basis, the closure of long-stay mental illness hospitals, together with the development of local mental health services based on the concept of treatability, has resulted in the exchange of one form of neglect for another.

AN EFFECTIVE COMMUNITY SERVICE

The task of an effective mental health service is to recreate the intended functions and responsibilities of the mental hospitals within the community, but in a way which values each individual and enables him to achieve his optimum level of functioning in the least restrictive environment possible. Although present treatments are not able to cure all psychological disabilities, there are a number of tried and tested interventions which can enhance people's social functioning and greatly improve their quality of life.

Many people with enduring disabilities lack basic coping skills. If they are to survive in the community without becoming impoverished, isolated and reclusive they will require assistance in obtaining welfare benefits, accommodation, daytime occupation and medical treatment. Substantially, the task is one of social rehabilitation and long-term maintenance. If mental health services are to prevent the withdrawal of long-term users from the service they must have the ability to maintain continuity of care and be sufficiently aggressive and persistent in style and far less dependent on the motivation and initiative of those to be served than hitherto. The failure of 'Care in the Community' initiatives is in part due to the fragmentation of statutory and community services as outlined by Sir Roy Griffiths in his report *Community Care—An Agenda for Action* (Griffiths, 1988). To be successful, mental health services will need the capacity to negotiate for accommodation, welfare benefits, daytime occupation and medical care across a range of agencies. Case management systems must therefore be integrated into the organizational structure and operational policies of a comprehensive service. The structure must clearly define which agency is responsible for the provision of each element of a full spectrum of services.

What is now required is a change in attitude and commitment by all authorities, together with positive financial incentives. Additional finances should be allocated in such a way as to improve joint planning mechanisms and facilitate the development of services for mentally abnormal offenders as an integral component of a comprehensive locality-based mental health service. Survival in the community for people with lasting disabilities, which includes mentally abnormal offenders, depends upon:

- Clear management responsibility placed with one agency
- Appropriate, often long-term, support from a worker trained to deal with the problems of these individuals and who will monitor them with considerable persistence and facilitate their receiving services
- Specialist treatment and long-term support
- Multiprofessional assessment
- Programmes of resettlement
- Appropriate living arrangements—for life if need be
- Purposeful and valued activity
- Food and opportunity for social contact
- Further education/adult literacy
- Income maintenance and welfare benefits advice
- Work rehabilitation schemes
- Support to families and carers.

These services will need to be developed in a way that they meet the particular needs of mentally disordered offenders, if inappropriate sentencing and hospital admission is to be avoided.

Additional training for staff should be organized, in order to create a pool of skilled workers who can be used directly, or to provide consultation and support to other workers in the locality. Effective multiagency working is urgently needed between the:

- Police
- Probation Service
- District Health Authority
- Social Services Department
- Housing Authorities

to inaugurate a system locally, which would: assist the courts in obtaining psychiatric/psychological/social enquiry reports, assessments and recommendations, which can assist sentencing decisions; a system which could mediate in the conflict between psychiatric hospital policy and the inability of the community to cope with people who display difficult or dangerous behaviour and give guidance in the instances of differing diagnosis between, for example, prison doctors and local psychiatrists.

In Hertfordshire, an 'assessment panel scheme' (Tonak and Cawldron, 1988) has been devised, which goes some way to meeting these requirements—despite the fact that the Home Office has refused funding for the scheme. Additional benefits identified when the scheme was evaluated in 1986 were that courts received more constructive reports than hitherto—both in terms of the quality of assessment and also the knowledge of what action will be taken. The various disciplines were working together instead of in isolation, therefore the case management was more effective. The offenders who were able to be contained in the community were judged to be receiving better care as a result of the joint approach to case planning, and the isolation and stigma attached to offenders had been reduced by organized group activity and therapy.

For those who cannot be cared for in the community, small units attached to, and administered by District Health Authorities should be developed as an integral part of local mental health services. These units would need to provide:

● Sufficient level of physical security
● High staff ratios
● Individual care programmes based on the principles of 'ordinary life'
● Active programmes of rehabilitation and resettlement to facilitate re-entry into the community
● Ongoing contact with, and support for, families and carers.

These smaller units would go some way towards de-stigmatizing secure facilities and, as an integral component of local mental health services, would afford continuity of care and of carers.

Those who are most disabled and most likely to reoffend should be allowed to live in some form of secure, good quality, homely residential care, local to the individual's community. It should be the least restrictive as is necessary to contain the situation, but does not put the individual in a position where they are likely to abscond or reoffend. This model of service aims to provide a maximum to minimum security within the mainstream provision of mental health care and attempts to forestall unnecessary segregation from family and community.

To date, the movement behind care in the community initiatives in the mental health field is seen by many as a cost-cutting exercise. Sadly, the development of the RSUs is now viewed as a very expensive mistake. As society continues to struggle with the need to distinguish between the 'mad' and the 'bad', there is a greater need for the development of specialist skills and specialist resources on a multiagency basis but within a framework of clear management responsibility. The growing concern over serious sexual abuse on very young children is illustrative of the need for greater clarity in assessment, legal powers and the nature of services needed to tackle the problem presented by the mentally abnormal offender. Now is the time for a re-think.

REFERENCES

Bean P. (1986). *Mental Disorder and Legal Control*. Cambridge: Cambridge University Press.
Better Services for the Mentally Ill (1975). London: HMSO.
DHSS Circular HC (88) 43 issued in July 1988. London: HMSO.

Gostin L., ed., (1983). *Secure Provision—Review of Special Services for Mentally Ill and Mentally Handicapped in England and Wales.* London: Tavistock Publications.

Gostin L. (1985). *Secure Provision: A Review of Special Services for the Mentally Ill and Mentally Handicapped in England and Wales.* London: Tavistock Publications.

Gostin L. (1986). *Institutions Observed: Towards a New Concept of Secure Provision in Mental Health.* London: King's Fund Publishing Office.

Griffiths R. (1988). *Community Care—An Agenda for Action.* London: HMSO.

Home Office and Department of Health and Social Security (1975). *Report of the Committee on Mentally Abnormal Offenders* (The Butler Report) Cmnd 6244. London: HMSO.

Lamb R. (1984). Deinstitutionalisation and the homeless mentally ill. *Hospital and Community Psychiatry,* **35** (9), 899–907.

Mechanic D., Aiken L. (1987). Improving the care of patients with a chronic mental illness. *New England Journal of Medicine,* **317** (26), 1634–8.

Mental Health Act (1983). London: HMSO.

Moving Resources for Care in England (1981). London: HMSO.

The Police and Criminal Evidence Act (1984). London: HMSO.

Third report of the Social Services Committee 1985/86 on the Prison Medical Service. London: HMSO.

Tonak D., Cawldron G. (1988). Mentally disordered offenders under courts—corporation and collaboration of disciplines involved. *Justice of the Peace,* 28 June.

16 *A probation service perspective*

ANNE E. MACE

INTRODUCTION

Probation service staff become involved in work with offenders suffering degrees of mental disorder at a number of different stages in the criminal justice system. Their role can be that of experienced adviser in decision-making processes, informant on the availability of suitable community-based provision and facilities for offenders, or direct supervisor of offenders subject to statutory court orders or released on licence from prisons or Special Hospitals. Thus, in the course of their work, probation staff can be involved with those suffering episodic bouts of mental illness which may or may not be associated with the commission of offences, through to some of the most seriously disordered offenders dealt with by the penal system or the Special Hospitals. These are offenders for whom decisions about transfer, release, or discharge, involve fine-balance and full consideration of issues of public protection.

THE OVERALL PROBLEM

The dilemmas for probation service staff in handling many cases falling within the category of mentally disordered offender—even when the mental disorder is in a mild form—are affected by wider social and cultural attitudes and make the need for expansion and development of interagency approaches and supportive networks very important. The probation service worker is embroiled in society's moral and ethical value systems. There are many taboos related to mental disorder, and many hostilities related to criminality. The worker responsible for giving advice, making a report or supervising a mentally disordered offender is very aware of strong public views, reactions and fears. Recent experience suggests a mounting unease and hostility related to the presence of increasing numbers of mentally disturbed or mentally handicapped people in the community. This follows the closure, or changing role, of hospitals and the discharge of long-stay patients into local communities, where day-care and accommodation facilities are often inadequate to meet the needs and demands.

The nature of the crimes committed by mentally disordered offenders can themselves pose problems for courts and for probation staff trying to assist in the individual sentencing process. Behaviour patterns featuring sexual offences, violence, repeated nuisance offending, minor thefts or bizarre incidents can create neighbourhood alarm and make accommodation placements in the community particularly difficult. In times of rising intolerance in the public mood and perhaps even a narrowing of the definitions of normality and abnormality, the boundaries of what will be tolerated without outcry, neighbourhood pressure or public campaign seem to be narrowing too.

For probation service staff called upon to handle such tensions, the very label of mentally disordered offender can increase the complexity of handling high-risk situations. Account has to be taken of public unease and the proper balance has to be achieved between the protection of the public and the rights, welfare and resettlement of the individual offender. Within the spectrum of professional practice skills, this can mean the necessity to think of the unthinkable possibility, to ask the unaskable and loaded question, to work with a high degree of suspicion and acute sensitivity, to exercise clear, decisive and finely balanced judgements in situations of emergency and potential risk, or to resist unjustified clamour to act, or provocation to succumb to pressure. The stresses of such a responsibility should never be underestimated, for even with the maintenance of close supervision and frequent contact in the handling of many cases, there will be periods of isolation, vulnerability and anxiety.

At a Home Office seminar held in 1987 on 'Issues for senior management in the supervision of dangerous and high-risk offenders', Herschel Prins referred to the course of progress in a case—or the lack of it—often being very clearly determined by the interventive activities of the probation officer and those giving support and supervisory back-up. He identified a hierarchy of anxieties that are born of dealing with highly uncertain and ambiguous situations that need to be addressed. These include such factors as the immediate supervisor's own fears and fantasies, the need for a full and detailed knowledge of the index offence and the total circumstances surrounding it to be available, well digested and regularly taken into account in the work. He highlighted the vital importance of keeping close enough knowledge of the individual and his or her current situation to identify increasing risks, 'trigger' factors or warning signs, or indicators of mental health deterioration. He also referred helpfully to the requirements on managers in any of the agencies involved to respond in as supportive a way as possible to those carrying direct responsibility for such cases; in doing so, and by providing an understanding sounding-board, the protection of the public and the interests of the individual may both be enhanced. Amongst such requirements, he cited the need to ensure that situations in which supervisors are finding it difficult to communicate and liaise with other key professionals—and with the medical profession in particular—are resolved, if necessary at the highest level of interprofessional contact. Experience confirms over and over again that the existence of a clearly defined case management plan and cooperative interagency approach to the handling of work with mentally disordered offenders underpins good decision-making and effective use of available facilities and treatments.

Amongst the most frequently reported problems encountered by supervising probation officers in practice are:

1. *Lack of a network of supportive facilities*
   It has not been unusual to hear a sentencer state 'We are reluctant to send him/her to prison. We are making a probation order in the hope that you might be able to arrange something helpful and get the right kind of treatment made available.' In such cases the problems manifested would be not so much associated with serious criminality, aggression or violence—but more likely paranoia, obsessive behaviour or persecutory activity which creates equally isolating and difficult placement and support issues.

2. *Poor communication between hospitals, the social services departments and the probation service*
   Thus, allocation decisions can still occur at the last minute and discharge plans be made too hurriedly so that they can be inadequate, lack contingency arrangements, or include inappropriate elements. This may result in placement in unsupported lodgings, bed-sit or bed and breakfast accommodation, or in an understaffed or under-resourced hostel facility after a desperate last-minute telephone enquiry.

3. *Difficulties in establishing good liaison with other institutions*
   Such liaison would establish networks of facilities and back-up arrangements which in a situation of emergency can be activated at speed, and without the interminable complications of getting funding responsibilities resolved.

4. *The yawning gap in provision for many offenders who are assessed as having a personality disorder* (Also discussed by Christopher Stuart-White in Chapter 5.)
   This group of offenders needs some kind of sheltered environment if they are to survive in the community. Appropriate accommodation is in short supply and many lodgings are far from satisfactory substitutes for the missing supportive hostels which are required. The most severe shortcomings of a 'Care in the Community' policy approach which is not sustained by an adequate network of community facilities are further exposed when there is an offending history to take into account as well.

   The social backgrounds of such offenders are often complex and methods of intervention used by probation officers range from simple single objectives, such as supporting and encouraging people to keep medical appointments, through to multiple approaches using group work, residential facilities and volunteer support. Difficulties over employment present common problems and it is an uphill struggle to find sympathetic employers or a sheltered workshop placement.

EXAMPLES OF GOOD PRACTICE

Communication, cooperation and co-ordination of actions and responsibilities are the key factors in getting a local network established that is capable of maintaining quite disordered or disturbed individuals in the community. There are some notable examples of good practice being established on the basis of an interdisciplinary approach.

Considerable experience and benefit can be gained from the establishment of close working relationships between members of the probation service and staff of a Regional Secure Unit, or forensic psychiatric team within an Area or District Health Authority. In West Yorkshire, for example, the appointment of liaison officers who can be actively involved as a member of a clinical team working with inpatients who have been convicted of criminal offences, and for whom continuing supervision may have to be arranged by the probation service, has been to the mutual benefit of the probation service and, undoubtedly, the patients. Such liaison has had the additional advantage of ensuring the willingness and availability of psychiatric consultation, supervision and assessment that can be offered more widely to probation service staff. For example, the working arrangements underpinned by the role of the Liaison Probation Officer to the Regional Secure Unit have been particularly useful to hostel staff, both individually and in teams, in increasing their skill and confidence in the handling of disturbed residents. This has enabled hostels in the Area to offer valuable contribution to through-care and discharge plans for Special Hospital and Regional Secure Unit patients.

A comprehensive multidisciplinary approach in the Hertfordshire Area was referred to in a series of articles in *Justice of the Peace* on the subject of 'Mentally Disordered Offenders and the Courts' by Anne Barker (Barker, 1987), and Dorothy Tonak and George Cawdron (Tonak and Cawdron, 1988). (Also discussed here in Chapters 4 and 15.) An assessment panel has been established to promote more effective liaison between agencies and offset the likelihood of inappropriate orders or disposals being made at court. In many courts it has not been unusual to hear a sentencer say: 'We are putting him/her on probation in the hope that you might be able to do something.' This frequently relates to the borderline mentally ill or mentally handicapped person, or an individual diagnosed as suffering from a personality disorder for whom no treatment is being offered under the definitions of the 1983 Mental Health Act. (A group discussed in Chapter 5.) The behaviour manifested is not necessarily aggression or violence: it can be paranoia, obsessiveness or persecutory activity which can pose equally difficult placement and maintenance problems unless there is a good range of available back-up facilities and supports. Without these, a supervising probation officer can be faced with an impossible task, have a sense of being used as a dustbin or feel total helplessness and vulnerability with the case. Worst of all, the offender may not receive the constructive help which can actually reduce the likelihood of further offending.

The multi-agency panel adopts a shared approach to assessments requested by the Courts. As a result of these interagency discussions, in which panel members each carry authority on behalf of their respective organizations, it becomes possible to identify programmes of treatment and support which can be recommended to the court either as a community-based package (operated under the terms of a probation order and containing a condition or requirement to participate in the programme), or on the basis of initial inpatient care with a follow-up plan identified. This can include designation of key-worker role, detail of the work to be done by each agency, and contingency plans to be operated in situations of crisis or breakdown. Defined arrangements of this kind can both promote a working relationship of understanding and trust capable of spanning different agency structures and responsibilities and enable difficult, perplexing cases to be handled with a greater degree of confidence and a sense of reciprocation. The furthering of such working partnerships as a basis for future work must be a priority for all the agencies concerned and would have the capacity to enable the probation service to extend the range of cases for which it could take responsibility within the terms of a probation order.

OBSTACLES TO GOOD PRACTICE

As indicated earlier, a probation order can include a requirement to receive psychiatric treatment on either an inpatient or outpatient basis and therefore offers a measure of flexibility, oversight and support which can be highly effective in responding to the needs of mentally disordered offenders as well as affording public protection. The successful implementation of such a requirement in an order is dependent upon close cooperation, consultation and communication between the probation service and local psychiatric services. It is obviously aided by the presence, at local level, of psychiatric staff with an interest in the field of forensic psychiatry. In the absence of such a specialist, there can be difficulties and blocks in the establishment of satisfactory and dependable liaison. Probation service experience indicates a very variable network of interest and back-up across the country as a whole for dealing with mentally disordered offenders in the community. A lack of continuity between inpatient treatment and preparations for discharge into the community can particularly bedevil and undermine the chances of successful transition and resettlement.

Residential placements, supportive lodgings and participation in day-centre programmes are facilities which the probation service has been increasingly able to offer in recent years. Obviously, such facilities remain limited and detailed account has to be taken of the degree of disturbance or demand on staff time which can be coped with. Opportunity to make use of similar facilities offered by the local social services departments or health authorities increases the range of suitable placements and supportive networks that can be considered. Where good, clear and dependable links are established with specialist units and community nursing staff, probation supervision can be a highly effective and flexible vehicle for work with mentally disordered offenders.

RETURNING TO THE COMMUNITY

So far this chapter has attended to the probation service's involvement with mentally disordered offenders whose behaviour does not require Special Hospital placement or incur longer-term imprisonment. Prior to the 1983 Mental Health Act, the legal position of the probation service in the supervision of Special Hospital patients was confused. The Act clarified the position in that it unequivocally placed the responsibility for after-care of such people on the local authority social services or the District Health Authority (Section 117). However, a subsequent statement from the Home Secretary stated that the probation service would be expected to be the agency nominated to supervise discharged Special Hospital patients whose criminal offences carried a life-sentence penalty where they had not been diagnosed as mentally ill and in need of hospital treatment. With this proviso, the legislation otherwise places Special Hospital patients clearly in the social work/medical field rather than the offender/penal system and it would be the exception rather than the rule for a probation officer to be nominated as primary worker in such a case. In other words it would only be likely to happen where the probation service has 'significant' knowledge or previous contact with a case.

What is absolutely essential is that consideration is given to the identification of a through-care officer, with proper consultation, at an early stage. There is too much evidence of discharge arrangements being made without sufficient team involvement and with the consequence that the after-care officer is not brought into the case early enough. Unexpected discharges from hospitals (special or otherwise) can leave probation officers with considerable problems of resettlement of discharged patients. It has to be borne in mind that the experience of supervising an ex-Special Hospital patient comes relatively rarely to individual probation officers, which can in itself create anxieties, and there are likely to be only a few probation officers in any one area with a comprehensive working knowledge of the legislation and procedures relating to this category of client. It is therefore vital that each probation area has an identified system of management and consultation procedures in respect of such cases (which usually come within Dangerous/High Risk Offender policy and procedures) on the basis of which appropriate practice guidance and staff supervision can be offered.

The problems of discharged mentally disordered offenders on their return to the community from the prison system or from hospital are acute and all possible assistance is needed to overcome the difficulties of transition. This transition highlights the obvious need for continuity in the treatment of the offender within the institution and the follow-up plans on his or her return to the community. An Interdepartmental Working Group of Home Office and DHSS officials on Mentally Disturbed Offenders in the Prison System in England and Wales referred to the importance of continuity of treatment in the institution and afterwards in the community (Home Office and DHSS, 1987). In furtherance of this aim, they identified the need for the development of the secondment of probation officers to undertake social work in prisons, and the need for the Parole Board to attend to after-care arrangements for prisoners released on licence. This kind of concern is shared by probation staff who have gained experience in work with mentally disordered offenders. Nevertheless, they remain concerned about the quality and availability of diagnostic facilities and about the patchiness of provision of appropriate facilities for treatment and management of the type recommended by the Interdepartmental Working Group.

PROPOSALS FOR IMPROVEMENTS TO SERVICE DELIVERY

There are a number of areas in which the service could be improved.

Training

Within the probation service, probation staff at all levels need to be familiar with the 1983 Mental Health Act and its implications. In particular, they need to be aware of the availability of forensic psychiatric services and how they can be utilized for the support and management of work with mentally disordered offenders. There is a great need for an extension of interdisciplinary training exercises and consultancy to improve oversight and decision-making, as well as to increase confidence in the handling of the most difficult cases. Training should include information on recognition of symptoms of mental abnormality, and classifications of mental illness, mental impairment and psychopathy—including the issue of 'treatability'.

Advisory panel

A regional or area interagency advisory panel should be established to have oversight of the management of the mentally abnormal offender in the community, or within the regional/local institutions which will require discharge arrangements to be planned and supervised.

Probation guidelines

Within each probation area it is important that a code of practice is devised for probation staff who will undertake supervision of mentally disordered offenders. It should include clear lines of responsibility, definitions of accountability and clarification of the respective roles of medical staff and probation officer when both services are carrying statutory responsibilities. Such a code of practice should provide for regular scrutiny of the handling of a case at appropriate intervals by a probation service manager, as well as opportunity for periodic consultation sessions with someone with expertise in the field of mental disorder who is 'external' to the case. It would undoubtedly be helpful for there to be formal guidelines setting out criteria for decisions about allocation of after-care of hospital patients between social services departments and the probation service as, for example, Section 37 of the 1983 Mental Health Act.

Community resources

Greater emphasis should be given to the utilization of a wider range of statutory and voluntary services within the community. Adult education, day centres and voluntary support groups are all needed to offset the isolation and rejection of the mentally disordered offender.

More use could be made of the guardianship order within the terms of the 1983 Mental Health Act—lack of local authority resources means that it is rarely used. Additionally, there should be willingness on the part of local authority housing authorities to provide, or ensure provision for, accommodation for former residents who may have been detained or in hospital outside their catchment area. This should include sheltered accommodation.

It is noticeable that consultant forensic psychiatrists are becoming more prepared to use the probation order with a condition of residence/ treatment rather than a Section 37 hospital order because it is seen that more advantageous after-care arrangements are possible, for example placement in approved probation hostels. (See too Chapter 5.)

Prison establishments

The probation service should consider a strategy for identifying the mentally disordered offender within the prison system namely those subject to Rule 43 with whom effective work could be undertaken, and a useful network of support established.

Transfer Direction Orders (Section 47/49 of the 1983 Mental Health

Act) have created many problems, especially when the patient is transferred close to the expected date of release (EDR). When the patient has reached the EDR, his status is changed to that of a *notional* Section 37 hospital order. It would be beneficial if C3 Division (Home Office) devised a mechanism whereby a patient subject to Section 47/49 transfer could be reviewed on a regular basis.

Life sentencers who come under the terms of Section 50(1)(b) of the 1983 Mental Health Act, combined with Section 61 of 1967 Criminal Justice Act, pose further problems. It is suggested that:

1. Life licence supervision should be undertaken by the probation service;
2. restricted patients with life sentences, released on Life Licence remain subject to recall to prison (Section 62, 1967 Criminal Justice Act)—but if their mental condition deteriorates and requires hospital treatment that they can be transferred again under the provisions of Section 47/49 of the 1983 Mental Health Act.

There are many areas of confusion within the operation of these decision-making processes and the fact of a recall or repeated transfers poses even greater dilemmas for the planning and management of after-care arrangements.

SUMMARY

Probation service staff working with mentally disordered offenders are inevitably caught up in some of society's most deep-seated dilemmas—such as the persisting taboos about mental disorder and hostility to offenders. Undertaking the supervision of mentally disordered offenders thus involves the exercise of skill and finely planned judgements which take account of both the protection of the public and the support and resettlement needs of individual offenders. The potential isolation of supervisors working with such dilemmas, particularly during periods of crisis or deterioration, strongly indicates the need for clear lines of management, responsibility and accountability. It also emphasizes the importance of good, reliable interagency liaison, networks of support, and community-based facilities which can be used to plan ahead for the discharge or release of mentally disordered offenders held in Special Hospitals or prisons. Where such working arrangements exist and can be depended upon, the probation service is capable of extending its capacity to deal effectively with a wider range of cases within the terms of a probation order. Certainly, it can handle more confidently cases involving pre-release planning and discharge on licence from an institution. There are good examples emerging of the way in which a multiagency approach offers both constructive care for individual offenders and the reliable kind of protection and reassurance which is sought by the community. This signals a way forward in the management of a significant group of offenders who pose concerns at all levels of the criminal justice system. Too often in the past, they have remained marginal in terms of provision in the community, and in some cases they have been subject to prolonged and unnecessary institutionalization.

REFERENCES

Barker A. (1988). Mentally disordered offenders and the courts: some aspects of the problem as seen by a beak and a quack. *Justice of the Peace*, **152** (4), 55–7; 71–4; 100–4.

Coker J. B., Martin J. B. (1985). *Licensed to Live*. Oxford: Blackwell.

Floud J. (1982). Dangerousness and criminal justice. *British Journal of Criminology*, **22**, 213–8.

HM Inspectorate of Probation and Home Office. (1987). *Issues for Senior Management in the Supervision of Dangerous and High Risk Offenders*. London: HMSO.

Home Office and Department of Health and Social Security (1987). *Interdepartmental Working Group of Home Office and DHSS officials on Mentally Disturbed Offenders in the Prison System in England and Wales: Report*. London: HMSO.

Norris M. (1984). *Integration of Special Hospital Patients into the Community*. Guildford: Gower.

Prins H. (1986). *Dangerous Behaviour, the Law and Mental Disorder*. London: Tavistock Publications.

Tonak D., Cawdron G. (1988). Mentally disordered offenders and the courts—co-operation and collaboration of disciplines involved. *Justice of the Peace*, **152**, 504–7.

17 *Treatment in the community: rhetoric, reality and the rear-view mirror*

IAN BYNOE

INTRODUCTION

Our Victorian forebears would have been bemused to learn that people were seriously discussing the subject of the mentally disordered offender in the community. For them, a combination of untreatable serious mental illness or handicap and criminal behaviour was quite enough to qualify someone for membership of those alternative communities constructed by them in rolling countryside and behind high physical and social walls. Removed from the hostile and harsh world, their lives could be lived in surroundings which were genuinely thought to be in accordance with their needs. Except, as we know, such people were not deemed to have too many needs. Thus in 1974, the Department of Health discovered that more than 24 000 long-stay hospital patients did not have full personal clothing of their own and many did not have a cupboard in which to hang their clothes (HMSO, 1975.)

It has been stated policy of successive governments during the last 30 years to abandon the values which led to the construction of such places, to dismantle the physical and personnel facilities which they required and to replace the whole with community based facilities providing individually tailored services in the least restrictive setting. The impact of this and other policies on the offender in the community is the subject of this chapter. It will describe in more detail the thinking behind the concept of care in the community, current changes proposed in sentencing policy generally which may contribute to changes in provision, and the reality as seen in relation to particular problems. This chapter will conclude with some suggestions for change for the offender being treated in the community.

COMMUNITY CARE

The Percy Commission (Royal Commission, 1957) in its proposed legislative changes, which were largely incorporated into the 1959 Mental Health Act, foresaw the time when the mental health services would be community based and more able to respond to individual needs for treatment and support. It even felt it right, where appropriate, to impose a duty on a local authority to take persons in the community into its guardianship, an idea which was, however, rejected in 1959. The Ministry of Health's Hospital Plan of 1962 (Ministry of Health, 1962) called for a wholesale reduction in beds in the large mental hospitals within a 15 year timescale. The results of the early efforts to implement this idea were seen by the Butler Committee when it came to survey the scene in the mid 70s (Home Office and Department of Health and Social Security (DHSS), 1974 and 1975). This Committee's radical proposal for the establishment of medium security units is, of course, well known and has shaped spending and policy in secure provision and forensic psychiatry these last 15 years. What the Committee uncovered regarding care in the community is less familiar. In its Interim Report it noted:

... although the scale of provision of community social services varied from place to place, in general the services that exist are as yet insufficient for the tasks they have to do and it would be unwise to expect too much of them for some time to come.

(Home Office and DHSS, 1974, para. 14)

And, in its main report, it returned to the subject of shortages of resources and inadequate or non-existent cooperation and coordination of services, reporting that it had been told by the Association of Directors of Social Services that:

Effective care and after-care of the mentally disordered can become a reality only when there is a sufficiency of facilities located in the community adequate to the task.

(Home Office and DHSS, 1975, para. 3.13.)

It concluded that there was no such sufficiency and recommended that the provision of trained social work staff, enough hostel accommodation to meet demand, better communications between health and social work authorities, and the involvement of psychiatry with the probation service would all address the unmet needs of the offender in the community (being either someone discharged into it or a person whose condition was never thought serious enough to warrant custodial treatment). Of significance was the identification by the Report of a group of persons routinely sentenced to imprisonment for trivial offences, whose mental vulnerability and 'inadequate' personality combined to produce in them a need for positive asylum or 'sanctuary'. It called on hospitals to revive what was considered to have been a former role of social carer for this group (Home Office and DHSS, 1975, Ch. 7). It did not decide that this was a job for social work authorities to undertake. Legal informality and the absence of individualized 'rights' to services still governed much social welfare provision at that time and the Report did not recommend even minimal legal duties on service providers to clearly assess need and make formal arrangements to meet it when persons were discharged into the community. But the fundamental principle underlying all of the Report's proposals speaks of the humanitarian values which should inform any care in the community provision:

Mentally disordered offenders should be put into the treatment situation which is best suited to their treatment needs, with proper regard for the requirements of safety.

(Home Office and DHSS, 1975, p. 53.)

As the Butler Committee was calling for the provisions of more resources for care in the community, the Government was publishing its White Paper 'Better Services for the Mentally Ill' (DHSS, 1975). This was a time when social policy might be floated on idealism, only to be holed fairly rapidly by the International Monetary Fund. With no special recommendations for forensic services, housing or employment, the document candidly commented:

Multiprofessional teamwork, adequate assessment, consultation and arrangements for after-care, and social work support are as yet sadly all too often theoretical ideals which bear scant relation to the practical realities. Inevitably patients and their families do not always receive the standard of care and support they should.

(Home Office and DHSS, 1975, para. 11.4.)

In view of the financial constraints affecting public spending, there was promised little further progress towards realizing the ideals which informed government policy.

Since 1959, mental health legislation had been concerned mainly with the provision, under detained conditions, of psychiatric treatment to the small proportion of inpatients needing compulsory intervention. Thus, the review of the 1959 Act which led to its substantial amendment in 1982 and 1983 brought little real change for forensic patients in the community. However, reforms to the provisions concerning guardianship were intended to make it a more attractive option for the mentally disordered person needing some control or supervised support in the community. The after-care duty provided by Section 117 of the 1983 Mental Health Act, and imposed on health and local authorities, was designed to ensure that adequate attention was given to community care needs on the discharge of the former detained patient. Hospital order patients would be included and were meant to benefit from the necessary assessment and joint working which this duty was designed to encourage. A more specialized and better trained social work profession was promised with the requirement that those using the law to arrange compulsory admissions should be suitably qualified—by being 'approved'—to do so. Lastly, for the detained patient or conditionally discharged restricted patient, the Mental Health Act Commission was established to monitor their conditions and expose any specific difficulties which they faced.

With regard to their social policy, the British appear to believe that if one repeats something enough times then somehow it will be willed into existence. So how has the oft repeated policy of 'Care in the Community' fared in the 1980s? With the Department of Health retreating from any interventionist role in mental health policy; with those local authorities prepared to spend on only essential social provision being financially penalized for their pains; and with some health service general managers balancing the books, it is not surprising that the gulf between rhetoric and reality began to widen before the public's disconcerted gaze. This was most pronounced in the field of mental illness. A private market, floating on Department of Social Security payments, was burgeoning to cope with the growing numbers of the dependent elderly. In the field of mental handicap, there had been closer and more effective attention to the need to build and resource facilities in the community before hospital closure and mass discharge took place.

The Government's response to the disquieting evidence that its mental health policy might be cruelly ineffective was first to commission a report from Sir Roy Griffiths (DHSS, 1988), then to prevaricate for nearly two years in the light of his recommendations, then to issue a White Paper (DOH, 1989), the limited legislative effects of which have been introduced in the National Health Service and Community Care Act, 1990. Most of the changes will be effected in non-statutory ways by Ministerial direction, government circular and code of guidance.

The White Paper promises much which is new without abandoning the fundamental thrust of earlier policy, but also without giving too many details on implementation and resources. What is in it for the mentally disordered offender in the community? It reaffirms the principle of matching services to individual needs, proposing a system of written assessments of community care needs; of written 'care programmes' for all those with mental health needs (not just those covered by Section 117 of the Mental Health Act and the as yet unimplemented Section 7 of the 1986 Disabled Persons (Services, Consultation and Representation) Act); a good practice guide from the Royal College of Psychiatrists in relation to discharges from hospital; and responsibility for the provision of social care to rest with local authorities. With these proposals is made available new money by way of a special grant to local authorities to spend in the discharge of their responsibilities towards the mentally ill. The Government has not decided to alter the arrangements for legal supervision of patients living in the community—that is, no compulsory treatment in the community is envisaged—and it promises initiatives in relation to those whose homelessness leads to them not receiving treatment and those whose

needs for emergency care are not being met. [Since this chapter was written it has been announced that the specific mental illness grant for 1991/2 will be £30 million.]

The baseline for any increase in spending is low. The White Paper candidly acknowledges that only 3 per cent of local authorities' expenditure is currently devoted to services specifically for those with a mental illness (DOH, 1989). The Office of Health Economics in a recent report preferred perhaps a more revealing comparison when it stated that by the end of the last decade, 80 per cent of spending on mental health was in hospital services not in social provision through community services (Office of Health Economics, 1989). Albeit the Government has now promised a higher profile for the local social work department in the field of community care, this is to be in an 'enabling' role rather than as an exclusive, or even a major, provider. Thus, the local authority will be placed under a statutory duty to draw up, publish and monitor community care plans which will define the community care needs of the area and the strategies and services in place or to be provided by other agencies to meet them. Also, various provisions appear in the legislation making it financially disadvantageous for the authority to provide residential social care through its own staff or facilities. It will be as likely to 'buy in' the services offered by the private or voluntary sector to meet the need which has been identified. Some argue that proposed changes to the financing and organization of other parts of the National Health Service threaten to marginalize still further the resources of staff time and money devoted to psychiatric treatment and rehabilitation (DOH, 1989).

CHANGES IN THE PENAL SYSTEM

Meanwhile, what has been going on in the penal system? What are the major new ideas here which may have an impact on the future for the mentally disordered offender? The direction of Home Office thinking is to be found in the 1988 Green Paper 'Punishment, Custody and the Community' (Home Office, 1988). This is an important document which could signal major changes in sentencing practice. The Government has had difficulties in the past in persuading sentencers to conform to guidelines and has changed the law to restrict their discretion (Criminal Justice Act, 1982 and 1988). It will be interesting to see if these radical ideas find their way into the White Paper and legislative changes promised for 1990. [Since this chapter was written, these ideas have found their way into the White Paper published in January 1990 and will no doubt appear in the legislative changes proposed.] Their importance to the offender with mental health needs is the stress, yet again, on disposal to community care unless this is intolerable to public safety or necessitated by the sheer gravity of the offence.

For, now:

Custody should be reserved as punishment for very serious offences, especially when the offender is violent and a continuing risk to the public.

(Home Office, 1988, 1990, para. 1.8.)

And

... for ... less serious offenders a spell in custody is not the most effective punishment.

(Home Office, 1988, 1990, para. 1.1.)

For, although it would restrict liberty it would also hamper the chances of the person learning the social skills and self-discipline which would, in the long term, reduce the chances of their re-offending.

If offenders remain in the community, they should be able to maintain their relationships with their family; their opportunities for work, training and education will be better; and they should be able to make some reparation for the harm they have done.

(Home Office, 1988, 1990, para. 1.7.)

A complex new sentence involving supervision, punishment and training suited to the circumstances of the defendant is proposed. The person who is adjudged to be dependent on alcohol or drugs may be ordered to attend for training or treatment in addition to being punished. It is optimistic about the chances of the courts and social workers training people out of crime. Where it is realistic is in predicting the money which will be saved with fewer defendants being sentenced to imprisonment. The writer recalls in times past the diffidence with which he drew to the attention of the lay magistrates the cost consequent upon their anticipated decision to imprison his client. Now we read:

If the courts are to have a wide discretion with powers to place a range of requirements on offenders, they should take account of the costs to the taxpayers of carrying out the requirements.

(Home Office, 1988, 1990, para. 3.37.)

In future, advocates obviously need have no such qualms. It is the probation service which fears that, over time, its social work tradition and skills will be replaced by some form of community policing role.

If the suggestion that punishment is more effective when in the community and that custody should be reserved largely for public protection has any worth, then it provides an interesting contrast with the way in which mentally disordered offenders are dealt with by the courts (Hodgins, 1988). It raises, too, the interesting discussion about whether or not the mental health offender, if placed in the community, should have more supervision, especially in the matter of a requirement to submit to compulsory medication. What, then are the powers which the criminal court possesses?

The court's specific options under the Powers of Criminal Courts Act 1973 or the Mental Health Act 1983 enable it to place the defendant in a number of different settings depending on the treatment needs or dangerousness posed by the person—or a combination of the two. A psychiatric probation order may be made with a condition specifying inpatient treatment, outpatient attendance, or treatment as medically directed. It can last as little as six months or as long as three years but must have the consent of the defendant before being made. The court has to be satisfied on the evidence of one doctor that the offender's 'mental condition requires and is susceptible to treatment but is not such as to warrant his detention in pursuance of a hospital order' (Powers of the Criminal Courts Act, 1973). Though it will be formally supervised by a probation officer who may return the matter to court in the event of breach or other circumstances, social work support and other treatment may be provided in the context of the order by a whole range of other professionals. The Hertfordshire Panel Scheme (referred to in Chapter 15) seems to be able to make the management of such an order a truly multidisciplinary affair with all the gains for the defendant and the court which that entails. For the offender who can be provided with support and treatment in a community setting, either now or when facilities are established, the probation order must be considered the first specific option which the court should entertain. It meets the defendant's needs without compromising public safety, often leaving the defendant in the community where treatment is likely to be most effective. (See too the arguments proposed in Chapter 5.)

Guardianship under Section 37 of the Mental Health Act 1983 is available to the court where a diagnosis of mental illness, psychopathic personality disorder, mental impairment or severe mental impairment is present. It is rarely used for mentally disordered offenders—perhaps the probation order being preferred in its stead. The most recent statistics show that in 1982/83 there were 41 persons under guardianship; the equivalent figure for 1986/87 was 120 and these included civil 'receptions' into guardianship under Section 7 of the Act (Mental Health Act Commission, 1989). The Mental Health Act Commission has concluded that the reasons the provision is so unpopular is that local authorities are unprepared to vote the resources to providing guardianship. Indeed some authorities refuse to take anyone under guardianship. Social workers complain that the 'essential powers' of the guardian (access and the prescription of residence and attendance for various purposes) are ambiguous or inadequate or both—there is no power to compel medical treatment. It must be said, however, that the alleged problems have not emerged after any extensive use of the order and it would seem sensible, before calls for more restrictive measures are heeded, for much greater use to be made of this provision.

After probation, a hospital order is the most likely outcome where the treatment needs of the defendant require inpatient attention, often where the sentencing court has concerns for the risk to public safety of treatment being given or tried in the community. The 'restricted' patient, of course, may in time return to the community still on a hospital order under the supervision and with the treatment provided as per the conditions attached to the conditional discharge which has been granted by Tribunal or the Home Office.

If supervision in the community is considered a desirable option to help maintain treatment and safeguard public safety, is there any place for a change in the law to permit compulsory medical treatment, particularly of those diagnosed as having schizophrenia living at home as opposed to being inpatients in hospital? The idea is not a new one. The British Association of Social Workers (BASW) suggested in 1977 that there be a new Community Care Order including this power and the Government also considered the continuation of the extensive 1959 Act guardianship powers which had already included this power (BASW, 1977). (In the event, the powers were reduced in 1982 so as to remove this one.) Since 1983, the proposals have been revived with a radical proposal for a preventive Community Treatment Order from the Royal College of Psychiatrists being endorsed by the National Association of Health Authorities but opposed from varying positions by MIND, BASW and the Community Psychiatric Nurses Association. No consensus or majority view has emerged in the Mental Health Act Commission. Guardianship has existed since 1959 for the person perceived to need supervised treatment in the community and yet it has been consistently ignored. By generally encouraging the authority which is guardian to be a local social services department and not a health authority, the law reflects the fact that care in the community has a crucial social dimension and that many of the stresses which lead to relapse derive from the absence of appropriate social and psychological support or training in coping skills.

When the Butler Committee looked at guardianship, the powers they suggested were much more extensive, including the power to compel treatment. But the responsibility was considered by local authorities to be too onerous for routine applications to be made. Butler resisted the suggestion that authorities be obliged to receive a person into guardianship—an idea that had been proposed earlier by the Percy Commission. But the author believes that this possibility should be re-examined before more restrictive and exclusively medical strategies are introduced. There could surely be some useful research undertaken in this field to explore attitudes to medication in the group apparently targetted for this new order and the contribution which supervision and assistance such as guardianship can bring to maintain consent to medication and prevent relapse.

GAPS BETWEEN INTENT AND ACTION

Although this latest White Paper is keen to describe the growth and expansion there has been in services, nevertheless there is some acknowledgement of the gap between intent and action in the matter of care in the community. An examination of just three specific areas of concern by way of example will emphasize the difficulties—and the distance—which still has to be travelled. They each relate to community care issues and are not referred to directly at all in the White Paper.

Discharge from secure provision into hostel accommodation

Numerous government reports and other documents have highlighted the need for specialized housing particularly to meet the needs of the person discharged from long-term hospital treatment under conditions of security. The Aarvold Report stated:

We have been told that in some parts of the country hostel accommodation is at a premium.

(Home Office and DHSS, 1973, para. 39.)

Butler's interim report has been quoted above. The Committee's final report called for a substantial increase in the general hostel accommodation and greater coordination between the agencies which provide the accommodation for the discharged offender (Home Office and DHSS, 1973, Ch. 8). In June 1980 the All-Party Parliamentary Penal Affairs Group stated:

there should be a substantial increase in hostel provision and other forms of accommodation for the mentally disordered. The range of voluntary after-care hostels for offenders grant aided by the Home Office should include some projects catering specifically for offenders suffering from mental disorders.

(Parliamentary All-Party Penal Affairs Group, 1980.)

So, what was delivered during the 1980s to meet this obviously pressing need? Reporting in its Second Biennial Report on the years 1985–1987, the Mental Health Act Commission said, of the shortage of social services facilities:

The provision of community care facilities for former special hospital patients is an area where there is still a great deal of work to be done, and although provision in some areas is good, in others it is to all intents and purposes non-existent.

(Mental Health Act Commission, 1987, para. 12.7.)

We are not considering here unsupported ordinary housing which might be available from the housing department (though there is even less of that after ten years' restriction of public housing). What is needed is supported and supervised accommodation of a type acceptable particularly to the Mental Health Review Tribunal and the Home Office. Has the position improved in the last two years? After drawing attention to the good schemes in operation in the Zulu Road project and the Mersey Region's cluster flats the Commission's Third Biennial Report goes on to record:

Community services particularly local authority services could play a much larger part in prevention and aftercare if they had more resources and were less overwhelmed by the demands of child protection. At present, their contribution particularly in respect of restricted patients is much less than it might be and there are no incentives of any kind for Social Services Departments to volunteer to participate in care for people who have been treated in security.

(Mental Health Act Commission, 1987, para. 11.9.)

Any Special Hospital patient who has won their deferred discharge will know the truth of that as the months pass by and no place appears willing to take him or her. A two-year wait is not unknown. Clearly, local authorities must now be required to include planning for such needs in their new community care plans. It is to be hoped that the Department of Health will ensure proper attention is given to such provision so that these can no longer be so ignored.

And what of the Home Office? As part of its overall drive to reduce the remand population, more bail hostel places are to be made available across the country but there are no definite signs that psychiatric bail hostels are envisaged. When inviting comments on the future shape and style of bail hostel provision in 1989, the Home Office asked for comments concerning these. It is to be hoped that the idea will see the light of day soon, since such facilities could serve a number of different purposes including rehabilitative ones though their main advantage will be for bail remands.

Section 136 and the psychiatric emergency

In the community, the manner in which the psychiatric crisis is handled, especially where this may involve the commission of a criminal offence and in a public place, will provide an acid test of the adequacy of the services in place to provide 'care' in the community. For the offender being supervised in the community, or for the person at risk of entering the criminal justice system, the response of the authorities to police use of Section 136 of the 1983 Mental Health Act 1983 provides an illuminating commentary on the undeveloped and often merely rudimentary resources which are available in the community. Reference can be made to recent research conducted by two researchers for MIND and published in 1987 (Rogers and Faulkner, 1987).

Under Section 136, a police constable has the power to remove to a place of safety anyone found in a public place appearing to be suffering from mental disorder and in immediate need of care or control, where to do so would be in that person's interests or for the protection of others. A 'place of safety' is defined in the Act so as to include a hospital, council home, or police station. It is not an admission Section but one legally justifying detention for assessment, and the power to detain lasts for up to 72 hours for the purpose of enabling the person arrested 'to be examined by a registered medical practitioner and to be interviewed by an Approved Social Worker' and for the making of any necessary arrangements for treatment and care of the person.

Health Department statistics which show, for example, that the Section was used 1523 times in 1986 are misleading since these only record the occasions when a hospital was used as the place of safety and the person's arrival therefore led to a technical 'admission' (Department of Health, 1989). In the absence of a reliable recording system to show when the police used it without involving the hospital in this way, the figure is unhelpful, although it seems generally recognized that the Section is most used in London.

The MIND research confirmed what some might have thought could easily have been predicted.

The police referrals tended to be young, the majority were male, social classes 4 and 5 were overrepresented, the overwhelming majority were unemployed and a substantial number were homeless ... the particularly disadvantaged position of the group may suggest that wider social and economic factors such as unemployment, type of housing and financial support are important factors in bringing about this type of psychiatric emergency.

(Rogers and Faulkner, 1987, p. 39.)

For many years, those bodies which have examined the use of Section 136 have drawn critical attention to the widely divergent practice in different local and health authority areas and police force districts. Butler referred to problems demonstrating the need for greater local consultation and mutual understanding (Home Office and DHSS, 1975). The 1976 Mental Health Act Review called for measures to alleviate the effects of poor practice (A Review of the Mental Health Act 1959, 1976). The 1978 Mental Health Act Review felt there was a need for national guidance to ensure acceptable implementation (A Review of the Mental Health Act, 1978). As one commentator on this subject has observed:

It is difficult to generalise, but one theme begins to emerge; that is the variability of the service offered to the police by social and medical allied staff.

(Bean, 1986.)

In its second report, the Mental Health Act Commission drew attention to the fact that the use of the Section was often treated as an admission to hospital and not as an assessment in every case requiring the attendance of and interview by an approved social worker as the law clearly required (Bean, 1986).

This only confirmed the results which Rogers and Faulkner had found in their study. They felt justified in concluding that:

... contrary to legislative intent, social workers were rarely involved in assessing referrals under Section 136.

(Rogers and Faulkner, 1987, p. 41.)

In the light of the replies to a London borough-wide questionnaire seeking some explanation for this fact, they further state:

It is likely that many social services departments do not recognise a legal obligation to provide assessments nor do they regard it as a priority, financially or otherwise.

(Rogers and Faulkner, 1987, p. 41.)

Locally negotiated and agreed arrangements between police and local and health authorities—a requirement of the Mental Health Act Code of Practice introduced in December 1989—should go some way towards ensuring that the Section is more properly applied. That this research reveals these discrepancies of practice and failure to create community based arrangements rather than hospital ones offers yet further evidence of the undeveloped state of available community facilities.

The Police and Criminal Evidence Act 1984 and the mentally vulnerable suspect

It is hard to imagine a more stressful and more significant experience for the mentally disordered person than to face arrest by the police and questioning when in their custody. In this situation, impaired communication and coping skills may combine with inappropriate mood to place the person at enormous disadvantage in the hands of even entirely scrupulous but accusatorial police officers. The Codes of Practice made under the 1984 Act provide limited protections for such suspects (Police and Criminal Evidence Act 1984: Codes of Practice, 1985). They depend for their effect on the identification by the police of the mental vulnerability in the first place and then the ready availability of an 'appropriate adult' to attend on and accompany the suspect during their time in custody and when interviewed by the police.

One would expect a society which took seriously the matter of community care to oblige the police to ensure the availability of such an appropriate adult particularly in the case of the mentally disturbed person who may suddenly leave home for another town where offending may occur. The police will not in such cases be able to draw on the assistance of those who know or care for the suspect. In some senses they will then be at their most vulnerable since, if charged, bail is likely to be refused and a remand in custody will follow unless rapid efforts can be made to arrange alternatives. Unfortunately, nothing in the Act or the Codes imposes any such simple duty and it is within the writer's knowledge that suspects can still be processed through the police station and into the court system without sufficient attention being given to their special needs even when these were clearly acknowledged to exist.

Research could usefully examine the extent to which the police are able to arrange the speedy attendance of someone to fulfil the role of 'appropriate adult' and the local resources which may be available to the police service in the event of efforts being made to coordinate arrangements. Frequently MIND groups are contacted to assist in this situation. Is this because the local or health authority cannot or will not help?

Home Office research has shown that of 5519 suspects arrested during a survey (in March 1987), 1 per cent were in the category of the mentally vulnerable (Home Office, 1989). However, this is a misleading statistic since the total which is represented included 43 per cent who were not arrested under the Police and Criminal Evidence Act at all but had been apprehended as 'missing persons'. But even if the true figure is nearer to half a per cent, this seems to the author to be surprisingly low when compared with the much higher incidence of diagnosis of mental disorder in the prison population (Gunn, 1985).

Research might usefully examine how the police decide that a person is mentally ill, handicapped or in some other way mentally vulnerable. It could assess whether they are accurately identifying the suspects at risk and demonstrate a need for training if they are not.

FURTHER SUGGESTIONS FOR CHANGE

Clearly, the next decade will be crucial for the success or failure of the policy of community care as it has been tried by successive governments. By the end of it we will know more clearly who have been the winners, who the losers. What changes would help to ensure that the mentally disordered offender will be found in the former group, not the latter?

We know little of the small print of the Government's proposals for community care plans and for detailed assessments. An exposure of the needs which people in the field have seen for years, both for individuals and groups as a whole, may lead to more extensive and better resourced services—or simply a better appreciation of what is not in place. The Department of Health, particularly through the Social Services Inspectorate, will be monitoring the preparation and implementation of the community care plans of the social services authorities. Health authorities will also be obliged to prepare similar plans in relation to their existing and projected needs. Will the Government insist on the creation and maintenance of minimum standards and services here, or will it allow the continuation of the dramatic countrywide variations of services from good, through poor to non-existent?

Also, there is no clear idea of the amount of any extra funding available to authorities for mental health which will permit the expansion of services in this area. Until the size and nature of the mental illness grant is known, it is impossible to predict what may now be feasible which was not before [see note on p. 209 re size of initial grants]. However, early candidates for additional expenditure must be the establishment of more supported or supervised accommodation, particularly for the former patients of secure hospitals or for the ex-prisoner with mental health needs. Also, the creation and maintenance of adequate and skilled social work involvement in crisis intervention work where the police may have an interest is a priority.

The health and social service authorities need to devote more time and resources to the creation of good quality housing which by its location, regime and staffing addresses the needs of those perceived by Butler to be 'inadequates'. Prison in the new era is apparently not going to be an option for them when they break the law. Will common lodging houses, shop doorways or night shelters have to carry on with this task? What, for example, will we see in the London Borough of Southwark's Community Care Plan for 1992 addressing the needs of this group and what will be the response of this government when the Councillors present their bill? Will 'positive asylum' within housing designed on the basis of normal patterns of living be available for those most disabled by long-term illness or institutionalization (British Medical Journal, 1989)? It is not inconsistent with the idea of care in the community if it is suited to the individual needs of the resident and is delivered in the least restrictive setting possible.

The mentally disordered offender carries a heavy burden of stigma and intolerance when in the community. The author knows of one ex-Broadmoor patient refused work in a sheltered workshop run by a large mental health charity. The reason? Not the view of his doctor that he posed no immediate threat to the public but the fact of his offence many years before. The treatment of the subject by the press and other media often still lacks balance and seriousness, preferring to play instead to a gallery which takes comfort in crude stereotypes and its accompanying messages of unbridled dangerousness, segregation and incarceration. These are the figures seen in the rear-view mirror by politicians, health and social work professionals, courts and tribunals wishing to place or keep the mentally disordered offender in the community and eyes can be distracted and nerves troubled by the sight.

Two developments may assist here: one more attainable than the other. Legal professionals involved in the representation of this group need to see it as specialized work, demanding particular skills and a body of both general and specifically local knowledge. Their profession, as much as any other, can fall into stereotyped and confused thinking about mental disorder and dangerousness and can fail its clients as a result. Lawyers regularly working in this field need to acquire the skills for interviewing such clients in police station, court or hospital, if necessary by role-play exercises. They need to have a detailed grasp of the community facilities available for the client to be able to encourage professionals and courts alike in a community-oriented approach where this is practicable. They need the same knowledge when it comes to pressing for discharge from security for a person who requires a place in the community. If judicial concern will concentrate on matters such as potential violence then the representative must be able to argue how services and staff skills will handle a client's potential instability.

The Law Society has established a specialist panel of solicitors approved for representing clients before the Mental Health Review Tribunal. A similar but far less rigorously vetted scheme is seen with the Duty Solicitor Schemes in police stations and in magistrates' courts. The writer's recollection of the latter scheme was that it often involved the representation of those with a mental health problem—other defendants had called out their regular 'brief', and the mentally disordered would rarely stick with one firm and would seldom get someone out to the police station. Surely, there is a place for more compulsory training of such duty solicitors in the special needs of the mentally disordered offender?

The other proposal may have to wait for the third millenium. Certainly, the current administration has set its face against the concept. This is the idea of legislation to combat discrimination on grounds of disability to include within that definition a person with a current mental disability, or someone with a past history of disability who is perceived to still have one. It is perfectly lawful to refuse someone a job because of their mental health history although medical reports may confirm no presenting symptoms and give an excellent prognosis. It affects particularly the entry or return to paid employment of the person who has been mentally ill, and legal protection may bring more equal treatment in the community for the person who can avail themselves of it. [This type of law is most developed in the USA where the recently passed Americans with Disabilities Act 1990 will substantially improve the status of the person seeking redress for unfair and unjustified treatment on grounds of disability.]

In due time, 1989 may be seen to be the year that the Government was made to realize that community care needed more than mere rhetoric on which to prosper and develop. Time will tell whether its response was equal to the task it was set. Those sceptical about the whole direction of the policy, as seen in that rear-view mirror, have certainly not left the scene. Calling for a review of the Institute of Psychiatry's innovative outreach work with Daily Living Programme teams, the Chairman of the House of Commons Social Services Select Committee stated: 'This project is letting people who are deranged out among the public.' [Frank Field MP quoted in *Hospital Doctor* 23 November 1989.] A more rational and realistic contribution to the complex debate about treatment in the community may be found in these words from a report of the Interdepartmental Working Group between the Home Office and DHSS on the Mentally Disturbed Offender in the Prison System. At paragraph 7.18 of its 1987 report it states:

The professions need to be encouraged to continue to give attention to the whole range of problems. In doing so they will make a necessary contribution to the development of a network of facilities to serve the diverse needs of mentally disturbed people, non-offender and offender alike. This will be a long, detailed process.

Whoever thought that having to replace the inheritance of 150 years of custodial treatment would call for anything less?

REFERENCES

DHSS (1975). *Better Services for the Mentally Ill* Cmnd 6233. London: HMSO.
Mental Health Act Commission (1957). *Report of the Royal Commission on the Law relating to Mental Illness and Mental Deficiency 1954–1957* Cmnd 169. London: HMSO.
Ministry of Health (1962). *A Hospital Plan for England and Wales* Cmnd 1604. London: HMSO.
Home Office and Department of Health and Social Security (1974). *Interim Report of the Committee on Mentally Abnormal Offenders* Cmnd 5698. London: HMSO.
Home Office and Department of Health and Social Security (1975). *Report of the Committee on Mentally Abnormal Offenders* (The Butler Report) Cmnd 6244. London: HMSO.
DHSS (1988). *Community Care: Agenda for Action.* London: HMSO.
DOH (1989). *Caring for People: Community Care in the Next Decade and Beyond* Cmnd 849. London: HMSO.
Office of Health Economics (1989). *Mental Health in the 1990s: from Custody to Care.* London: HMSO.
Home Office (1988). *Punishment, Custody and the Community* Cmnd 424. London: HMSO.
Criminal Justice Act. (1982). London: HMSO.
Supervision of Punishment in the Community (1990). Cmnd 966. London: HMSO.
Hodgins S. (1988). An aftercare programme for mentally disordered offenders. In: *Trends in Law and Mental Health* (Koenraadt C., Zeegers R., eds.) Arnhem: Gouda Quint bV.
Powers of the Criminal Courts Act. (1973). London: HMSO.
Mental Health Act Commission (1989). *Third Biennial Report 1987–89.* London: HMSO.

British Association of Social Workers (1977). *Mental Health Crisis Services.*

Home Office and Department of Health and Social Security (1973). *Report of the Review of Procedures for the Discharge and Supervision of Psychiatric Patients Subject to Special Restrictions* (The Aarvold Report) Cmnd 5191. London: HMSO.

Parliamentary All-Party Penal Affairs Group (1980). *Too Many Prisoners.* London: HMSO.

Rogers A., Faulkner A. (1987). *A Place of Safety.* London: MIND.

Department of Health (1989). *Legal Status of Patients—KH15 and KH16 England Financial Year 1987/88.* London: HMSO.

A Review of the Mental Health Act 1959. (1976). Cmnd 7320. London: HMSO.

Bean P. (1986). *Mental Disorder and Legal Control.* Cambridge: Cambridge University Press.

Police and Criminal Evidence Act 1984: Codes of Practice. (1985). London: HMSO.

Home Office (1989). *Detention at the Police Station Under the Police and Criminal Evidence Act 1984.* Home Office Research Study 104 (by David Brown). London: HMSO.

Gunn J. (1985). Psychiatry and the prison. In: *Secure Provision* (Gostin L., ed.). London: Tavistock Publications.

Section 6
Resumé

18 *Some concluding reflections*

MICHAEL MUSTILL

INTRODUCTION

Anyone charged to write the concluding chapter of a compilation such as this is likely to adopt a strategy on the following lines. First, he or she will look for common themes, ideas, motives, aims and methods. Once identified, these unifying notions can be spliced together to form the framework of the subject. Material drawn from the various contributions may then be rearranged upon this framework to yield (the author hopes) a solid intellectual construct. This can be exploited to reveal and illuminate any gaps in knowledge, loose ends, areas of disagreement, divergences in technique and possibilities for development. With luck, all this will leave the author well-placed to wind up with a rousing six-point plan of action.

A study of the preceding chapters shows that this idealized scheme will not work in our chosen field. The value of the contributions lies not only in their individual strengths, but in their diversity. The drawing-together of different disciplines, the assault on problems from different angles, has been an enterprise never previously attempted, the momentum of which it is vital to maintain. A plan of action must certainly be devised, but the very diversity of the material with which the reader of this book is presented makes it impossible to derive such a plan from a unitary view of the field.

The problem announces itself with the title of the book. *The Mentally Disordered Offender* was a useful, and perhaps indispensable, label for the colloquium and for the initiatives which it must profoundly be hoped will follow, for it signals an intention to mobilize all available skills and agencies in a concerted attack on the scandalous neglect of so many fellow-beings. Furthermore, the attention of ministers must be captured, the imagination of donors fired, the ignorance of the public remedied, the interest of practitioners aroused. For this purpose *The Mentally Disordered Offender* is as good a banner as any under which to march.

Nevertheless, it is imperative that those who carry out these tasks should bear constantly in mind that 'the mentally disordered offender' is an artificial construct, not corresponding to any objectively determinable section of the population.

It is undeniably convenient to regard those with whom this book is concerned as occupying the area of intersection between two groups comprising, respectively, all mentally disordered people and all offenders. It may then be assumed that the occupants of this area form a distinct population and that generalizations may be made about the best way to promote their interests. Useful as it may be, this assumption can mislead in ways which must be recognized. There are two principal sources of trouble.

In the first place neither of the two overlapping populations is homogeneous. In each case the characteristics of the members vary radically in both kind and degree. The mentally disordered extend from the totally deranged to the rather eccentric. The degree of disorder may not be quantifiable, except in some instances in terms of conventions based on batteries of tests, but few would, I believe, doubt that some very general hierarchies can be established, at least within the confines of each individual disorder. Again, the patients will differ greatly amongst themselves as to the type of disorder with which they are afflicted.

So also with the population of offenders. England has not yet gone as far as the United States towards the construction of a sentencing grid, formally ranking various groups of crime in order of gravity. Nevertheless, it is obvious that the law does regard some offences as more serious than others, and a glance at the median sentences imposed for different crimes is enough to confirm that this is so. It is equally obvious that within the confines of a single offence some are more serious than others.

Equally significant is the great multiplicity of types of criminal conduct. Persons who have pleaded guilty to (say): a killing under grave provocation; the robbery of a sub-post office without a weapon; a rape with no features justifying a sentence in excess of the norm; and the distribution of Class A drugs on a smallish scale, might find themselves leaving the Crown Court for prison with sentences in roughly the same range, yet this does not mean that there is any kinship between the individual offences.

A second ground of error is the assumption that because the two populations somewhat overlap, there is a direct relationship between them. This is not so. In reality the coupling between the two groups is very loose.

Only infrequently will the factors that make a man mad also operate directly to make him offend. Some burglars may be disordered, but few burgle because they are disordered. Even where there is a link between the disorder and the mental processes which cause the person to commit the criminal acts, the disorder may only be a trigger or an aggravating factor, whilst other perfectly rational motives may be engaged at the same time. This means that in general it is impossible to isolate subgroups of the disturbed and identify them with subgroups of offenders. It is true that at the extreme ends of the spectra there may be some correspondence. The authors of very serious crimes tend to be seriously ill; but this is not always so, and on occasion the offender who was once seriously ill has passed completely out of the group of mentally disordered by the time he has entered the judicial system. Indeed the very act of committing the crime may have cured his illness. Equally, although people who are mildly ill usually commit mild crimes, if they commit any at all, it is, clear that there is a large middle ground where the correspondence does not hold good.

Thus, although it is convenient to regard the groups as if one were evenly painted yellow and the other blue, so that when the two areas are made to overlap, the result will be a uniformly green area representing the subject for study, the image is quite misleading. One mentally disordered offender may have nothing whatever in common with another, save that according to the current definitions of disorder and offence each person finds himself a member of the two superimposed groups.

This prompts reference to another source of difficulty, which is nonetheless important for being obvious: namely, that neither population is static. Each is determined by a definition which is constantly revised; the agencies whose function (not infrequently self-appointed) is to establish degrees of deviation from the norm which qualify someone for the labels of mentally disordered and criminal are not the same; the definitions are of a different kind; and the methods by which the definitions are applied to the individual case are totally different. This is not the place—although there most emphatically is a place—for a discussion of the philosophies of medicine and penology, and of the interaction between the two. Nevertheless even a glance at successive editions of the textbooks is enough to show that in relation to each group there are persons who in one generation might fall within it, and in the next might be outside: and vice versa. How much the more so in the case of the mentally disordered offender, whose possession of the label depends on the opinions of two quite distinct bodies of standard-setters, and indeed also of those who enforce the standards set by others.

Thus, the active male adult homosexual became a member of both groups successively, and left each successively, making his exit from our field of study, possibly for ever. The active paedophile by contrast still seems to be a member, at any rate if one adopts the standpoint of those doctors who believe that such offenders can be 'cured'.

Many persons who according to the standard-setter fall within our chosen field are in practice extruded from it on practical grounds. Thus, a great deal of conduct which in reality amounts to an offence is effectively de-criminalized; as, for example, in the case of small repeated offences by 'inadequates', whom the law-enforcing agencies do not have the resources, or the inclination, to pursue through the courts.

All this being so, we shall muddle ourselves and our audience alike if we do not constantly bear in mind that there exists no idealized figure of the 'mentally disordered offender'; and that in the case of each activity upon which we engage we should take care to identify not only the particular type of mentally disordered offender with whom we are concerned, but also the reasons why we assign him or her to this category at all.

MAD OR BAD?

The problems of the mentally disordered offender are almost always assumed to have two aspects—the medical and the legal—and two alone. This is natural enough for the term itself is composed of two elements, and the agencies who confront the offender can be divided broadly into two categories. Nevertheless, it is a mistake to make the assumption too readily, for it ignores the possibility that there exists a third group, further superimposed on the two which we have already identified: namely, the group of people who are bad, or (if one prefers) of people who have done bad things. The choice between these two formulations is of great importance, for it reflects the stance of the observer towards the offender and the offence. But we must leave it for another occasion. What matters for present purposes is that the public at large believes that this group exists, that it is distinct both from the group of offenders and from the group of the disordered, and that of all the three groups it is much the most important. It is distinct from the group of offenders because whatever the jurisprudents may say, the distinction between *malum prohibitum* and *malum in se* is recognized by all of us, even if we would not all agree on where the line should be drawn. It is distinct from the group of the disordered through the quality of the acts which the individual has done. Everyone acknowledges that people who are not bad sometimes commit criminal offences; that not all offences are bad, except to the degree that it is almost always wrong not to obey the law; and that some acts are wrong but not criminal. This third group is regarded by the public as important, because the unarticulated penal policies of the majority of citizens are in a real measure truly penal in nature. The utilitarian aims of sentencing would, I suppose, be acknowledged by very many, perhaps with some prompting. It would be recognized as a good thing that offenders should be persuaded not to reoffend; that they should be deterred from doing so; that they should have their social techniques improved so as to make the idea of offending less compelling; that if all else fails they should be locked up so as to make offending impracticable. Much deeper than any of this, however, is the notion that wrong deeds ought to be marked as such by the way in which the system deals with the person who has done them.

The professionals dealing with the mentally disordered offender overlook this third element at their peril. Even in strictly technical terms they will find it hard not to take account of it. Every lawyer learns at college about the effect which mental disorder may have on what lawyers like to call the mental element in offences: for example, in relation to the M'Naghten defence. Much more important in practice is the impact, often deadened by layers of fudge, which the mental disorder has on the perceived ethical element of the offence. Although the reasoning is not often spelt out, it is widely felt that an offence associated with mental disorder is not so wrong as one which is not. Combined with the tacit assumption that the formal gravity of an offence ought to bear some relation to its apparent wrongfulness, this notion may in the most extreme case cause the offence to be entirely recategorized: as in the notorious instance of 'diminished responsibility', where the perversion of the logic of the offence of murder has created the most serious problems of sentencing and trial. Much more commonly, the effect of the disorder on the apparent moral content of the offence is an important element in sentencing, since it serves to make the sentencer, speaking for the public, regard the offence as occupying a different part of the range of badness, or on occasion as not being bad at all.

Furthermore, even if it were possible for those seeking a better-made framework for dealing with the mentally disordered offender to ignore the ethical element it would be a profound mistake to do so. Of course, the professionals have no business to be docile camp-followers of inflamed and uninformed public opinion. But prudence as well as humility demands that the moral principles of the majority should not be too brusquely thrust aside. If any real progress is to be made in our chosen field we shall need the widest understanding and support. An acknowledgement that a diagnosis of mental disorder is not a signal for switching off all notions of culpability is, I suggest, essential if we are not to alienate our potential backers. Understanding without sentimentality is the note to be struck.

This is easier to propose than to achieve. One obstacle is that rankings of wickedness by any individual are influenced by many factors, peculiar to the individual who performs the ranking, including age, economic status, locality, racial grouping and religious persuasion. As the influence of the last of these, which has tended to impose some degree of consistency on received moral standards, continues to wane, public perceptions of wrongfulness, whilst still strongly marked, are becoming ever more fragmented and volatile. Thus, whereas it is possible to be sure, after all the wheels have turned, whether or not an individual is to be ranked as an offender, and also possible in many cases to be reasonably confident whether or not he is disordered, the boundaries beyond which his conduct is regarded as wrong are much more blurred and unstable.

The problems of assimilating ethical questions into the management of the mentally disordered offender are, I believe, liable to be felt most acutely by members of some 'caring professions' (an expression to which I return in a moment) whose instincts and training dispose them to regard it as unprofessional and indeed objectionable to allow moral judgments to intrude. It is true that causing a mentally ill patient to recognize a need for self-judgment according to ethical norms may be a part of treatment, on a par with the gaining of an acquaintance with the generally accepted norms of others. But this is part of the task of fitting the patient to interact more effectively with the world at large. The carers do not, as I understand it, thereby acknowledge the intrinsic validity of the existing or any other ethical system, or see it as their function to rank the patient and his actions in any scale of rightness or wrongness established by such a system. It is a practical aspect of practical treatment. But when their patient comes into contact with the machinery of criminal justice, a term which through the word 'justice' insists on the recognition of ethical norms as valid and appropriate, this moral neutrality ceases to be germane. In terms of his or her own training the carer may feel obliged to maintain it but he or she would not be right to insist on the same detachment in others who also have the interests of the mentally disordered offender at heart. Recognizing this fact is liable to be a painful process, but it must be gone through if the carers and those with whom they are associated in this common task are not to forfeit the support of that large body, sympathetic but not sentimental, to whom the problems of the reaction between criminality, illness and wrongdoing are so far unknown. The first step must be to work out where we stand.

THE PROFESSIONALS

Just as the mentally disordered offender is a member of two distinct groups so also is there a deep divide amongst those who determine his fate. In the 'mentally disordered' aspect of his existence the offender will be in the hands of an organism which is essentially a system of support staffed by psychiatrists, psychologists, nurses, social workers, hostel wardens. These are members of the 'caring professions'. The term has irritating overtones, since it implies that other professionals do not care. It is also misleading, since it suggests that nothing more is required of these members than a genial benevolence: a quite unfair picture of what are often some very tough jobs. Nevertheless, it will serve well enough, since everyone knows what it means. Yet at the same time the same individual, in his character as an offender, finds himself consecutively, and on occasions simultaneously, given over to those who are concerned to support, not an individual, but society as a whole: the agents of the criminal justice system. These include police officers, lawyers, judges and magistrates, and prison officers.

Certainly there are some professionals whose duties require them to straddle the two disciplines: for example, prison doctors, forensic psychiatrists, and probation officers. Even in these instances, however, the individual professionals would probably accept, if pressed, that their allegiance is committed primarily to one camp rather than another. Almost everyone in the field would regard (incorrectly, for the reasons which I have tried to show) 'mentally disordered offenders' as a subset of 'mentally disordered' or as a subset of 'offenders', and would see their relationship with the individual as being crucially determined by the perspective in which they view him. The groupings which, for immediate purposes only, we may label as 'carers' and 'lawyers' (in the latter case, named after their most publicly visible representatives) differ fundamentally as to: the nature of their relationships with the patient/offender; the aims which the professional sets out to achieve; the formal structure of the tasks which the professional is called on to undertake; and the continuity or otherwise of the relationship between the professional and the individual.

All question of aims, policies, training and preconceptions apart, the 'carer's' vision of his relationship with the offender is quite different from that of the 'lawyer'. The good doctor sees his patient, not as an object but as a subject, with whom (not upon whom) he can work to improve his patient's life. The lawyer cannot think in these terms. The offender is of course the centrepiece of the judicial process. He or she is a human being, as any decent lawyer will recognize. All the same, the offender is distanced from those who deal with him, if only because the process is concerned with the social order, not with the individual. The doctor wants to find out what is wrong with the patient, so that he can decide how best to care for him. He should and will glance over his shoulder at the general interests of society, and will on occasion prefer them to those of the patient. Nevertheless, the instinct of the doctor is to look to the patient first. So also with the carer and his client. This is not at all the approach of the lawyer. The structure within which he works, and the attitudes which pervade his training and experience, unite to invest the offender with a passive role. At the stage of guilt or innocence the mental make-up of the offender is often quite immaterial: he is simply a human who has acted in a particular way. At the stage when guilt has been established, his individual history, characteristics and mentality do become relevant. Thus, they may help to explain if not excuse the offence, and hence may blunt the edge of the sentencer's determination to mark a morally objectionable offence with a severe punishment, and also because (at the lower end of the scale of seriousness) they may encourage the sentencer to chance his arm with a method of disposal which might otherwise have seemed inappropriate. English penal policy, so far as it is discernible, does recognize among the elements in the delicate and often unarticulated business of sentencing, a desire if possible to cure the offender of his predilection to offend again. But where this factor is in play the benefit to the offender's well-being is a side-effect, the object of the cure being to ensure that other members of society do not suffer the detriment of further offences.

The working methods of the two groups of professionals are also quite different. It is true that in some instances the mental health legislation requires the doctor to reach and express a formal conclusion on diagnosis or prognosis; but in the main such conclusions are neither immutable nor an end in themselves. Rather, they are interim and often tentative elements in a broad analysis of the ways in which the patient can be cared for and, if possible, cured. For the lawyers, and the agencies roughly grouped around them, the procedures are altogether more sharp-edged. The police officer decides whether there is sufficient evidence to justify charging the suspect and handing him over to the prosecution service. This service then decides whether the case is strong enough to justify handing the suspect over to the trial process. At the trial the judge makes procedural rulings according to principles which he is bound to apply. The magistrate or jury decides yea

232 The mentally disordered offender

or nay upon guilt, and hence upon whether the defendant should be handed over to the sentencing process. The sentencer decides yea or nay whether to hand the offender over to the prison service, or to other authorities.

If the defendant is committed to prison, another body or agency decides according to established principles whether he should be released before the time fixed by the sentencer. In most cases, the decisions are not provisional or tentative, nor are they mere elements in a general design, whereby the doctor in partnership with the patient endeavours to help the patient to a goal which is predetermined, by methods which are essentially continuous, variable or pragmatic in nature. The criminal justice system operates more like an electronic circuit, in which the successive operations of switches 'gate' the subject into or out of the next stage of the circuit. Much of the system operates without reference to a primary goal, of which the well-being of the individual is the centrepiece. Often one may feel that the system operates without any explicit goal at all. The relevant agency simply performs its allotted function according to prescribed rules, and either moves the subject further into the system, or moves him out of it. Having done so, the agency switches off, awaiting the next signal. It is only at the extremity of the system, where the offender is compulsorily kept in contact with a penal or social agency, because that is what the sentencer has ordered, that there is any continuity of contact between himself and the system, and any purposive relationship directed in part at least to the welfare of the individual.

All this being so, it is, I believe, essential that any attempt by the 'carers', on the one hand and the 'lawyers' on the other, to appraise and solve the problems raised by the mentally disordered offender should recognize that they do not occupy the same professional universe. Nothing can change this, and nothing but good can come from a frank recognition of the fact, and from a magnanimous determination to recognize the apparently opposing points of view and to understand the reasons why they appear to be opposed.

A PHILOSOPHY OF CARE

The foregoing sketch of the conceptual difficulties underlying our subject may already seem too long for the practitioner. There can be few professions less given to reflection than those which we have just examined. Perhaps men and women with a bent towards abstract thought are not drawn to study medicine or the law. At all events such people will not find much intellectual nourishment in their education. A law student has a fair chance of completing his studies without hearing the words 'bad' or 'wrong', and without even being asked to consider the meaning of 'law'. His medical friend will be in a similar position, making contact with the philosophy of medicine, if at all, in the very narrow field of medical ethics.

So also when the time comes to practise. The demand is for on-the-spot solutions to individual practical problems. The patient or offender appears on the conveyor belt, is adjusted in the best way the professional can manage, and sent off again on the belt, which brings up another to take his place. The demands made by this process, enhanced because the subject-matter is not a piece of machinery but a fellow human being, give no opportunity for rumination, and indeed actively discourage it. The professional pursues established aims by established means, and those who seek to give their utmost to the community assume that they can best achieve this by working harder and perfecting their technical skills. Few pause to ask themselves whether the time-honoured processes are soundly based, or whether some quite different method would be more efficient, or more fair, or more morally acceptable. Most professionals are impatient with these questions, regarding them as suitable only for 'academics' who lack the fortitude to endure the heat of the kitchen, and whose efforts serve only to rock the frail craft which the professionals are struggling to keep afloat. Even if not ill-disposed to reflection, most professionals simply do not have the time to engage upon it, or to study the reflections of others.

This gulf between those who do and those who think about doing, when each ought to participate in both, has stunted intellectual growth in certain areas of English law; I cannot speak for the medical and social sciences. The consequences have not always been harmful, for the absence of fully developed theoretical formulations makes for flexibility. But in our chosen field the need for rigorous thinking is imperative for, as we have seen, the amorphous group whose well-being we seek to promote is defined by simultaneously applying criteria of wholly different kinds, and is in the hands of an alliance of alien professional cultures.

SOME QUESTIONS DRAWN UPON AT RANDOM

We thus need to start by asking ourselves what are the relevant questions, before we proceed too far on the assumption that the answers are obvious. Simply to indicate the kind of questions which ought to be asked, here are a few suggestions:

1. Is a prison hospital part of the medical system or of the penal system?
2. Does the divide between the medical and penal systems reflect a divide between illness and culpability? It scarcely seems to do so in practice, since prisons contain many who are mentally ill, and hospitals contain many who are culpable? If the answer is 'No', then what is the rationale for the existence of two separate systems?
3. It is often regarded as axiomatic that the medical system is concerned with care and treatment alone. For instance, if a disordered offender is restrained, this is said to be in the interests of the public and of

himself, not in furtherance of any penal policy. Should this necessarily be so?

4. If an offender is in prison because his conduct is regarded as culpable, and if it is then found that he has become mentally disordered, or was mentally disordered all along, so that he is transferred to hospital under Section 47 of the 1983 Mental Health Act, what happens to his culpability? Does it disappear, or does it simply cease to be relevant? If he is transferred back again under Section 50 (1) (a) does his culpability revive? What is the intellectual basis of this notion?

5. If the justification for extracting the mentally disordered offender from prison and inserting him into the quite different environment of a hospital is that his illness is thought to eliminate his culpability, why is it that an untreatable psychopath goes to prison and a treatable psychopath goes to hospital? Surely treatability and blame have nothing to do with one another?

6. Is it perhaps the case that illness, or at least serious illness, in some way is seen to 'trump' all other reflections of an individual's deviations from the norm? If so, why?

7. The uncharitable might say that for many offenders it is often a question of luck whether they happen to come into contact first with the penal or the medical sections of the regime. Might the uncharitable be right?

8. A graph plotting the criminality of an individual's acts against the degree to which they deviate from the norm would remain at zero for some time; then climb steadily; and then suddenly plunge back to zero at the point where mental illness is conceived to be engaged — except in the case of homicide, where the return to zero would be less steep, reflecting the diminution of 'responsibility'. A similar plot of culpability would have much the same shape. This looks very odd. In terms of society's perception and treatment of the offender it seems that the worst thing for him to be is fairly deviant. Is there something wrong with our ideas of criminality or of mental illness?

9. The concept of what may be called in non-technical language 'dangerousness' is rightly of concern to the public. Ordinary people think that the risk that an offender may, if given the chance, cause harm to someone other than the victim of the crime which has made him an offender outranks the risk that he may be kept in custody for longer than the risk demands. Are ordinary people right?

10. In many instances involving disordered offenders someone (a doctor or a judge) has to forecast whether the offender is now dangerous and will continue to be so. How is the prognosis of risk to be carried out?

11. Where the offender is mentally disordered the concept of dangerousness appears in two different contexts: in the assessment of protection of the public from serious harm under Section 41 of the

1983 Mental Health Act, and in the decision by the Review Tribunal on whether the continued detention of the offender is necessary for the protection of other persons. Are these criteria the same? If not, what are the differences, and why do they exist?

12. A and B are before the Crown Court for sentence on the same day, each having been convicted of a violent offence. Neither has expressed any form of regret. Defendant A is sentenced purely as an offender, and having forfeited the only available ground of mitigation (namely expressions of remorse) is made the subject of an informal diagnosis of dangerousness by the judge, who sentences him to a long term of imprisonment in the interests of public safety. The legal representatives of offender B have obtained medical evidence which, on the basis of precisely the same factors which have aggravated A's offence, including lack of remorse (sc. 'lack of insight') conclude that B is mentally ill. Some time later, the doctors in charge of B conclude that he is no longer mentally ill, although they believe that he is still a risk to the public. The review tribunal therefore feels obliged to discharge him. Thus, of the two dangerous people one is at liberty and the other is not. There seems to be something wrong here, but what is it? Should the judge have abstained from his informal diagnosis in case A? Or was he wrong to accept the medical diagnosis in case B? Or have the doctors misunderstood the criteria of public safety? Or is the legislation misconceived?

13. Just as grossly aberrant behaviour may (if the offender is lucky) lead to his being treated as ill, so, too, certain types of mildly aberrant behaviour may lead to the same conclusion. But only certain types. If a young man persistently takes motorcycles the court is liable to treat him as the sort of person who, in his own interest and the interests of the public, needs to be taught a lesson by being locked up. If he persistently takes ladies' underwear from washing lines he has a better chance that a doctor will say that he is ill, and that a judge will accept that he needs to be handled in the medical rather than the penal system. Is there really a difference between the two cases which justifies the difference between a prison sentence and a probation order? If not, what is it in the training and preconceptions of the doctor and the judge which appear to justify this result?

14. 'At what point, in any given case history, should persistent quirks or multiplying phobias be officially diagnosed as delusions of grandeur or manifestations of paranoia?' [H. Levin commenting on the jury's verdict 'of unsound mind' on Ezra Pound: New York Review of Books (1986), No. 17, p. 47. Pound was ultimately released without trial.]

15. Is it possible to cure paedophilia? What does 'cure' mean in this context, and what are the criteria for success?

16. Underlying many judicial decisions in this field is the assumption

that disposal in the medical system is more humane than disposal in the penal system. Is this always right?

17. Are we doing the 'inadequate' any favours by treating him as ill?
18. Should we own up to the fact that there are not two populations, identified crudely as 'bad' and 'mad', but three, and recognize that instead of trying to force every individual into one or the other, we should recognize that he may be a member of the third? And if we do recognize this, what next?

There are many more questions than these, which were drawn more or less at random; and some of them are extremely elusive. I firmly believe that the long-term success of any general assault on the practical problems cannot be answered except in the context of a methodical and intellectually remorseless exposure of the conceptual problems—problems which are, in my opinion, both more numerous and more profound than those which afflict the tasks of healing patients and dealing with offenders, when these tasks are uncomplicated by the interplay between the two. This is not to say that practical efforts to put right the more glaring deficiencies in practical provision for offenders should be held up during the gestation of theses which the practitioners may not have the time or the inclination to study, even when published. Rather, that a purely piecemeal attack will make the existing fragmentation worse. The marshalling of many disciplines will be for the good, but there must also be some common perception of the intellectual framework within which the solutions are intended to work. We cannot wait for the answers, but we should not delay the asking of the questions—and, as a first step, we should encourage the professionals to accept that questions are there to be asked, and to start discussing amongst themselves what they might be.

TOO MANY REGIMES—OR TOO FEW?

At the beginning of this chapter, I ventured to refer to mentally disordered offenders as the subject of scandalous neglect. This is not hyperbole. Far too few people and institutions understand the special needs of these human beings, or want to understand them; far too few are able or willing to recognize the special ethical, legal, medical and administrative problems they pose for society, or the extent to which these problems are currently going unsolved; and far too few think it their business to see that something is done about them.

This is not to say that there are too few institutions or groups of professionals whose work touches our field of study. A glance through this book will prove the contrary, for the number of groups and bodies who may come into contact with mentally disordered offenders easily overtops a dozen. (One of the many features which makes this subject so interesting and surprising to the newcomer is that every penetration below the surface of the problem reveals the involvement of some other agency or group of workers. For example, who would have predicted that the Department of the Environment might have an important part to play in our particular sector?) Yet the problems are not being satisfactorily solved, and indeed are likely to get worse as these offenders are herded back to the community at large. Why is this so? A shortage of resources forms part of the answer, but there must be something else. (Judges are rightly required to abstain from public political comment, and I am not here making a political point. The scale on which public funds are raised and the priorities according to which they are disbursed is a matter for Parliament. Nevertheless, it is obvious that if more money is spent on the mentally disordered offender the problems will be eased, although they will certainly not go away.)

Another part of the answer is that provision for the mentally disordered offender is dispensed by two mutually exclusive regimes: either the offender is in the criminal justice system, with all that that implies as to aims, philosophies and methods, or he is in the sociomedical system, whose aims, philosophies and methods are inconsistent with those of the other system. The offender never inhabits both worlds at once, except to the very limited extent that he is, for example, remanded to hospital pending trial or sentence.

Having made this statement, I must immediately contradict it, for there is in truth an unacknowledged third regime: namely, the non-regime of an unsupported life in the community.

I believe that everyone concerned with trying to make this bi- (or tri-) polar system work regards it as deeply unsatisfactory. To call it a system is indeed a misnomer, for the way in which it operates is not systematic. Thus, for example, the point of entry into the system is often a matter of chance, depending upon whether the disordered person is diagnosed as such before or after he is identified as an offender. Once absorbed into a particular regime, there is a very fair chance that the offender will stay there. Also, there is the very interesting and perhaps important practice, to which a previous contributor has drawn attention, whereby police officers intercept mentally disordered offenders short of the judicial system, and either return them to life in the community, or discreetly steer them into the world of healing and caring. (We seem to know very little about this practice. More information is needed, and thought should also be given to its ethical and constitutional aspects.)

Once the offender has been received into one regime the decisions on whether he should be removed to another, or to a different part of the same regime, are lacking in method. Not because there are no rules, or because the professionals do not try to operate them diligently and sincerely, but because there is no true interface between regimes: they are simply too different in kind. Moreover, the criteria for retention or transfer are too much dependent on imprecise concepts for the process of applying them to be predictable and consistent. Here again, a great deal depends on the capacity of the individual who has immediate control of the offender—

doctor, probation officer, judge, ministry official, etc.—whose primary allegiance is to one regime, to appreciate the aims and idiosyncrasies of the other regime, to appreciate the techniques, strengths and vulnerabilities of those who practise in it. Paradoxically, error may also follow through excessive susceptibility to the attractions of other regimes. Judges and prison officers do not want to keep people in prison who might be better off in hospital. Doctors and staff do not want people in hospital who might be better in the community; and on occasion they may feel unease about patients who might be safer in prison. Thus, for good reason or bad, the mechanism may simply consign the disordered offender to the wrong part of the system; and when it is recognized that this has happened, the procedure of transferring him to the right place tends to work very slowly. Yet again, it may happen that the practitioners of every regime will feel, in relation to a particular offender, that they have nothing to offer him, so that he is handed over from one to another, and handed back again, to the distress not only of himself but also of those who are trying to do their best for him and for society.

This polarization has another unhappy consequence, namely the semblance of confrontation between the practitioners of the two systems: and also a real risk of misunderstanding. I believe that the confrontational aspect is much exaggerated, and that when it does come to the surface this happens because the representatives of both regimes are unwilling to recognize that they are engaged in incompatible tasks or to make the intellectual compromise necessary if the process is to work at all. More often, a genuine problem arises because the professionals of one discipline are at a loss when forced to adapt their modes of thought to those traditional in the other. A doctor whose aim is to develop a relationship with his patient as an individual, as a step towards the betterment of the patient's individual life, may feel distaste for the abruptness and dispassion of an adversarial process conducted as part of a judicial system directed primarily towards the interests of the community as a whole. The judge may be exasperated and sceptical about judgements which to him may seem founded on slender evidence and couched in terms of categories of disease which lack objectivity and precision. These attitudes are not limited to the lawyers and doctors alone, but extend to others participating in the two systems. This is not of course to suggest that there is incomprehension in every case, or that where there are difficulties they always lead to injustice; but the fact that practitioners of the two regimes speak a different language does require a degree of flexibility and forbearance on both sides if the lines of communication are to be kept open.

If one turns now from the major intellectual and practical regimes to the individual agencies which deal with the offender, a different source of dissatisfaction is found. One might think that, with so many bodies involved, the offender would find one which could take the responsibility for his welfare. In one sense, there are indeed such agencies. A court must take a decision if an offender appears before it; the hospital or prison authorities must receive the offender if, in accordance with the rules, the courts require them to do so. But amidst all the ministries, courts, hospital authorities, probation services, local government dependencies, social services, housing departments and prisons, there is not one with the task either of planning and executing general measures capable of reconciling the needs of disordered offenders and of society, or of taking an individual offender in charge from the very outset and steering him towards the best available means of disposal. Consequently, there is no trace of coherence in our policies; no strategic thinking; no safety-net to catch those who slip through the gaps between agencies.

THE OUTSIDER

These conceptual and administrative deficiencies combine to increase the isolation of the mentally disordered offender. He is already a misfit. The incidence of mental illness is high enough for many ordinary citizens to have within their immediate acquaintance someone who is mentally ill; like it or not, they are forced to recognize mental disorder as a fact of everyday life. So also, in a rather different way, with criminality. But the combination of criminality with irrationality is much harder for people to accommodate, and much further removed from their own personal experience. Occasionally, a disordered offender can be viewed by the public in a sympathetic light, particularly if the medical, social and judicial agencies choose so to present him. But ordinarily he is a figure of whom it will be hard for the ordinary citizen to think: 'There, but for the grace of God . . .'

The mentally disordered offender is also a piece of grit in the wheels of State. His presence in prison makes life difficult for staff and inmates alike. He cuts across the grain of a judicial and penal regime designed to deal with orthodox criminality. He disrupts the carefully poised balance of the general psychiatric hospital. His fecklessness or violence makes him unwelcome in supportive accommodation designed for those who are offenders, or for those who are disordered, but not for those who are both. He is out of tune with everybody. The professionals do their best, but they would prefer to see him somewhere else.

A NEW BRIDGE

For sure, the neatest solution would be to create an agency with powers over all disordered offenders, to take them in charge and cater for their special needs from first to last. Compelling as this vision may be, it is surely a pipe-dream. In theory, one could start again from scratch by assuming either that all disordered offenders require treatment and care, or that with the exception of those whose mental condition at the time of the offence was such as to disqualify them altogether from blame, all offenders ought to be dealt with in the penal system. One could then have a unified regime system in which proper medical care could be provided within the penal system, or some kind of punitive element (in the widest sense) could be incorporated where appropriate into the medical system. In practice, there seems no possibility of dismantling the existing bi-partite regime, or of persuading either the public or those who work in it that this would be just. So we must accept that disordered offenders will continue to be distributed between the two parts of the system, whilst hoping to blur the sharpness of the distinction between the two by enhancing the level and quality of care within the penal system and, if this is not too much of a heresy, to incorporate at least some recognition of moral responsibility within the treatment of the individual offender in the medical system.

There may, nevertheless, be ways of bridging the divide. One approach would be to work towards the establishment of an agency, created and funded by the State, yet standing outside the two elements of the existing regime; charged, as is neither of these elements at present, with controlling and safeguarding mentally disordered offenders and nobody else. In whatever part of the system the offender might be, he would, from the outset, be the special responsibility of this new agency, which would follow his case throughout. This would minimize the risk that the offender would be lost through a gap between the services. It would also make him the primary responsibility of an ascertained group of professionals equally interested in his status as a mentally disordered person and his status as an offender; whereas at present in practice, however hard everybody tries, one role is regarded by a particular group of professionals as subordinate to the other.

Whilst this is an attractive idea, it scarcely seems an immediate practical possibility. The new body would have to be detached from the existing lines of ministerial responsibility. It would cost a good deal of money. The times are scarcely propitious for the launching of such a new venture. Moreover, the integration of what would essentially be an interdisciplinary service into the long established regimes would require the utmost skill to avoid the creation of resentment and the confusion of roles and responsibilities.

Nevertheless, if this ideal solution must be rejected, it does not follow that nothing can be done. A body with similar but more limited aims could be created in the voluntary sector. The aims would necessarily be more limited, because the body could not have any responsibility for the disposal of individual offenders. Nor would it be practicable to track the individual offenders through the system, except perhaps on a sampling or research basis, given the large numbers involved, and the problems of access to confidential information and documents. All the same, if the membership of the body could be made wide enough the very fact of its entering upon a largely deserted field would immediately make it a focus of attention; and if persons of expertise and prestige in the public services, the voluntary sector and academic life could be persuaded to take an active, and not simply supervisory part in its work, the body would be enabled to take the high ground and exercise a powerful influence on the shaping of policy.

This new body could also be a vehicle for concerted, measured and dispassionate thinking about the ethical and conceptual foundations of problems whose existence is already well known. Certainly, there have been valuable individual contributions to the debate by doctors, academic lawyers and others, but these are not enough. Public pressures are too broad and too insistent, parliamentary and ministerial time too short, for such efforts to strike home. A body which has the opportunity to conceive, and the authority to bring forward, a battery of questions which have to be addressed and the repertory of possible answers could by this act alone perform a great public service.

The new body could do more than this. Straddling the disciplines, outside the orthodox lines of report and command, with no specialist axe to grind, it would be well placed to study the existing provision for the disordered offender in all its aspects, identifying gaps and keeping a beady eye on shortcomings in performance. It could promote research and promulgate its fruits; stimulate the diffusion of knowledge and understanding within and between the professions; conceive and perhaps initiate practical projects.

If something on these lines is worth entertaining, it will, I believe, be of great importance to devise an effective structure for the new agency. This will not be an easy task. In particular, it may be too ambitious an aim to conjure up an entirely new and entirely autonomous organization, having as its object the tackling of all the different challenges which exist in this field. At the moment, competition for public and private funds may be too intense. On the other hand, it would be setting the sights too low simply to create a committee, of whatever degree of eminence, to ruminate and publish the occasional communique. Some intermediate solution must be devised, almost inevitably within the framework of an existing voluntary organization or consortium of organizations. But whatever the precise form, the essentially unifying role of the new body must be at the very centre of its mandate.

TROUBLES IN COURT

Nobody could claim that the English judicial process in its current shape furnishes a satisfactory framework for examining the three questions which arise whenever a mentally disordered person comes before the court: should there be a trial and if so, what part should the defender play in it; has it been proved that the defendant committed the offence with which he is charged; if so what sentence should be passed?

To some degree this is inevitable, given the imprecision of the concepts of mental disorder, and the irreducible conflict between care and punishment. Nevertheless, the position is worse than it need be. The mental condition of the accused bears critically upon, amongst other things, the intent with which he does the prohibited acts, and the moral culpability attached to the doing of them in his individual case. As to the former, the tangles into which the law has led itself as regards the need for intent, the meaning of the concept, and the manner in which it is to be established have by now been so intensively discussed that there is no point in rehearsing the topic here. It is sufficient to observe that if the lawyers cannot clarify to their own satisfaction what is meant by intent, even in the case where the defendant is in good mental health, it is not surprising that attempts to marry it to the vitiating effects of mental disorder have not been successful, or that these attempts have been accompanied by so much friction amongst the professionals involved. As for the moral perspective, the absence of any unequivocal stance on the relevance of the concept of wickedness to the sentencing process means that the part to be played by mental disorder in the mitigation of the apparent turpitudeness of the defendant is correspondingly hard to pin down.

Elsewhere, there is need for a review of those processes whereby an accused person is diverted from the criminal justice system into the medical regime without a trial ever taking place: notably, by a finding of what is misleadingly called unfitness to plead, or by virtue of an order by magistrates under Section 37(3) of the 1983 Act. The former is deservedly unpopular amongst practitioners, because the jury is called upon to try what is not really a jury question, and also because a verdict of unfitness leads inexorably to detention under a restricted order without limitation of time. Furthermore, the absence of a trial means that the question whether the accused actually did the acts complained of, and if so whether he had at the time a sufficient moral responsibility for what he did to be justly punished for a crime, may be a cause for resentment on the part of the accused and of that neglected figure, the victim. The power (under Section 4(2) of the Criminal Procedure (Insanity) Act 1984) to postpone the determination of the question of fitness until the close of the prosecution case is only part of an answer. On the other hand, whilst it is easy enough to assert that the procedure is objectionable, to find a better alternative is more taxing.

In particular, I am troubled by the idea of extending to the Crown Court the existing power of magistrates to make a hospital order, without recording a conviction, if satisfied that the accused did the act charged. This may be well enough if the offence is trifling and the accused was caught in the act. Humanity and expediency combine to make it undesirable to mount a trial simply for the purpose of recording a conviction. With more serious offences the position is quite different, since the establishment of whether or not the accused did the act charged may have a vital bearing on his treatment after he ceases to be an accused and becomes a patient. The process to decide this cannot be skimped. It is not an answer to say that the court should decide whether the evidence adduced by the

Crown is sufficient to establish a *prima facie* case. The defendant's accusers must test the evidence by cross-examination, which will be difficult if they cannot establish enough rational communication with him to discover the nature of his case—or indeed whether he has got a case. Again, they could not in such circumstances properly advise him to enter a plea of 'no contest', or whatever the equivalent of 'not guilty' might be. What is to happen when, as so often, an important element in the prosecution case is an alleged confession, which at once engages the question of the accused's mental condition, not at the time of the offence or at the time of the trial, but at the time when he is said to have confessed? Perhaps most importantly, there are many cases where in the ordinary way counsel would find it essential to call the defendant on his own behalf. This cannot be done if the defendant is irrational, yet without him the trial will be incomplete. The whole topic needs to be thought out afresh.

The same can, of course, be said of the important issues which arise when the trial has actually begun. These are at their most conspicuous in relation to offences of homicide. At a time of intense political controversy on the nature of the offences classified under this label, and on the issue of the mandatory life sentence, it would be inappropriate at this stage and in this place for me to express my own strongly held views. Meanwhile, it is surely permissible to hope that whatever else happens we shall see the back of 'diminished responsibility'. The shortcomings of this misbegotten compromise are too well-known to need elaboration here. Those which have attracted most professional attention relate to the processes for establishing the defence. This is not surprising, since it is often thought in the particular case that the procedure is too confrontational, with the adversarial system forcing psychiatrists, advocates and judges into roles which they are not best fitted to perform; although it may be noted that on other occasions there is room for believing that the process is not confrontational enough, with the doctors, prosecutors and judges propelled by the mandatory life sentence for murder into a too-ready acceptance of the plea of guilty to manslaughter. Less well aired, but equally serious, are the problems of sentencing. The judge is required to select a sentence on the basis of only two established or admitted facts: that the defendant suffered from an 'abnormality of mind' at the time of the offence; and that his 'mental responsibility' for the offence was somewhere between full responsibility (which would make him guilty of murder) and nil. Even if the judge is sure that he knows what is meant by the expression 'mental responsibility', and even if he is sure that his understanding of it is the same as that of anyone else involved in the case, he will receive no guidance on the extent of the diminution of responsibility. He must make up his own mind on whatever material is placed before him, in most cases without an opportunity for any prolonged personal scrutiny of the defendant, as to which of the available options, ranging from instant liberty to prolonged confinement, is appropriate to meet the responsibility of the defendant for the particular acts which he has committed. At this point, 'mental

responsibility' tends to be surreptitiously translated to 'moral responsibility', until what is eventually an ethical judgment is disguised as a
medical diagnosis. Such a process is bound to be erratic, and all the signs
are that the public is coming to recognize it as such, and demand
something better. Every effort should be made to think of something
better, before public opinion propels the legislature into something worse.

It is also, I believe, permissible to mention the very unsatisfactory state
of affairs concerning restriction orders under Section 41 of the 1983 Act.
The tightening of the criteria for such orders, welcome as it was in some
respects, has served also to sharpen the dilemma of the court when
choosing between a restriction order without limitation of time, which may
cause the patient to be detained for too long, and an ordinary hospital order
under Section 37 which in an appreciable proportion of cases will result in
a person who has culpably killed another being released within a very few
months of appearing in the Crown Court. Many people would regard this
as wrong, yet a conscientious application of the 1983 Act often leaves the
sentencer with no choice. The problem is compounded by the fact that the
legislation imposes on the judge, and not on the medical practitioner, the
ultimate responsibility for deciding whether the offender is too dangerous
and will remain in the future too dangerous, to make an ordinary hospital
order a responsible choice. The judge has no qualifications for making such
a prognosis, beyond his experience as advocate and judge in seeing
dangerous people sentenced by the courts: and since in neither capacity
does he usually receive the kind of follow-up information which enables
him to know whether the sentencing option chosen actually turned out to
be right, the value of such experience is debatable. Moreover, in the
majority of cases where the offender fails to be sentenced for manslaughter
upon a plea of not guilty to murder accepted by the prosecution, rather
than after a trial during which the judge can study the offender, his
prognosis will normally have to be formed in the course of a hearing lasting
an hour or two at most, during which the offender does and says nothing at
all. It is not hard to see why, once the legislative decision had been taken to
leave the disordered offender within the existing sentencing framework, it
was thought essential to give the judge the last word, but in my opinion the
way in which this works in practice is not wholly satisfactory.

At the other end of the scale the picture is even more clouded. An uneasy
alliance of humanity and expediency has led to something of a consensus
that minor offenders should if possible be kept out of prison. It is beyond
the scope of this book to consider whether, as regards the 'normal' offender
(if there is such a person),this ideal is intrinsically capable of being realized,
at least to the degree which some of its proponents would desire, let alone
realized with the resources currently available. What does seem clear, to
the writer at least, is that the adoption of unspecialized measures to deal in
the community with the mentally disordered offender will simply result in
his being condemned to a life of aimlessness, isolation and social nuisance
in which he will be constantly recycled through the courts, until ultimately

the magistrate or judge is driven to conclude that enough is enough. There is nothing humane about this, nothing to promote the interests of either the offender or the public. A better choice is hard to devise, but I would certainly commend for further thought a practical possibility referred to in earlier chapters of this book. A fully developed forensic psychiatry service, drawing upon a wide range of disciplines, could provide informed and coherent support for the offender, who is currently rejected by the fact of his offending or because of the personality traits which have caused him to offend, from participation in the mainstream social and medical regimes. I believe it important for the offender, as well as for the victim and society at large, that his status as an offender should be explicitly and formally acknowledged. Here, the revised form of guardianship order has much to offer.

Now, whether this particular combination of measures promises to be the most effective is debatable, but the need for some form of provision which simultaneously recognizes the disorder (or the 'inadequacy', or whatever) and the criminality is self-evident. Time is short for devising the right mixture of skills, support and sanctions. Uncoordinated proposals for penal reform, particularly at the lower end of the scale, are being fired off in all directions, at a time when the vanguard of the failures of mental heatlh care in the community will quite soon be moving from the streets into the courts. Here, as everywhere in the field covered by this book, there is need for hard unsentimental thinking, followed by strategic planning. Who is going to do it?

INFORMATION AND EDUCATION

Whilst studying the previous contributions in preparation for this final chapter, I had jotted down areas for possible research, with a view to producing a consolidated list. It soon became clear that this was unnecessary, and indeed discourteous to the reader, who will have recognized without prompting that in virtually all the areas we know too little about the most elementary facts and figures. What is worse, we do not even know what is known, so that valuable work may have gone unnoticed or duplicated. This is a fatal obstacle to any but a haphazard attack on these urgent and important problems. We cannot execute efficiently without planning: and we cannot plan without knowledge.

I believe that steps should therefore be taken without delay to:

1. Make a comprehensive survey of the research which has already been done in this field.
2. Identify the gaps in current knowledge.
3. Commission research to fill at least the most important gaps.

This survey should not be limited to the United Kingdom. Penal systems differ, and so does provision for the mentally disordered, but the problems raised by the mentally disordered offender must be much the same everywhere. The United States' experience will have much to offer. (It is no doubt unfair to suggest that penal ideas tend to be promoted as innovations in the UK just when they are in course of being discredited in the US, but there is much we can learn from the failures as well as the successes of American initiatives.) But we should cast the net wider. English is not the only language of penology, and a comparative study of five or six jurisdictions would be of great value. The material must exist; all that is needed is to find it.

The purpose of gathering information of this kind is to establish a firm base for planning and action. Much of it will be too indigestible for general dissemination. There are, however, three important respects in which knowledge already to hand could and should be put into wider circulation.

First, the practitioners are not in general well enough informed about the relationship between the mentally disordered offender and their own disciplines. For example, magistrates, judges, clerks and advocates are very busy people, struggling to keep the individual cases moving through an overloaded system. They simply do not have time to give private study to all the technical aspects of the problems with which they may have to deal, and to a great extent have to rely on learning by experience. This is not easy, so far as mental disorder is concerned, since the occasions when the individual practitioner comes into contact with the disordered offender may be infrequent. The result is, I believe, that many participants in the criminal justice system simply do not know as much as they should about the bare bones of the subject: the repertoire available to the courts, the consequences of using particular powers, and the considerations which should govern the choice of remedy. Circulating pamphlets and fact-sheets is unlikely to help, given the flood of paper with which the practitioner already has to cope. Direct training at all levels seems the only solution. Perhaps the Judicial Studies Board, the magisterial training bodies, the various professional in-service training organizations and the universities can be persuaded to find room in their courses and seminars for instruction and discussion on the problem of the mentally disordered offender. Whether a similar initiative is called for in the medical and social spheres is not something which the author is qualified to assess.

Second, professionals in one field do not know enough about those who work in other fields: what they are required to do, what they try to do, what their methods are, and in what perspective they view the disordered offender. Direct training here is of little value. There is no substitute for meeting those from other disciplines, discussing problems both within a prepared structure and informally, and if possible seeing others actually at work. The kind of grand forum which I propose for the increase of mutual understanding at the planning of nation-wide initiatives could well be echoed at the local level. It is too much to hope that with such a fissile subject everyone's views will be perfectly in harmony, but at least those involved will afterwards have some idea of what their counterparts are talking about and trying to achieve.

Finally, there is the paramount need to inform the general public. Opinion is coming to the boil about the penal system, and concern about the mentally disordered is bound to increase as the implications of community care start to make themselves felt in everyday life. The mentally disordered offender is not an attractive subject; the double problems of dealing with him are not readily understood; the need to divert resources from other obviously deserving causes is not obvious. Great alertness will be needed if these awkward customers are not to be swamped in the rising tide of public demands to have something, anything, done about criminal and antisocial behaviour. As an essential first step we must somehow bring home to the citizen who is neither mentally disordered nor criminal that he is fortunate to be so; and that although some disordered offenders may deserve censure or punishment, all of them alike deserve understanding, support and an opportunity to put themselves back in tune with the social order. Education in the widest sense, aimed at all and using the widest battery of methods, must be the key to lasting success in the endeavours to which this book is devoted.

CONCLUSION

I am conscious that there are no clarion-calls here; very little to win votes or attract private giving. Even if these proposals were put into effect, nobody could point with joy and pride to a single offender whose life had been transformed. It would be foolish to postpone by a day the taking of new practical initiatives so as to produce immediate tangible gains, to broaden the base of experience, and to promote public interest and support. Nevertheless, this dry work must be done, distant from the firing-line though it may be, if provision for the mentally disordered offender is not to remain as incoherent, and its success so intermittent, as it unhappily is today.

Index